I0028070

'This book is an absolute treasure. Drawing on his wealth of experience, keen insight, and clinical wisdom, in this marvellous collection of essays Vincenzo Bonaminio has taught us an important lesson. He has shown us how one can integrate Winnicott's seminal ideas and innovative approach to treatment with the knowledge gained from long immersion in Freudian and Object Relations theory and practice to create new and effective ways of thinking and working. This is an invaluable contribution to our field. *Playing at Work* should be required reading for all practising therapists.'

Theodore J. Jacobs, *Psychiatrist at the Albert Einstein College of Medicine and the New York University School of Medicine, and analyst at the New York Psychoanalytic Society and Institute*

'There is a lot of Italian creativity in this new book by Vincenzo Bonaminio: together with his recognized psychoanalytic competence and his special knowledge of Winnicott's thought (but not only...), the author's ability to play unfolds here with all his happy freedom of observation and theoretical-clinical reflection, well known to those who have attended his stimulating live seminars, as well as his writings. Bonaminio is a truly original interpreter of the profound continuity that exists between the childhood, adolescence and adulthood of human beings, and manages to grasp with fresh and precise intuition the possible points of contact with the patient even in very difficult situations. I strongly recommend his book as a special reading experience that is at once thoughtful, lively, and authentically innovative.'

Stefano Bolognini, *Former President of the International Psychoanalytic Association*

'With a vibrant immediacy that rings ever true, Bonaminio brings the bewildering uncertainty of analytic engagement fully to life. This is a clinical page-turner, not a theoretical pronouncement illustrated by custom tailored vignettes. The work is playful, perhaps because Bonaminio's own spirit is playful, yet it is suffused with profound thoughtfulness. Here, theory grows from experience, not the reverse. And how profoundly valuable is the theory, centrally shaped by Winnicott's thinking but with that of many others coming to life. The result, Bonaminio's unique contribution. To our generations of struggle to understand, Vincenzo Bonaminio adds fresh clarity. This significant work is the playful expression of a deeply serious thinker.'

Warren S. Poland, *author of* Intimacy and Separateness in Psychoanalysis

Playing at Work

Playing at Work offers a thorough guide to the innovative psychoanalytic practices of Vincenzo Bonaminio, as he draws on the work of Winnicott, Bollas, and Tustin to demonstrate an effective method for working with adults, adolescents, and children in clinical settings.

Using several clinical cases, the book explores central psychoanalytic concepts such as transference and countertransference, identity and self, embodiment, anxiety, and the role of parental influence on psychic development. By providing extended commentary on his case material, Bonaminio illustrates the significance of writing about clinical practice to the development of techniques that address patients' varying needs. Simultaneously, this text offers a method that cultivates each patient's capacity for intuition and the use of metaphor to form their own interpretations, and thereby invests a sense of freedom into the analytic situation.

By its deeply reflective insights, and its emphasis on the contribution made by the analyst as an active participant in the therapeutic situation, *Playing at Work* forms essential reading for all practicing psychoanalysts and psychoanalytic psychotherapists who wish to improve their clinical practice with patients of any age.

Vincenzo Bonaminio is a training and supervising analyst of the Italian Psychoanalytic Society and works in Rome in a private practice with adults, adolescents, and children. For over 25 years he has been Director of the D.W. Winnicott Institute, and is Director of the Winnicott Center, Italy.

THE NEW LIBRARY OF PSYCHOANALYSIS

General Editor: Alessandra Lemma

The *New Library of Psychoanalysis* was launched in 1987 in association with the Institute of Psychoanalysis, London. It took over from the International Psychoanalytical Library which published many of the early translations of the works of Freud and the writings of most of the leading British and Continental psychoanalysts.

The purpose of the *New Library of Psychoanalysis* is to facilitate a greater and more widespread appreciation of psychoanalysis and to provide a forum for increasing mutual understanding between psychoanalysts and those working in other disciplines such as the social sciences, medicine, philosophy, history, linguistics, literature and the arts. It aims to represent different trends both in British psychoanalysis and in psychoanalysis generally. The *New Library of Psychoanalysis* is well placed to make available to the English-speaking world psychoanalytic writings from other European countries and to increase the interchange of ideas between British and American psychoanalysts. Through the *Teaching Series*, the New Library of Psychoanalysis now also publishes books that provide comprehensive, yet accessible, overviews of selected subject areas aimed at those studying psychoanalysis and related fields such as the social sciences, philosophy, literature and the arts.

The Institute, together with the British Psychoanalytical Society, runs a low-fee psychoanalytic clinic, organizes lectures and scientific events concerned with psychoanalysis and publishes the *International Journal of Psychoanalysis*. It runs a training course in psychoanalysis which leads to membership of the International Psychoanalytical Association – the body which preserves internationally agreed standards of training, of professional entry, and of professional ethics and practice for psychoanalysis as initiated and developed by Sigmund Freud. Distinguished members of the Institute have included Michael Balint, Wilfred Bion, Ronald Fairbairn, Anna Freud, Ernest Jones, Melanie Klein, John Rickman and Donald Winnicott.

Previous general editors have included David Tuckett, who played a very active role in the establishment of the New Library. He was followed as general editor by Elizabeth Bott Spillius, who was in turn followed by Susan Budd and then by Dana Birksted-Breen. Current members of the Advisory Board include Giovanna Di Ceglie, Liz Allison, Anne Patterson, Josh Cohen and Daniel Pick.

Previous members of the Advisory Board include Christopher Bollas, Ronald Britton, Catalina Bronstein, Donald Campbell, Rosemary Davies, Sara Flanders, Stephen Grosz, John Keene, Eglé Laufer, Alessandra Lemma, Juliet Mitchell, Michael Parsons, Rosine Jozef Perelberg, Richard Rusbridger, Mary Target and David Taylor.

A full list of all the titles in the New Library of Psychoanalysis main series is available at https://www.routledge.com/The-New-Library-of-Psychoanalysis/book-series/SE0239

For titles in the *New Library of Psychoanalysis* 'Teaching' and 'Beyond the Couch' subseries, please visit the Routledge website.

Playing at Work

Clinical Essays in a Contemporary Winnicottian Perspective on Technique

Vincenzo Bonaminio

Translated by
Gina Atkinson

Routledge
Taylor & Francis Group

LONDON AND NEW YORK

Cover image: © By permission of The Marsh Agency Ltd., on behalf of
The Winnicott Trust CIO 1174533

First published 2022
by Routledge
4 Park Square, Milton Park, Abingdon, Oxon OX14 4RN

and by Routledge
605 Third Avenue, New York, NY 10158

Routledge is an imprint of the Taylor & Francis Group, an informa business

© 2022 Vincenzo Bonaminio

The right of Vincenzo Bonaminio to be identified as author of this
work has been asserted in accordance with sections 77 and 78 of the
Copyright, Designs and Patents Act 1988.

All rights reserved. No part of this book may be reprinted or
reproduced or utilised in any form or by any electronic, mechanical,
or other means, now known or hereafter invented, including
photocopying and recording, or in any information storage or retrieval
system, without permission in writing from the publishers.

Trademark notice: Product or corporate names may be trademarks
or registered trademarks, and are used only for identification and
explanation without intent to infringe.

British Library Cataloguing-in-Publication Data
A catalogue record for this book is available from the British Library

Library of Congress Cataloging-in-Publication Data
Names: Bonaminio, Vincenzo, author.
Title: Playing at work : clinical essays in a contemporary Winnicottian
perspective on technique / Vincenzo Bonaminio.
Description: Abingdon, Oxon ; New York, NY : Routledge, 2022. |
Includes bibliographical references. |
Identifiers: LCCN 2021053243 (print) | LCCN 2021053244 (ebook) |
ISBN 9781032132563 (hardback) | ISBN 9781032132556 (paperback) |
ISBN 9781003228332 (ebook)
Subjects: LCSH: Winnicott, D. W. (Donald Woods),
1896-1971--Influence. | Psychoanalysis. |
Psychoanalysis--Methodology.
Classification: LCC BF173 .B636 2022 (print) | LCC BF173 (ebook) |
DDC 150.19/5--dc23/eng/20220201
LC record available at https://lccn.loc.gov/2021053243
LC ebook record available at https://lccn.loc.gov/2021053244

ISBN: 9781032132563 (hbk)
ISBN: 9781032132556 (pbk)
ISBN: 9781003228332 (ebk)

DOI: 10.4324/9781003228332

Typeset in Bembo
by KnowledgeWorks Global Ltd.

To the late **Andreas Giannakoulas,** my teacher
and mentor, who recently passed away.

To my patients, children, adolescents, and adults who by
responding to my errors, more or less serious, of poorly
focused interpretation, have taught me what it means to
practice psychoanalysis and to be a psychoanalyst.

To **Christopher Bollas,** who visited our clinic for many
years letting us absorb his deep thinking on Winnicott and
who – through his individual supervision with me – opened
my mind to the creative thinking in psychoanalysis.

To **Glen O Gabbard** from whom I learned how clinical
psychoanalysis should be adapted to the analysand's needs
and not vice versa.

To **Ted Jacobs** and to **Warren Poland** with whom on various
occasion I have touched, almost concretely, what a consummate
clinical wisdom means.

Similarly, I learned a lot from the seminars and the individual
supervisions by **Frances Tustin,** who as visiting Professor made
me understand how the minds of autistic children work.

I am grateful to my wife, Mariassunta Di Renzo, also a
psychoanalyst, who has generously assisted in editing some of
the most critical points in the book, and to my children Angelo
and Giulia, who have enthusiastically supported my work.

Contents

Contents

Presentation

I have known Vincenzo Bonaminio for over 40 years. When I first met him, he was one of the next generations of Italian psychoanalysts, following a tradition established by the Gaddinis and the Chilean transplant, Matte-Blanco. His mentors – Adriano Giannotti and Andreas Giannakoulas – had created a remarkable program in child psychotherapy at the Institute of Child Neuropsychiatry at the University of Rome. Uniquely, they hosted and made 'use of' analysts from Great Britain, many of whom would visit the Institute again and again over the years.

Paula Heimann, Marion Milner, and Frances Tustin had transforming effects upon Bonaminio and those of his generation. So too did his senior colleagues at the Institute, especially Noveletto, Giuliana de Astis, Marco Lombardo Radice, Grimaldi, and Teresa Carratelli, Paola Natali.

The glue that held them all together in the same potential space was the work of D.W. Winnicott. The staff at the Institute and their students did not merely study Winnicott; they lived him. Although deceased, his thinking thrived in another country, given a remarkable new life by young people who took him to their hearts. He became their Winnicott. Their subjective object.

Reading Bonaminio here, I find a remarkable mind and spirit, a thinker who writes like no one else I have known. There is an indescribable combination of deft uses of psychoanalytical theory and theoreticians, clinical descriptions that are both deeply moving and intellectually challenging, and a reflective voice that is unique in psychoanalytical writing.

His readers will discover this for themselves, right from the very beginning. Some pages into this book you may get the feeling that instead of reading an ordinary psychoanalytical text, you are on a magical mystery tour, a roller coaster that rides through theory, clinical realities, and personal confessions. It would be dizzying were it not for some invisible track in the author's mind that carries you from one sight and insight to another and another, in what we might think of as a Roman journey.

The book is almost a piece of theatre, the author a sort of composite of Virgil, Boccaccio, Dante, Fellini, and Dario Fo. This fusion of traditions and perspectives forms a perceptual system that grasps the work and the spirit of D.W. Winnicott in unprecedented ways. While other writers refer to the work of Winnicott and quote him, Bonaminio lives Winnicott in his writing.

All the psychoanalytical roads travelled by Winnicott lead to Rome. This book reflects the very particular sensibility of the Italian mind, illuminating with intelligent passion the way Italian clinicians think about and create psychoanalysis.

Christopher Bollas
December 2020

Foreword

In the opening line of his introduction to this outstanding contribution to the psychoanalytic literature, Vincenzo Bonaminio begins by asserting in boldface type that "This is not a book on Winnicott." This assertion reminds me of a patient who came to my office many years ago, and said, in his first session, "This analysis is NOT about my mother—she was a great mom and we don't need to talk about her." In a similar vein, Bonaminio, in his denial, tells us that the book is very much about Winnicott. And that is certainly fine with me, because to some extent, Bonaminio and Winnicott are inseparable, and the reader of the book will benefit from this connection.

While it may not (officially) be a book on Winnicott, Bonaminio knows that Winnicott is coursing through his veins every time he is sitting with a patient in his consulting room. Each time he exhales, a touch of Winnicott is set free in the air that passes between him and his patient. If Bonaminio writes a book, you can be sure that Winnicott is center stage in one way or another. In fact, one of the most compelling features of this new and thoroughly engaging book is that the reader becomes absorbed in the way that Bonaminio's ideas interact with those of Winnicott. We are all enriched as a result.

Bonaminio writes with an engaging style that draws you into the consulting room with him. He has an impressive knowledge of those thinkers that share his psychoanalytic interests. He emphasizes, for example, a key distinction between Winnicott and Bion, namely, while the latter focused on the unconscious internal objects that must be taken into account and brought into the light of day,

Winnicott, by contrast, focused on the totality of the self and its oscillation between integration and non-integration. Moreover, he stresses correctly that the notion of authenticity is central to the construct of true self/false self. Bonaminio points out how Winnicott's notion of the "environment mother" is part of his view of what constitutes analytic technique. This may be expressed most clearly in Winnicott's 1963 paper on "Communicating and not communicating leading to a study of certain opposites." He was appalled at how his need to make interpretations had prevented deep change in his patients. Like Winnicott, Bonaminio is judicious in his interpretive comments.

One of the most impressive features of *Playing at Work* is the detailed clinical material provided by the author. Readers will find themselves drawn into the mind of the author, understanding his countertransference and his use of theory, but also gaining an understanding of what is happening inside the patient. I highly recommend this superb contribution to psychoanalytic theory and practice. It will be of value both to psychoanalysts and to psychotherapists. It will illuminate landscapes of the mind to the reader that will be of great value in clinical work.

Glen O. Gabbard, MD
February 2021

Acknowledgments

The papers in this book were translated by Gina Atkinson, MA, whom I would like to thank sincerely for her exceptional dedication and accurate work.

I would like to thank Alessandra Lemma for her support, editorial guidance, and for introducing me to Phillip Birch. In him I found a patient, tireless, acute, and attentive copyeditor. He has managed to achieve a uniform style across the papers in this book, given that they had been written at different times and for different purposes. I would like to express my sincere gratitude to him.

I am also very grateful to Carlo Zuccarini, PhD, who translated the lengthy introduction to this book from Italian to English. Through his patience, willingness, and professionalism, he managed to achieve the "almost impossible task" that I set before him (like the title of one of my chapters, in this book: "A Task Which Can Never be Accomplished"); he took what was an ambitious *mélange* and helped to structure an introduction designed to take readers in hand, especially readers who may not be familiar with my work.

I cannot fail to express acknowledgment for this work to Ana Rita Nuti Pontes at Ribeirao Preto (Brazil), as if by magic, arose a book, for which I am very grateful, *Nas margens de mundo infinitos* (Imago Editora).

The final attention of my close friend Tracy D. Morgan, PhD, a smart and brilliant American psychoanalyst and editor of the podcast "New Books in Psychoanalysis" added my 'voice,' albeit in English, to the introduction. As only a close friend could be entrusted to do, she captured and conveyed my humor, my sense of the absurd, my way of working, in short, my idiom.

Last but not least to Adam Elgar, M.Sc. To him my special thanks and gratitude because he translated some additional parts of the book, generously offering support, patience, and a capacity to understand my 'crazy; last-minute requirements, so that through the continuous email exchange between us we became close friends.

But long prior to this, and in addition, I would like to recognize my wife, Mariassunta di Renzo, a psychoanalyst herself, who, after many years of life shared together, has not only contributed to the thinking behind some of the papers, but also to the creation of the psychoanalyst I have become. To my beloved children, Angelo and Giulia: watching them grow has transformed what I know about life itself. Angelo, a young psychotherapist, expert in the treatment of very disturbed adolescents in institution and in private practice, and Giulia, a clinical psychologist, both of them aiming to be trained as IPA analysts

All of them have had to endure my absences which goes against the grain of the Abruzzese style of close family life. I hope they are pleased with what I have done with my time while they were eating *maccheroni alla chitarra* during Sunday lunch.

"I am most grateful to the Winnicott Trust for their generous financial support for the production of this book".

Permissions Acknowledgments

Bonaminio, V. (2017) Transference Before Transference. *Psychoanalytic Quarterly*, 86:795–810. Reprinted by permission of the publisher (Taylor and Francis, Ltd., http://www.tandfonline.com).

Bonaminio, V. (2017) Clinical Winnicott: Traveling a Revolutionary Road. *Psychoanalytic Quarterly*, 86:609–626. Reprinted by permission of the publisher (Taylor and Francis, Ltd., http://www.tandfonline.com). Portions of an earlier version of this paper were previously published in Portuguese as part of an earlier contribution, Bonaminio, V. (2011). "Nas margentes de mundos infinitos … : A presença do analista e do analisando no espaço transicional em uma perspectiva contemporânea do pensamento de Winnicott", ed. A. R. N. Pontes. Rio de Janeiro, Brazil: Imago.

Bonaminio, V. (2008) The Person of the Analyst: Interpreting, Not Interpreting, and Countertransference. *Psychoanalytic Quarterly*, 77:1105–1146. Reprinted by permission of the publisher (Taylor and Francis, Ltd., http://www.tandfonline.com).

Bonaminio, V. & Di Renzo, M. (2014) "These Anxieties are Not Mine": Adolescence, the Oedipal Configuration, and Transgenerational Factors. *Psychoanalytic Quarterly*, 83:595–632. Reprinted by permission of the publisher (Taylor and Francis, Ltd., http://www.tandfonline.com).

Statement on Privacy

As the author of this text, I take full responsibility for its content.

While the theoretical and conceptual part is available to anyone who wants to draw on what has already been published, the clinical part is a more delicate problem.

In introducing my book, I emphasized that my intent is primarily clinical and the reader will find the explanation of this choice in the opening pages.

The clinical narration of cases in analysis or in psychotherapy poses a particularly difficult dual challenge: protecting the privacy and intimacy not only of the analysand's narrative but also of the analyst's thoughts and interpretation.

I only sought explicit verbal consent with regard to two patients, the adolescent and the child. For the child I received the parents' enthusiastic assent which I have tried to respect.

I showed one adult analysand the entire paper, asking him for specific permission to mention one of his dreams. He told me to change a minor mistake, adding, "if things are done, they should be done properly."

The patient I have called Bernard also gave me his consent.

It was impossible for me to seek the other patients' consent because, having successfully terminated their analysis some years before, they either moved abroad or to other regions of Italy without informing me of their new locations.

It was as though I were passing between Scylla and Charybdis; my anxiety level was very high. I carefully re-read the text many times and made the greatest possible effort to ensure that my patients were unrecognizable.

INTRODUCTION

An Unconventional Introduction for an Anglo-American Readership

This is not a book on Winnicott. You will find instead 12 chapters containing clinical essays that are based on my psychoanalytic work with adult patients, as well as two adolescents and one child. Although this is not a book on Winnicott, which I purposefully wished to avoid, this does not mean that I want to downplay his influence on me or that I do not appreciate recent books treating the concepts of Winnicott.

After many years of relative silence about him, it warms my heart to see the current resurgence of interest in his thinking. Nevertheless, this is not a book about Winnicott.

In this brief overview of the recent revival of interest in Winnicott, I cannot fail to mention the precious volume by Jan Abram (2007), *The Language of Winnicott*. The research data for the book was funded by the Winnicott Trust. Abram's book, which is scholarly and rigorous, contains many references to Winnicott's work. The book greatly stimulated the revival of interest in Winnicott because it brought order and clarified his disordered array of concepts. I would say that because Abram's focus is primarily on the central themes that traces a coherent line of development in Winnicott's thoughts, mainly the developmental growth of the individual, she leaves somewhat in the shadows his clinical and technical contributions, which are mentioned. Perhaps Abram coherently with her task could not avoid this, but her book is nonetheless extremely valuable.

The instructive book *Reading Winnicott* (1991) by Lesley Caldwell and Angela Joyce consists of a collection of key papers by Winnicott with a detailed examination of them. Mention should also be made

 DOI: 10.4324/9781003228332-1

of the four volumes that resulted from the international conferences on Winnicott organized at the University of Milan by Andreas Giannakoulas, Max Hernandez, and Mario Bertolini. Only one volume has been translated into English – the other three volumes have only been published in Italian.

Thanks to an epic effort by Lesley Caldwell and Helen Taylor Robinson, an eminent, monumental, and superbly edited 12-volume set was published in 2016: *The Collected Works of Donald W. Winnicott* (Oxford University Press). This publication is another milestone in the renewed interest in Winnicott, but it also marks a starting point. It makes available to the interested reader a complete and rigorously edited version of the large number of works by Winnicott intended for both psychoanalytic colleagues and the lay readership. This was in keeping with his desire to make psychoanalysis accessible to everyone.

The brilliant foreword by Christopher Bollas concludes with the following words:

> This publication presents the works of England's greatest psychoanalytical thinker and writer. An impish wonderful human being, irksome but charming nonetheless now lives in this text. He would, no doubt, to be "used as an object" by those who read him now and in the generations to come.
>
> (2016, p. L)

Bollas is implicitly referring to the last work by Winnicott "The Use of an Object" (1969).

The exceptional book *Winnicott* by Adam Phillips (1988), which is short yet rich in content, is unconventional in its structure. This is characteristic of the author. He provides an admirable summary of Winnicott's essential work in 140 pages with a rare depth of reflection. As it was published in 1988, this book by Phillips can be considered the first in this renewed interest in Winnicott.

A text that really allowed me to understand the essence of Winnicott was written earlier by Masud Khan (1975) as an Introduction to the new edition of *Through Pediatrics to Psychoanalysis, Collected Papers* (Karnac, 1975).[1] This text is so condensed, yet flowing and meaningful in every word, that it summarizes brilliantly in just a few pages, as only Masud Khan could do, the essence of Winnicott's thought. It is a brief piece that I recommend to my students at the University and the Institute.

André Green is another authoritative figure, a rigorous and consistent custodian of the Freudian word in his work. In the last years of his life, he opened the doors to the value of Winnicott's work. Somewhat ambivalent towards it at first, Green subsequently recognized the worth of Winnicott's work, contributing significantly to clearing the way for his writings in France. Even before Green, there was an increasing interest on the part of the French beyond their national psychoanalytic confines, which they and many francophones considered to be 'genuine' psychoanalysis. Fortunately, the current interaction that occurs between the various national psychoanalytic traditions has broken down these barriers. Significantly, one of Green's last books was entitled *Play and Reflection in Donald Winnicott's Writings: The Donald Winnicott Memorial Lecture Series* (London: Routledge, 2005), which also includes writings by Cesare Sacerdoti and Brett Kahr. The book essentially revolves around two exceptional works by Green about Winnicott: 'Play and Reflection in Donald Winnicott's Writings,' which is actually the memorial lecture, at The Squiggle Foundation and 'Addendum to Lecture.' These writings feature Green's consistent rigor and authoritative style, but also a greater openness and 'playfulness.' The original French edition is entitled *Jouer avec Winnicott* (2005).

Among the many others, I have a first personal memory of André Green. As a novice with a hunger for psychoanalysis, I tried to attend as many scientific events as possible (I am now much more selective). I recall the first IPA international congress that I attended decades ago, which was held in Rome. I was on the point of leaving the conference after a particularly intense day of sessions when I happened across a room so crowded that people were overflowing into the hallway. I stopped to investigate and, being tall enough to see above the crowd, I caught a glimpse of André Green. He was sitting at a table and concluding his talk with the following words:

> After Freud, whose work is still today – and even more so – ineluctable, Melanie Klein's revolutionary work gave birth to two wonderful and brilliant children: Winnicott and Bion.

That said, this book certainly does make use of Winnicott, and does so in the way he intended to be used as illustrated in "The Use of an Object" (1969). This paper was his last act and final bow, bequeathed to my generation of analysts. It articulated his vision for the future of psychoanalysis, a future in which I have been deeply involved.

3

The contents of this book – which I think is representative of my work – consists of a collection of papers spanning more than 25 years.

Although I have written many more papers than are contained in this book, I have selected these particular 12 papers because they were presented at IPA Congresses and other IPA events, and so many of their translations to English were readily available.

My intention in writing this book is to explain the way in which I understand and practice psychoanalysis.

This book also reflects the desire of someone who has read deeply, and in English, the work of British and American analysts, to share his thinking, to return the favor as it were. I want to show what an Italian analyst, whose training has been disciplined and yet ineluctably hybrid, has made of all that he has absorbed.

Initially, I wanted to organize the papers that follow chronologically. However, at the last moment, I made the radical and unusual decision to present my most recent paper first. I surprised myself.

To introduce you to how my mind works, I want to explain how I understand my inclination to shift the order in which this book is organized. The most recent essay that now comes first, 'Transference Before Transference,' explores the impact of an unexpected and rather violent intrusion on the analytic setting: as one patient was lying on the couch, an initial consult, having made a 'mistake' regarding the time of our appointment, rang and rang the bell to my consulting room, creating a bit of chaos in an otherwise uneventful session. So, at first, I wondered, am I following in the footsteps of the initial consult, engaging in some countertransference enactment? But on further reflection, I believe my decision to begin at the chronological end is based on the realization that the nature of this case highlights aspects of an underlying theme that recurs throughout my work, namely, the analyst's countertransference, is a phenomenon that exists prior to ever laying eyes on the patient.

Only when the analysis of this aggressive and violent patient proceeded could I understood, in *après coup,* that the unexpected intrusion was not simply a 'mistake' but a meaningful gesture, a *mise en scène,* in a highly condensed form - unrepresentable at that initial moment – of the core problem facing this patient. But his actions aroused, as you could imagine, a strong force field of feelings in me: I was frightened, and I was furious. And I had not even met him.

While this theme may not be original – others have dealt with it in a much more skillful and detailed manner – it remains significant for me, having developed within and through my own experience.

With the very first contact and often even before the patient's transference, the analyst's countertransference emerges. From the initial telephone call, email, or referral from a colleague, the analysand, as Christopher Bollas (1995, p. 27) tells us, impacts and transforms the analyst's self, perhaps in a way similar to Winnicott's claim that the mother hates the baby first (1947, p. 66–67). The analysand's initial words, tone of voice, manner of speaking, and so forth, impact the analyst. In turn, the analyst's countertransference structures the analysand's transference from the moment he steps into the consulting room, a place where two physicalities experience each other.

The analysand is asking for help, wants to get better, but does not know what the treatment involves. The analyst's initial perception of the analysand sets up a loose structure that inevitably affects the analysand's transference towards the analyst. Naturally, as the analytic process unfolds, things will change, and the transference will become that of the patient.

However, the analyst's initial feelings toward the patient will inevitably leave their mark. If the analyst is able, the early countertransference can be captured for future use.

"[What] is justified in the present setting," writes Winnicott, "has to be sorted out and kept in storage and available for eventual interpretation" (1947, p. 61).

I hope you will see in what follows many examples of how I work with the countertransference and that they may be of some help to clinicians reading this book.

Now, without wishing to appear arrogant or presumptuous, a quotation from Winnicott, whom this book is not about, mirrors some of what I have discovered about myself in compiling the papers for this book:

> I cannot presume, of course, that the way in which my ideas have developed has been followed by others, but I should like to point out that there has been a sequence, and the order that there may be in the sequence belongs to the evolution of my work.
>
> (Winnicott, 1969, p. 86)

Why emphasize the vicissitudes of the clinical?

Any writing on the subject of psychoanalysis reveals something about its author. You will have ideas about me on the basis of how I have arranged chapters, my foci, my clinical examples, my choice of words. Any writing, moreover, be it a novel, a historical text, or a work of psychoanalytic theory, is only complete when it has been read and interpreted by readers.

In selecting the material for this book, my intent has been to emphasize a personal dimension, trying to remain as close as possible to what was said in the consulting room and what work was carried out therein.

In what I consider to be an epistemological pearl, Bion addresses our clinical reportage:

> In the first place, I do not attribute to memory the significance it is usually given. The fact of involuntary distortions is so well established by psychoanalysis itself that it is absurd to behave as if our reports were somehow exempted from our own findings. Memory is born of, and only suited to, sensuous experience. As psychoanalysis is concerned with experience that is not sensuous – who supposes that anxiety has shape, color or smell? - records based on perception of that which is sensible are records only of the psychoanalytically irrelevant. Therefore, in any account of a session, no matter how soon it may be made after the event or by what means, memory should not be treated as more than a pictorialized communication of an emotional experience. The accounts of cases in this book, though sincerely supposed by me at the time to be factually correct... have been now regarded as verbal formulations of sensory images to communicate in one way what is probably communicated in another.
>
> (Bion, 1967, pp. 53–54)

It is furthermore my impression that in the contemporary psychoanalytic literature, detailed clinical descriptions of psychoanalytic practice are declining. In their place we find 'vignettes' intended to support theoretical conceptualizations, whether they serve to buttress what are thought to be established truths or recent innovations. However, this 'support' is somewhat precarious, as you would like to know more about the relationship between the patient and the analyst, or the patient's history.

While a 'snapshot' can tell you a lot, a 'film' can tell you much more. Of course, I am not exactly Fellini, Pasolini, Rossellini, or Moretti (forget De Sica), in what follows I will try to bring the clinical experience to life from multiple points of view.

Bollas (2007, p. 100) argues, and I agree, that an excessive insistence on "the here and now" risks flattening the depth and substance of analytic sessions, and even the entire analytic process itself. Perhaps this clinical tendency, very popular in England and also Italy, does not lend itself to seeing from multiple points of view? While working with what emerges in the moment has undoubtedly contributed to the clinical advancement of psychoanalysis, I also believe that "here and now" work is like a Polaroid taken on Christmas morning: it can only ever tell but a part of the story.

The need to elaborate upon our technique

In the turn away from clinical writing, we also run the risk of becoming technically redundant, if not also clinically ineffective. At the end of 'The Aim of Psychoanalytical Treatment' (1962) Winnicott addresses technique:

> In my opinion our aims in the practice of standard technique are not altered if it happens that we interpret mental mechanisms which belong to the psychotic types of disorder and to primitive stages in the emotional stages of the individual. If our aim continues to be to verbalize the nascent unconscious in terms of the transference, then we are practicing analysis; if not then we are analysts practicing something else that we deem to be appropriate to the occasion. *And why not?*
>
> (1962, p. 288, my italics)

There is certainly something more, "something else," to analytic work than verbally interpreting the patient's unconscious conflicts but how do we represent this technical "surplus?" And what does engagement with it proffer?

Let me first say that technical innovation does not involve abandoning the analytic setting or reneging on the structure provided by the frame.

Michael Parsons (2000, p. 19 and p. 148) compares psychoanalysis to a martial art, arguing that while the foundations of the setting are unassailable, the rules for clinical engagement, he calls them "combat moves," must be particularized.

From Glen Gabbard, my friend and teacher when he was visiting my clinic plenty of times, I have learned that while the basic psychoanalytic setting does not change, the analyst must adapt the setting to the patient's needs rather than forcing frequency, the couch, and so on so as to feel that one is being a psychoanalyst (*personal communication*).

In shying away from writing about the clinical, how can we develop techniques that help to free the patient to speak both evermore and anew?

I have learned from Winnicott many things, primary among them to value the power of *transitional space* when with my patients. I have learned how to loiter and to slouch, whatever is necessary, to stay a few steps behind rather than to march out in front of the analysand, leading the way. I have become comfortable with my role as the supreme dupe – the one who doesn't know much at all! On a good day, I am the one in the corner wearing the dunce's cap. And what has my embracing this stance yielded? Like a person who thinks he is taking the train to Milano only to discover he is seated on a train to Napoli: I find myself deeply surprised.

When my technical approach veers in the direction of this "something else," my patients develop the capacity for intuition, finding ways to represent the previously unrepresentable, and far better they do this than that I do it to or for them. While patients are not always ready for our interpretations, when they can interpret themselves, using metaphor to transform what has been psychically unwieldy, I think the analysis is operating in a "good enough" form.

A remarkable shift in my countertransference usually accompanies these moments. And as my countertransference shifts, so does the transference, and the treatment overall. As such, I have decided it is far better for me to endure being on the wrong train than that I throw the patient onto the tracks.

What psychoanalysis means to me

I consider psychoanalysis to be fundamentally a method of treatment. Metapsychology or theories can only be devised – or to be more polemical, 'authorized' – if they are based, firmly grounded on, clinical experience and not *vice versa*.

I have read or listen to metapsychological elucidations of clinical pathology that are so 'aesthetically' perfect and refined that the patient and her suffering appear to stand in the way of the author's need to look intelligent. The patient seems reduced to a hindrance or an obstacle.

That said, it would be arrogant of me, in spite of my cleavage to the clinic, to claim as irrelevant many books that primarily deal with theoretical issues posed by psychoanalysis.

I would just like to say much more humbly to anyone reading this book that my interest is primarily clinical and therapeutic. Naturally, I have not avoided dealing with theoretical concepts, as it would be absurd and lacking in depth to do so. However, I hope I have been able to strike a good balance between the metapsychological and the theoretical whilst favoring the psychoanalytic clinic.

A light-hearted selfie, or: Why Winnicott?

As can be gleaned from the title of this book, this collection of clinical papers is strongly influenced by Winnicott's work. It is also influenced by the British Independent tradition (Giannakoulas, 2010; Kohon, 2017) and, above all, by what I learned selectively during my official psychoanalytic training in Rome within the Società Psicoanalitica Italiana (SPI), and, primarily, from my analysis with Dr. Giulio Cesare Soavi. The motto that I secretly attributed to him was: *"suaviter in modo, fortiter in re,"* i.e., "Pleasant in manner, but powerful in deed," describing his delicate manner and respect for me as a person, but also his steadfastness and inner strength.

At that time, the 1970s, the orientation of the SPI reflected a loose Kleinian tendency, where the influence of Paula Heimann, Donald Winnicott, Marion Milner, Michael Balint, Masud Khan, and others who had metabolized the object relations revolution yet stood to its left, could be felt. As I was in Europe, we were also working through the thinking of the French – which meant, at that time, certainly Jacques Lacan but also André Green, Jean Laplanche, and the early psychosomaticists. Both of my supervisors while in training identified with a modified Kleinian or object relations orientation approach.

But, of course, I am an Italian analyst, endeavoring to communicate how I came to occupy that position to an English-speaking audience. I assume that the creation of an Italian psychoanalyst, as opposed to a British, French, or American version, may be a bit of a mystery that I will try to shine some light on.

My task was made a bit easier first, because for almost 20 years I had the privilege to join the editorial board of *The International Journal Psychoanalysis,* at the beginning under the directorate of

David Tucket, then of Glen Gabbard and Paul Williams, and currently of Dana Birksted Breen.

A challenging work that of reading carefully anonymous manuscripts for possible publication, but at the same time an inexhaustible source of information, ideas, theories, clinical descriptions at the edge of the latest and most recent reflections in psychoanalysis. A hotbed was the debates during our board meetings that enriched me immensely and made me get in contact with many analysts from all over the world.

For four years overlapping this long period at the IJPA I was also Vice President of the European Psychoanalytical Association – promoted in this charge by David Tucket to whom I am grateful – because this very hard job added further contacts with many analysts.

However, everything was not so simple because politics was overwhelming and, frankly, I do not think I am particularly cut out for politics when it happens at high levels.

The last 20 years have been especially fertile ones for Italian psychoanalysis. The translations of Antonino Ferro's and Giuseppe Civitarese's books in English, just to mention a few, have created a kind of sea change. We Italians are finally more firmly locatable on the psychoanalytic map.

With the election of Stefano Bolognini to the presidency of the IPA from 2013–2017, coupled with his publications and, among others, the books of Franco Borgogno, Franco de Masi, Domenico Chianese, and Borgogno, Luchetti & Coe's tome, *Reading Italian Psychoanalysis* (2016),[2] Italian psychoanalysis is no longer simply *"cosa nostra."*

After the first breach had been broken, and the barrier - above all linguistic - became progressively less rigid - many of us have been invited abroad for seminars and conferences, in Europe, in North America, and in South America.

Integrated fragments, or the cohesive bits incorporated

Bollas (1995) describes the analyst seated and listening to the patient as being introduced to significant figures, fantastic and otherwise, in the past and present life of the patient. The analyst becomes familiar with these figures. They populate the patient's dreams and his myriad interactions in the consulting room. These figures come to feel like characters in a play who move across a stage. We feel their dramatic impact. It seems apposite to now bring to the fore my "significant figures."

I want to also share the milieu, the setting, where my formative psychoanalytic development initially took shape. I want to convey something about myself and also to convey something about a moment in time. I am hopeful that you can hear me.

In a chapter on the development of psychoanalysis in Italy, in the already mentioned book *Reading Italian Psychoanalysis,* Anna Ferruta (2016, p. 24) suggests that the linguistic isolation of Italians "has become an advantage; it has favored receptivity and the wish to learn from others with no hesitation and no prejudice." I am in complete agreement with this statement for reasons that will hopefully soon become clear.

I was introduced to psychoanalysis in a country that embraced and relished ideas from elsewhere. Additionally, it should be remembered that the Freudian *opus* was not fully available in Italian until 1980, thanks to the hard work of Professor Cesare Musatti, a mythical figure of Academy and psychoanalysis. As a result, the development of Italian psychoanalysis has a beautifully chaotic history. We learned Freud through others, and these others were at times rapidly transforming the ideas of Freud. And yet, with our own eventual translation of Freud, which reflects Italian semiology and semantics, we have made him our own. The Italian translation of Freud's works is more faithful to Freud's original Viennese German and certainly does not claim to be the "standard edition."

Because I read Freud in my native tongue later than some others, it was as if I walked into the middle of a film and had to surmise what had happened the moment before I entered the cinema. This might be read as a disadvantage, but I see it differently; perhaps this beginning in the middle is also responsible for the creativity that seems to be at the heart of the Italian psychoanalytic project? And perhaps my generation of analysts could tolerate missing the first part of the "film" because Freud demonstrated his love for us very much, making over 15 visits to Italy in his lifetime, drawing inspiration from the Italian way of life? I like to think that Italy's exposed layers of history inspired him to think topographically, and given our notorious passions, also to think about the drives, though who knows.

Around 1970, when I decided to put both feet into the sea of psychoanalysis (I had previously trained at the "Instituto Winnicott" in Child and Adolescent Psychotherapy), I had already completed my studies in child and adolescent psychotherapy and was working as a clinical psychologist at the University of Rome after a graduation in "Epistemology of Science" (Psychoanalysis), and a Specialization in Infant and Child Psychology (non-psychoanalytical).

Stepping onto the scene in the eternal city, I encountered what could only be described as a Bionian earthquake.

I joined a group run by Dr. Francesco Corrao, a legendary and learned figure[3] in Italian psychoanalysis, and with him many of us read Bion quite closely. Our study group was rather youthful, and I recall we were wanting to show Dr. Corrao our brilliance, but I honestly found myself struggling to understand much of what we read. It seemed experience distant rather than experience near. Bion seemed to me – at the time – to explain *obscura per obscuriora*. Now I understand him much better and appreciate his intuitions and innovative vertex of thinking.

On the contrary, my daily life at this time was spent working with troubled children in the University Clinic and their families, contending with their newly emerging psychic problems. I literally immersed myself in these troubled waters and was caught up and fascinated by clinical practice.

I had also entered into a personal analysis with Dr. Soavi. It would be fair to say that through my participation in Dr. Corrao's group I discovered I was more interested in clinical experience than I was in theoretical formulation, though of course both are important.

When I learned Dr. Andreas Giannakoulas would be coming to my University Clinic in Italy from London to teach as Visiting Professor, I found a way to also attend his group.

It was there that I found my people. Dr. Giannakoulas trained at the British Psychoanalytical Society and had been exposed to both the work of Freud and his followers as well as the work of Winnicott, Klein, and their coterie, not to speak of his native Greek culture, which added a lot to what I had learned from Corrao.

During the last years of Winnicott's life, Giannakoulas was among the happy few summoned to his home to freely discuss clinical issues.

Giannakoulas was invited to Rome by Professor Adriano Giannotti, an SPI psychoanalyst and the Chair of one of the divisions of the Department of Child Psychiatry at the University of Rome La Sapienza, where I held the position of clinical psychologist.

Professor Giannotti was a most generative and forward-thinking man. Fortunately for us, Dr. Giannakoulas spoke both English and

Italian. We received him with open arms, as if he was bringing us the seeds for new and exotic flora and fauna, which, in a way, he was. Moreover, being Greek, he increased from his original source our culture for ancient philosophers, poets, and Greek tragedy.

After the premature death of Professor Giannotti, Dr. Giannakoulas took over the Department's Training Course and in short order began inviting psychoanalytic mavericks and psychoanalytic royalty to teach and work with us.

As both of these men's names begin with the word in Italian for already – "gia" (già) – I must say that indeed, they were "already" ready to teach us. And I felt especially receptive.

I was privileged to be supervised by Giannakoulas for many years. If I could summarize his way of working with me, I would describe it thusly:

> Vincenzo, you have to stick to the patient, accurately following every word, every hidden meaning, everybody movement but without intruding on their privacy. Interpretation can be a catastrophe if given inappropriately or poorly timed. That said, from time-to-time interpretation is mandatory because if you do not interpret when you have to, it can be a catastrophe as well because the patient will feel lost and alone, not cared for but thrown away.
> (personal communication)

I think that this conveys the essence of this great clinician's way of working. My long and intimate relationship with Andreas Giannakoulas in supervision and what I leaned from him gave me the privilege of becoming his successor to the Directorate of the *Winnicott Institute*, which I have maintained for over 25 years.

In the late 1970s and 80s, I had the great pleasure and advantage to learn from Christopher Bollas, Paula Heimann, Frances Tustin – invited by Andreas Giannakoulas – and a long list of many others.

If I mention Bollas, Heiman, and Tustin it is because they were invited as Visiting Professors for decades at the *Winnicott Institute*, and not occasionally. It goes without saying they left a relevant imprint upon us as trainees and staff members.

They offered us a psychoanalytic cornucopia, or as we say in Italian, a *macedonia*. They came to our department regularly to teach and to supervise and were delighted to do so because of their affection for Dr. Giannakoulas.

From Bollas's supervisions I have learned to listen closely and silently without interfering with the patient's free associations. I have learned to not prioritize my need to understand the analysand's *logic of the associations*, (the logic of the sequence) holding back and thinking silently. To paraphrase Bollas's concept, the impact of the object modifies the subject. Reading Bollas is always a surprise.

In 2017 Sarah Nettleton published an incredibly acute – and at the same time – concise overview of Bollas's *oeuvre* that I recommend this book as the best introduction to his work.

By Heimann, I was encouraged to be natural, authentic, and most especially honest with the patient without ever hiding the truth from him while doing so with care. With my heart, I heard Paula Heiman uttering to me with her authoritative voice her famous sentence:

> when a patient starts a speaking laying on the couch, you have to listen carefully and ask yourself "why the patient is saying this to me in this precise moment?"
>
> (personal communication)

From Tustin I learned to deepen my interest in primitive *a-symbolic* bodily experience with autistic children; some of them I supervised with her: I learned to be delicate, human, and careful with autistic children but at the same time to use firmness in conducting clinical work.

> You do not need to lay down on the pavement with the illusion to be closer to him.
>
> (personal communication).

Moreover, in my frequent attendance to the APSaA winter meeting in New York I was fortunate to become close friends of Ted Jacobs, Warren Poland, Jay Greenberg, Melinda Gelman, Henry Smith, Harry Friedman, Fred Busch, and many others.

During the many free conversation with them, in the dinner I was invited in, I had the possibility to follow their discussions on psychoanalysis having the wishful thinking of being one of that group. But in spite of this illusion, I breathe the spirit of part of British and American psychoanalysis: I learned a lot from them.

In the conversations with Ted Jacobs and Warren Poland I had the sense to be in front of two exceptional persons, the two "grand old and wise figures" of American psychoanalysis whose clinical wisdom went far beyond any theory or current.

In reading Poland's last book and in discussing with him about it, I had the impression that some of the concepts of paradoxical nature of psychoanalysis were perfectly fitting with Winnicott's view. Moreover, it seemed to me that the poetic writing of the author, his clarity, explained some paradoxical concepts in Winnicott. It is worth mentioning it at length:

> Clinical psychoanalysis serves as our best laboratory for exploring the riddle of what it is to be a person, and how a person is at once singularly unique while always a piece of the interpersonal fabric of humanity. In Intimacy and Separateness in Psychoanalysis, Warren Poland casts a freshly erudite eye on this paradox, resisting individual or intersubjective bias and avoiding the parochial allegiances common in our age of pluralism.
>
> (from the book's back cover)

Similarly, what I absorbed by reading Ted Jacob's book and discussing it with him was an optimistic view of psychoanalysis for psychic change. In his last book, *The Possible Profession* (2013), the author takes a fresh look at the many forms of unconscious communication that take place in the analytic process.

My immersion in psychoanalysis during this time period can best be compared to the overwhelming experience one has as a guest at a wonderful Italian hotel that shows a breakfast buffet offering all that his heart desires: *bomboloni di cioccolato, salmone affumicato, ricotta fresca, crema di mandorle, cornetti con marmellata, cappuccino, frittata di verdure, uova con latte, spremuta di arancia rossa e prosciutto.*

Like the hotel guest, all of my powerful hungers for knowledge, supervision, and collegiality found themselves satisfied under one roof. I consider myself very fortunate to have been in the right place at the right time.

I mentioned earlier Winnicott's seemingly disorganized approach to writing and presenting his thoughts. Yet he covered psychoanalysis comprehensively, including the area that we now call "outreach psychoanalysis." He is certainly not an 'organized' or consistent writer. Winnicott liked disorganization, or rather, he did not concern himself with being systematic. The valuable book *Between Reality and Fantasy. Transitional Objects and Phenomena* (1978), which I feel has been rather undervalued, contains a statement that was made by Winnicott during a conference at the Tavistock Clinic in London towards the end of his life: "What you get out of me you will have to pick out of the chaos" (Grolnik and Barkin, 1978, p. 37).

How could Winnicott worry about being systematic when his creativity sprang from chaos? Yet in his paradoxical thinking, we can also find the exact opposite in the following statement:

> I cannot assume, of course, that the way in which my ideas have developed has been followed by others, but I should like to point out that there has been a sequence, and the order that there may be in the sequence belongs to the evolution of my work
>
> (Winnicott, 1968b, p. 86)

Winnicott was perfectly aware that his observations and his resulting clinical ideas had a precise line of development. As P. Fabozzi and I have mentioned elsewhere, Winnicott's exceptional essay 'Primitive Emotional Development' from 1945 contains the seed of a sort of master plan. It foreshadows the trajectories that his work would follow and touches upon his main themes. Thomas Ogden (2012) – an eminent and exceptional contemporary scholar whose readings of Winnicott cannot be overlooked – in his paper on this subject also notes this peculiarity in Winnicott's essay, which was ahead of its time. It was written a year before 'Notes on Some Schizoid Mechanisms,' in which Melanie Klein integrated into a consistent theory her discoveries from previous years, introducing the concept of projective identification.

There here has indeed been a surprising resurgence of interest in Winnicott, outside Britain his theories and terms had been widely misunderstood for many years. This was true even in the anglophone United States, with its thriving and productive atmosphere in all matters psychoanalytic.

There are relevant exceptions to this assertion: Grolnik and Barking have contributed a lot to the revaluation of Winnicott contribution in the States. Unfortunately for limited space sake I can't, even briefly, discuss their contribution.

In the same line from Australia Margaret Boyle Spelman contributed with a set of books on Winnicott and his *oeuvre*. We met in São Paulo and Paris on the occasion of two meetings organized by Professor Zeljco Loparic, who also founded an International

Winnicott Association. So, Brazil and Argentina as well show an increasing interest in the work of Winnicott, sometimes with relevant contributions.

This rapid – all too concise – bird's eye view of the surprising spread of Winnicott's thought in vast areas of psychoanalytic world after years of near-silence does not diminish the fact that the cornerstone of the deepening of Winnicott's thought is firmly located in Europe and in part of the United States, primarily for the language – however idiosyncratic his English was – and then because Winnicott was a central figure of the mainstream of psychoanalysis, never abandoning the foundations of psychoanalytic thought. It could be said that Winnicott has two inalienable characteristics: he was one of the major figures of the English independent tradition and he was unique.

It was through the filial devotion and affection of Masud Khan, who edited some collections of Winnicott's work, that order was introduced into Winnicott's writings.

Anyone who has had the privilege – as I have, thanks to Dr. Giannakoulas – of reading some of the correspondence between the two men can see Masud Khan's critical acuity in encouraging Winnicott to clarify his concepts before publishing them. Khan advised Winnicott not to present one of his last papers at the Freudian Society of New York, where Khan felt it would be widely misunderstood and severely criticized. This did in fact happen and caused a deep narcissistic wound in Winnicott, who was already suffering from a heart condition that required him to be admitted to Bellevue Hospital in New York before being able to return to London.

The articulation and complexity of this paper has yet to be understood, in my view, in terms of its implications for new paths in psychoanalysis being opened up in the future. Since that time, after being wounded, Winnicott's health gradually declined, even though he continued to work until his death.

Clare Winnicott quotes in a fragment from Winnicott's diary: "Prayer: Oh God, may I be alive when I die." This phrase can be linked to Winnicott's well-known statement: "In doing psychoanalysis, I aim at keeping alive, keeping well, and keeping awake. I aim at being myself and behaving myself" (1962, p. 285). The presence of the psychoanalyst, of the mother with her child, was fundamental for Winnicott even as an adult: he implored to be present at his death.

The last volume of *Complete Writings* (Winnicott, 2016) contains two great works by Winnicott, *Human Nature* and *The Piggle*, which were published posthumously. They convey the feeling that Winnicott, who was by then suffering ill-health, had reviewed them over and over, given the abundance of notes in the margins. While reading *The Piggle*, we can observe the interaction between a two-and-a-half-year-old girl, rather troubled by persecutory anxieties due to the birth of her sister, and an elderly Winnicott, who accepted the request from two colleagues to see the troubled little girl. He adopted the approach of *psychotherapy on demand*. Elderly and unwell, we get the impression that this may have been the only clinical work that he could manage, yet he did not hold back. There is a strong feeling that Piggle's liveliness brought out the energy Winnicott still had within himself and that allowed him to respond promptly and with presence.

Notes

1 Masud Khan writes in a note: "This is a revised and an enlarged version of my introduction to the French edition of Winnicott's *Therapeutic Consultation in Child Psychiatry*, which he had wished me to write. I would like to thank J.-B. Pontalis, editor of 'Connaissance de l'Inconscient' (Gallimmard), the series in which this book appeared, for his persistent encouragement which enabled me to get it done. I am indebted to Mrs. Clare Winnicott for reading my text with diligent care and helping me to correct significantly certain imbalances of tone and texture" [p. *XI*].

2 All the authors referred to above have written more than the books quoted, as shown on the book *Reading Italian Psychoanalysis*. For brevity's sake I mention only the those which I consider more relevant to me.

3 His ample and deep culture was impressive. He was more than an academic expert in Greek philosophy, which he quoted in ancient Greek: Thales, Anaximander, Anaximenes, Socrates, Plato, Aristoteles.

References

Abram, J. (2007). *The Language of Winnicott*. London: Karnac.

Bion, W.R. (1967). Second thoughts. Selected papers in psychoanalysis. In: *The Complete Works of Wilfred R Bion*, Volume 6. Edited by Chris Mawson. London: Karnac, 2014.

Bollas, C. (1987). *The Shadow of the Object*. London: Free Associations Books.
_____ (1995). *Cracking up: The Work of Unconscious Experience*. New York: Hill and Wang.
_____ (2007). *The Freudian Moment*. London: Karnac.
_____ (2016). Foreword. In: *The Complete Writings of Donald W. Winnicott*, Volume 6. Edited by L. Caldwell & H. Taylor Robinson. Oxford: Oxford University Press, 2016.

Borgogno, F., Luchetti, A. & Coe, L. M. (eds.) (2016). *Reading Italian Psychoanalysis*. Abingdon: Routledge.

Caldwell, L. & Joyce, A. (1991). *Reading Winnicott*. London: Routledge.

Ferruta, A. (2016). Themes and developments in psychoanalytic thought in Italy. In: *Reading Italian Psychoanalysis*. Edited by Borgogno, F., Luchetti, A. & Coe, L. M. Abingdon: Routledge.

Giannakoulas, A. (2010). *La Tradizione Psicoanalitica Britannica Indipendente*. Roma: Borla.

Green, A. (2005). *Play and Reflection in Donald Winnicott Writings. The Donald Winnicott Memorial Lecture*. London: Routledge.

Grolnick, SA. & Barkin, L. (eds.) (1978). *Between Reality and Fantasy: Transitional Objects and Phenomena*. Lanham MD, Aronson.

Jacobs, T. J. (2013). *The Possible Profession*. Hove: Routledge.

Khan, M. (1975). Introduction. In: Winnicott, D. W. *Through Pediatrics to Psychoanalysis, Collected Papers*. London, Karnac, 1975.

Nettleton, S. (2017). *The Metapsychology of Christopher Bollas: An Introduction*. Abingdon: Routledge.

Ogden, T. (2012). *Creative Readings: Essays on Seminal Analytic Works*. Hove, Routledge.

Parsons, M. (2000). *The Dove that Returns, The Dove that Vanishes: Paradox and Creativity in Psychoanalysis*. London: Routledge.

Phillips, A. (1988). *Winnicott*. Harmondsworth: Penguin Books, 2007.

Poland, W. S. (2018). *Intimacy and Separateness in Psychoanalysis*. Abingdon: Routledge.

Smith, H. (2000). Countertransference, conflictual listening and analytic object relationship. *J. Am. Psychoanal. Assn.*, 48:95–128.

Winnicott, D. W. (1945). Primitive Emotional Development. In: *Through Paediatrics to Psycho-Analysis*. London: Hogarth/Inst. of Psychoanalysis, 1975.
_____ (1947). Hate in countertransference. In: *The Complete Writings of Donald W. Winnicott*, Volume 5. Edited by L. Caldwell & H. Taylor Robinson. Oxford: Oxford University Press, 2016.
_____ (1955). Clinical varieties of transference. In: *The Complete Writings of Donald W. Winnicott*, Volume 4. Oxford: Oxford University Press, 2016.

_____ (1960). Ego distortion in terms of true and false self. In: *The Complete Writings of Donald W. Winnicott*, Volume 6. Edited by L. Caldwell & H. Taylor Robinson. Oxford: Oxford University Press, 2016.

_____ (1962). The aim of psychoanalytic treatment. In: *The Complete Writings of Donald D. Winnicott*, Volume 6. Edited by L. Caldwell & H. Taylor Robinson. Oxford: Oxford University Press, 2016.

_____ (1968b). The use of an object and relating through identifications. In *Playing and Reality*. London: Tavistock, 1971, pp. 86–94.

_____ (1969). The use of an object and relating through identifications. In *Playing and Reality*. London: Tavistock, 1971, pp. 86–94.

_____ (1978). DWW: A reflection. In: *Between Reality and Fantasy: Transitional Objects and Phenomena*. Edited by S. A. Grolnik. New York: Aronson.

_____ (2016). *The Complete Writings of Donald D. Winnicott*, Volume 6. Edited by L. Caldwell & H. Taylor Robinson. Oxford: Oxford University Press.

1

TRANSFERENCE BEFORE
TRANSFERENCE

Scene 1. Paola. A Tuesday in March, not long after 6:30 pm, some years ago

Paola arrives on time as usual. It is the first session of the week. She is 38 years old, an only daughter, and has an elder brother. She has recently separated on a trial basis from her boyfriend, with whom she had a son who is now a year and a half old. The child is mostly cared for by her parents, who retired early. She is a teacher in a middle school.

Paola begins to speak softly of "the most important thing" that happened to her and bothered her over the weekend. Her child, Luca, with whom she could finally spend some time (she also feels like an inadequate, immature mother), "moved into the background ... it was as though he didn't exist. I behaved like I was in a trance, and only now and then was a little bit there."

She told me she had felt great discomfort in regard to Luigi, a school colleague of hers, with whom she seemed to be able to "construct a sentimental story." The principal chose her to accompany the students to a school camp in Northern Italy for almost the whole week. "By the way," she said hurriedly, "next week I won't be here for at least three sessions ... unless you might be nice enough to move my session from Friday to Saturday."

She felt bad, she said, because Luigi would have been the obvious choice to go to the school camp, given that he is a male and the physical education teacher, and without a doubt he is nicer in the

 DOI: 10.4324/9781003228332-2

boys' eyes. But the principal, "on one of her whims," seemed to have thought it would be better for Paola, a woman, to spend "especially the nights – in the hotel," with the children. "You know how parents are ... Maybe something would happen, and we'd be in the middle of it ... A woman is more attentive to certain things ... and then with these stories of molestations ... the principal will have thought of that."

But this wasn't what tormented Paola. It was the look Luigi fixed on her, amazed, waiting for her to say it was his turn, that in any case he was more suited. And in contrast, she remained silent and tried to avoid Luigi's gaze. She nodded obediently to the principal, like a schoolgirl, but inside she felt happy: happy to be free for a week, free of Luigi, who was a "bit of a bore," free from her parents and from Luca, too. She imagined the joy, the relaxation, of being able to smoke in peace, without being judged by Luigi, the health fanatic, or by her parents. But afterwards she felt like a worm for having "stolen" Luigi's place, for not having uttered a single word, for having rejoiced at what the principal said. She had also felt guilty in relation to me, because of the skipped analysis, but then she thought that wasn't really so serious, and of course I would understand her need.

Many characters and themes (Bollas, 1995; Ferro, 1996; 1999) presented themselves in my mind: the principal, the children, the parents, adolescent sexuality, molestations, phallic competition, the need to be alone (a withdrawal from the transference?). Inevitably, I could not be anything other than selective (the *selected facts* of which Britton and Steiner [1994] speak), about what I feel to be most meaningful to me, partly based on previous themes that I cannot specify here for brevity's sake.

Consequently, after listening to her words, I began to formulate an initial comment about what she had told me, then said, "certainly, you are using the analyst, supposing that he is on your side, in order to mitigate your sense of guilt, because you think he is 'understanding your needs,' but of course this is what you like to think ... in order to keep him on your side, an ally." Then I was interrupted by a loud, unexpected, and annoying ringing at the main entrance to the building.

That certainly doesn't concern me, I thought immediately. It might be a mistake, or the patient who sees my colleague with whom I share the office. But as far as I know there is no patient whom she sees at this hour. Besides, I continued to myself, we have staggered hours precisely to avoid overlapping each other ... it must be the janitor … that creep who, since we're getting close to Easter is being especially accommodating. He delivers books that arrive for me instead of leaving them with my colleague, as he has been told, because he knows I will definitely be in the office and thinks he'll pocket a more generous tip. He thinks he's clever, he does! He's like the mayors of the Christian Democrat party, who repair the streets on the eve of the election so they will gain more votes. He thinks that he will extract some big bills, much higher than customary. But he's a pain, let's face it. I'll reduce his tip rather than increasing it! People like him understand only through actions.

These were my *free associations,* or *countertransference thoughts,* those that, in an illusion, we would like to think of as always focused on the patient but have an "evocative resonance once disentangled from the analyst's accumulated thoughts"[1] (Fabozzi, 2002).

The janitor was not only the real janitor, the man of flesh and blood, but also my 'internal janitor,' who was having some difficulty filtering all this psychic material coming from the patient and the annoying and unexpected doorbell. This internal janitor certainly corresponded to the character in an unconscious script who doesn't do his duty and *represented* a deficit or a failure in my capacity to contain and give a preliminary meaning to the material.

While I was preoccupied with these thoughts, the famed *evenly hovering attention,* the much-exalted *reverie* of the analyst, was lost.

Listening, as Smith (2000) clearly says, is like every other psychic formation, a compromise. The analyst's listening certainly cannot escape the inexorable *work of the unconscious,* and at times – one could say ironically – the compromise is more in the analyst's favor than in the patient's!

I tried to get back on the same wavelength as the patient. I said, "Certainly, it is difficult to tolerate the feeling of having taken something away from Luigi … also to have done it without intending to, but maybe you feel so guilty because, deep down, you rejoiced a little: the principal preferred you to Luigi. Luigi is always in the middle of things and believes he is 'the cool one,' as you say … an athlete, a health nut, an ecologist, one who is always kind to children … and then there is the possibility of your taking a vacation from the analysis, well protected by the excuse of the greater necessity of work …"

Just as I was concluding my comment there was a second, then a third, loud ringing of the bell downstairs. I became irritated. *Who the hell is it?* I thought. *Is it possible that he doesn't understand? If someone doesn't answer a bell, they're not in, right? It's not rocket science.* Then it occurred to me that it could be the priest who wants to bless the house for the coming Easter festivities. *He carries on with his duties ... and is a pain in the neck to people who are working ... for heaven's sake! ... He can ring for as long as he wants... he'll figure out that some atheists live here ... I'm not going to open the door ... he'll get tired in the end.*

All this went through my mind, while my irritation increased together with my inevitable distancing of myself from Paola's narrative.

"Maybe it's someone who wants you," Paola said. "I wonder ... a messenger, the janitor ... maybe something serious has happened to your children." (*She wants to reassure me and instead makes me more anxious, I thought.*) "... maybe it's a mistake – maybe you made an appointment that got forgotten. Go answer it, don't worry about me."

In a falsely calm way, I answered: "there's no need, it must be an error, nothing to worry about, it will stop sooner or later." But then, after only a few seconds, given that the bell continued to ring, I contradicted myself. I became *disorganized*, just as Paola's narration was getting progressively more disorganized. Standing up from my chair, I said: "I'm very sorry, perhaps you are right. It's better to answer ... otherwise we risk having our eardrums perforated. It must be an error ... it's better to go and see."

I went to the intercom and said, "Yes?" clearly irritated, though I tried to control my tone. From the other end of the line a very loud masculine voice said, "I am Stampeder, Massimo Stampeder[2]... I have an appointment with Dr Bonaminio for 6:30. Excuse me, Doctor, I couldn't find the correct main door, will you let me in? Shall I come up? What floor are you on?"

"No, no!" I said. "The appointment is for 6:30 p.m. *tomorrow*, Wednesday. Wednesday at 6:30, I had told you ... Do you remember? Wednesday at 6:30." I felt like a boring old professor or an office clerk. I over-articulated the syllables: *Wed-nes-day.*

I did not even have time to finish my sentence before I noticed that Stampeder had already gone away. Perhaps he left with his tail between his legs, full of shame, or perhaps was furious at me, which became apparent in his own tortured analysis.

When I sat down once again, and attempted to resume our interrupted conversation, Paola said she understood my irritation and tried to console me. "It can happen, what do you expect?" she said.

"Mistakes can be made ... at any rate, it didn't bother me ... don't worry about it."

She spoke in a manic way, as though she were responsible for the event and wanted to placate the "furious mother." Then she added, and here really infuriated me: "Poor guy, he felt excluded, who knows how bad he feels about it ... I have nothing to do with it, I know; this is my hour ... but I feel guilty, as though I had taken his place ... but look here – this is my hour, and I'm thinking I've done something wrong to him! ... I'm strange, aren't I?"

I thought to myself, but look here at you, worrying so much about the poor guy, after you've just told me that you treated that other poor fellow, Luigi, like an old rag.

Contact with the patient was recovered, despite my 'hate in the countertransference' (Winnicott, 1947), which I recognized as objective, felt towards Paola and the unknown 'Stampeder.' This was not something one or the other of them made me feel, like the projection of their anger or aggression; however, a few minutes passed before I felt that the strong emotions were quietening down, so I was able to speak to her in a tone that seemed coherent and calm.

"Well, it is as though that person were Luigi, from whom you felt you had stolen a place even though you didn't want to. But profiting from a situation that was to his disadvantage made you feel guilty ... a little like now, when you feel guilty because of the person you imagine pacing around furiously downstairs, like a *beaten wolf*.[3] It is your hour, certainly, and this mistake has nothing to do with you; just as the principal's decision had nothing to do with you. But it is difficult for you to tolerate being the 'privileged one,' the 'chosen one' ... and who among us would not like to be 'that chosen one,' without, however, feeling the guilt of having taken away that place from someone else, perhaps a brother? It seems to me that this may be a plausible motivation for your otherwise incomprehensible sense of guilt. Your sense of commonality with Luigi, who remained excluded, and with that 'poor guy,' that you imagine wandering around downstairs."

Thus, I based my interpretation, like a 'selected fact,' on sibling rivalry *for* the mother. Is there an explanation for this? I mean: is there an explanation for the fact that I chose an interpretation to do with sibling rivalry, which had never appeared in her history or in

25

her relationship with me up to that point? I commented on rivalry with a brother whom I knew nothing about. Is there an explanation for the fact that I chose precisely that complex link in Paola's narration in response to the intrusions of Massimo Stampeder? It was as if the analyst were unconsciously acting as a bridge between two patients who of course didn't know each other.

The fact that countertransference may precede transference, preorganize and structure it, is a notion that was put forward a long time ago in psychoanalytic literature by some, although not many psychoanalysts. But more extreme is to say that understanding a patient's transference may be guided, however casually, *by the analyst's transference feelings toward another patient,* one who hasn't yet presented himself. Going even further, this common experience among three protagonists may have modelled – without the analyst knowing it – the second patient's transference, which was in turn modelled by the countertransference reaction of the analyst who was disturbed in his relationship with the first patient – with Paola, in the situation I've just described.

We see that, early on, the positions and attitudes of all the participants can be outlined with a certain precision. Each character takes various positions, without anyone yet knowing what kind of drama is being played out.

Reflections from 'behind the scenes'

The expression 'understanding the transference' is particularly apt because it definitively shifts the emphasis onto the analyst's predisposition to welcome what is not seen, if one is not predisposed to welcome it; in that case, it doesn't exist.[4]

That the countertransference may be a 'reply' to the patient's transference is, we might say, a useful fiction for psychoanalytic work. On an epistemological level, however, I maintain that this does not mean that the statement that "countertransference always precedes transference" is, so to speak, ontologically true. This is because, once the psychoanalytic process is set in motion, the receptive quality of the countertransference is, in effect, a way of welcoming, of modelling what the patient brings. Here, however, we are talking about the origins of the transference, and – however difficult it is to explain this and to understand it in depth – how it is structured by the analyst's countertransference. Without a doubt we owe to the *British independent tradition* in particular (Heimann, 1949/1950; Little, 1951; Winnicott, 1957; Racker, 1968) the identification of the analyst's countertransference as a priority – that is, as a basic position that precedes transference.

I intend to emphasize how this interpretation of sibling rivalry given to my patient was perhaps driven by an *unconscious attractor* (the 'psychic intensities' of both the patient's and the analyst's unconscious, of which Bollas (1995) speaks). In the *avant-coup,* this unconscious attractor anticipates, so to speak, a theme that will be present at a later point, much later in Massimo Stampeder's narration, a theme that seems to "look at the original scene through the *nachträglich* sight of a second period that refers to the first, attributes to it meaning, and in it finds its own meaning"[5] (Marion, 2010). As I emphasized some time ago (Bonaminio, 2004) I am speaking of that unpredictable and unavoidable *presentation* of the unconscious in intersubjective communication, of the emergence of the id from within us, which Freud described in its multi-faceted appearances in 'Jokes and Their Relation to the Unconscious' (1905).

More in general, I am referring to that *unconscious communication* between two subjects, which lies at the base of psychoanalytic work: that is, a direct communication *from one unconscious to another.* Without a doubt, this type of unconscious communication corresponds to conceptions of projective and interjective identification rooted in the theory of object relations (Bollas, 1995). We might think of Freud's metaphor of radio equipment that receives a transmission or of his statement that the unconscious of one person can react to the unconscious of another while eluding consciousness.

The current concept of the analyst's *dreaming activity* (Winnicott's "unending dreaming," Khan's "dreaming Ego," and Bion's "reverie") are nothing other than, if anything, an accentuation and a re-evaluation of this type of communication, returning to *dreaming* the centrality that Freud assigned it. More recently, Bollas (1995) described this complex psychic movement as a sort of *countertransference dreaming,* and Ferro has elaborated (since 1999) the concept of *oneiric activity* in the waking state of the analysand and the analyst in the consulting room. Bollas captures this process in extremely evocative words:

Freud's unconscious receiver, the dream set of countertransference, processes the patient's unconscious communications on its own terms: one dreamer to another. Dreaming the analysand during the hour, bringing the patient to another place, transformed into other persons, events, and places, the analyst *unconsciously* deconstructs – displaces, condenses, substitutes the patient.

(1995, p. 12, italics in original)

Following Bollas's argument, which seems to me particularly enlightening, we can say that the patient "senses that he contributes to the analyst's dreaming, affecting the analyst's unconscious but not reaching his consciousness as such – so privacy is assured" (Bollas, 1995, p. 15). As Freud wrote, "the *Ucs.* is alive and capable of development ... accessible to the impressions of life" (1915, p. 190). And on the "visibility of the unconscious," on its concreteness and the transformation in metaphor, Bion expressed himself as follows (Quoted in Resnik, 2006):

> The unconscious is a notion that is often mystified, considered unreal and immaterial; but for me, in contrast, the unconscious exists and is real, real and alive like a tree. The globality of the tree is made up not only of what appears to the observer, but also includes what is underground, the roots.

In the analytic situation, both the protagonists "are in fact *developing the unconscious,* creating a theatre for its enactment, providing a safe place for its plays, and thereby increasing its effectiveness in the therapeutic process" (Bollas, 1995, p. 16, italics in original).

One could ask why I affirm, together with Bollas, that this augments the efficacy of the therapeutic process. This is relevant because the communication that is achieved between the two (or more) unconscious minds detaches, so to speak, the individual's unconscious from his fixations, mobilizing in one and the other, the tendency to present and to know each other. One could say in this 'secure' place the *analytic ecology* constitutes for both patient and analyst, the two 'beasts', paraphrasing Bion, who come out of the lairs in which they have been curled up, believing themselves protected. They study each other, scrutinize each other, and get to know each other, and precisely because of this, they change the positions they were in. They see themselves in the other; they reflect each other; and in this reflection they acquire knowledge about each other and specific aspects of themselves.

The centrality of the mirror function – described fundamentally by Winnicott (1967), even before by Lacan (1949), then by Kohut (1971), and most recently conceptually extended in the same way to psychotherapy by Wright (1991) – cannot be undervalued as an unconscious communication. As Resnik (2006, p. 28) observed, Winnicott's mirror is a "mirror that speaks, as in fairy tales. In a certain way, Bion's idea of reverie is already present in Winnicott."[6]

The act of mirroring is thus a way through which the unconscious works and puts itself into contact with the other, *before* it places itself in relation to the other. It is a transference in the sense of a transfer of the unconscious, which happens *before* the transference as the unfolding of an object relationship. I will return to this topic later, claiming, so to speak, the priority and the primacy of primary identification[7] with respect to projective identification.[8]

Scene 2. Some central aspects of the analysis of Massimo Stampeder

My having referred to this patient as a beaten *wolf* instead of the more common expression, a beaten *dog,* is a clear irruption of the unconscious onto the earlier scene. We will follow this beaten wolf that appears suddenly and ends up being Massimo. As a matter of fact, Massimo was a beaten wolf in the communications he brought to analysis; many times, his bitter, resentful, irritated, and conflictual narration took the form of the following words: "I can't take it anymore, I can't take always being slapped in the face by everyone, being beaten."

Isn't it impressive that an adjective and a noun that have been put together in an unusual way – *beaten wolf* – disarticulating the "logic of the sequence" (Bollas, 1987), or better, the logic of semantics, *may forecast* something of which nothing is yet known? And that, furthermore, this forecast pertains to Paola's experience and certainly not to Massimo, who in that moment was merely the one who, demanding and insistent, rang the bell and felt himself excluded, expelled, rejected – anticipating in a traumatized way his basic problem, repeating it outside and *before the transference?*

It was certainly not in doubt that the analyst, subjected to the intense emotional turbulence aroused in him, identified with Massimo *before meeting him.* But Paola made a link in some way, became a *transponder* between two unconscious minds – if we accept the Freudian metaphor of the radio receiver (1915). My unconscious presented itself and, without my knowledge, caused me to represent Massimo as a wolf – a figure that came to me directly in the transference, in the improvised *mise en scene*.

Actually, in the *après-coup*, Massimo's transference toward me was frequently colored by ferocious tones, which re-enacted a very old anger toward the object and the primary environment, both in the here-and-now of the individual session, and in certain phases of the psychoanalytic relationship.

One could visualize the analysis with Massimo as the shore at which a shipwreck victim lands, exhausted, tossed by the ocean's waves. This shore constitutes at the same time both the place where he can deposit his original traumatic, unrepresentable experience, and the only possibility of transforming these primitive and raw elements – of rejection, of expulsion – and of elaborating them, thus rendering them human. But it is not an easy task either for him or for the analyst, because every act that happens on this shore contains both these aspects – that is, the *unthought known* that Bollas (1987) speaks of, and the *symptom of hope* described by Winnicott (1957).

Caught between Scylla and Charybdis, that is, between his incessant search for a fusional experience (which also implies his feeling influenced and thus taken over by the analyst, as though by the mother whom he had been idolizing and idolized by [Bollas, 1987; 1989]) and his experience of being violently expelled, Massimo was without doubt the most difficult and demanding patient I had in analysis during this period. In particular, the undifferentiated mass of mental content that he put forth in an almost delirious way was extremely difficult to disentangle from the good fusional aspects, narcissistically nourished, which were generative of growth for the self. I felt that this deliriousness placed him at risk of a malignant regression that Balint (1968) speaks of.

Then, in the course of one of my interpretations, the patient felt himself 'disproved.' The event is literally a trifle and, in my view, had no such meaning. Massimo came to the session, angry as usual with his father, who kept on finding jobs for him that Massimo considered demeaning. This time, his father has managed to put him into a group of candidates for the position of assistant to a famous Italian politician, about to found a new party. He said he was not ready for this offer and was not dressed for the interview, as he was wearing a sweater and not a suit. My comment was, "I don't think showing up in a tie is a 'must' to impress in a job interview." But I couldn't even finish my sentence before he stood up from the couch, enraged, and said in a very violent way, "I always knew you were a Communist pig, like all you analysts!" I was startled by this unpredicted reaction. His anger increased and he threw his wallet at me, which bounced off an old radio behind me that I keep as a very beloved memory of my past. At the beginning of the analysis, he had noticed it, appreciating and envying it. He went towards the radio, lifted it with one hand. I was afraid that he wanted to throw it at me; however, he only wanted to recover his wallet that this time was thrown with disgust at my feet, as if to say *you are only interested in money, you pig Communist!* and he left the room, slamming the door.

During his sudden explosion of violence, I felt somatic fear, which I managed to contain and limit. Progressively I calmed down, even though I feared he may come back, even more aggressive than before. Finally, I was able to achieve, could realise, that my comment was felt by the patient, *de facto,* as an intolerable separating maneuver: one of my violent evacuations of him that repeated his expulsion from "earthly paradise," or the regressively idealized mind and body of his mother on account of her pregnancy and the sister who had replaced him.

In his next session, surprisingly he turned up. I opened the door and he looked exactly like a "beaten dog," staring at his feet and breathing heavily. He crossed the door without saying a word and went directly to the couch. I sat down quietly on my armchair, silent for a while, and then I had a serendipitous, inspired *interpretation,* like those Meltzer (1978) speaks of. I said a little anxiously: "We shared a big fear the other time …" His first reaction was a sudden quieting of his heavy breathing. I added, "Yesterday we both felt a great fear of what was happening to us, a fear that could not be expressed in any other way." After this communication of a shared sentiment, it was possible for Massimo to accept the interpretation of the event and its significance, which became the dominant theme for the subsequent period of the analysis. However, apart from the contents of the interpretive work that was activated, what seems important to me to emphasize was the transformation of a fusional fantasy, almost delusional, into a common experience, starting from the sharing of a basic emotion like fear. I don't think I have ever felt, in analysis with a patient, such a vivid sense of a "shared mutative experience" (Giannakoulas, 1996). The situation of almost reaching a breaking point, precisely because it was emotionally contained and rendered thinkable, can gradually transform a regressive symbiosis that risks becoming malignant into a good fusional experience that maintains the tie, and in the meantime nurtures the separative processes as well.

Transference, as Winnicott writes in his paper (1956), *puts forward again, in toto,* the subject's unconscious movements and positions toward the object and environment, but also the unconscious positions of the object and the environment toward the subject. Transference, then, is a *staging* of the totality of the primal scene, and contains perhaps more than the subject's unconscious positions (Klein) – but also its unconscious reactions, its adaptations to the object's impingements and failures. It *reveals* and, in some way, contains fragments of the object's unconscious, too (Winnicott). There is, then, a way of communicating *something of the unconscious of the other through the intermediary of the unconscious of the subject,* which, so to speak, contains it.

On a technical level, this is related to the fundamental question already posed in the early 1950s by Paula Heimann (1949/1950): "Who speaks in this moment in the session, who is the patient speaking for, and to whom is he speaking?"

Having contemplated the first and second scenes – in *après-coup,* of course – one could ask oneself: Was Massimo's transference, what was brought into my presence with that irruption and will then be *represented* in the transference of the psychoanalytic relationship, revealing itself? Or, alternatively, was the *unfolding of the transference* already predetermined by my response to the patient's violent eruption? Was this a sort of Bionian *pre-conception* that subsequently found its actualization in the transference, and influenced it from the beginning?

The unconscious thus presents itself via an irruption and is represented in the transference through displacement and condensation. Both are forms of transferring, of transporting. One chooses the short path, irrupting, highly irrational, with disorganizing and 'traumatogenic' effects; the other, the path of the object relationship, of concealment, of innermost meanings, of displacement and condensation. But there is a transference before the transference, which precedes it and probably gives to it form, even if the first is shapeless and not formulable.

For many years (from the middle 1980s onward), I have been interested in the mysteries of this *work of the unconscious* that deposits into the child something to be worked through that belongs to the parents and to the preceding generation. Certainly, the transgenerational challenge is complex, not so much because we are amazed that psychic contents can be transmitted from one generation to another, but more because we still know little about how this happens, how it is accomplished, and by which means.

Many think of projective identification in this context, a concept that by now is omnipresent and ubiquitous. Now, however, I am convinced that these phenomena are better explained by *primary identification* – which pours content into the adjacent other by contiguity, the "osmotic pressure" (Rosenfeld, 1987 of the mother-fetus (child) intra- and extra- uterine proximity. Frances Tustin had elaborated the same concept in terms of *a flowing over at oneness* (1981). I have intentionally introduced the theme of the trans-generational because the temporal leap of unelaborated psychic elements implicit in it, is analogous in some way to the leap of emotional contents that bounced back and forth in the triangle made up of Paola, Massimo, and myself.

None of the 'actors' in the first scene knew about this. Indeed, like Massimo's finger on the intercom, and like Massimo Stampeder himself – who pushed his way in to communicate something to the analyst, to take a space and a time that was not his – these elements are 'acted out,' so to speak, by the unconscious: which is a kind of undesired, or perhaps no-longer-desired, guest. This 'no-longer-desired or undesired' element is Massimo's vexation, his central theme, a theme that will gradually unfold.

Let us go back now to the Massimo Stampeder of the second scene, in order to give further meaning to the story: some years later, when his analysis was in full swing and there were no shortage of tensions, which were sharp, at times intolerable, then receded, thanks to some ameliorative *coup de foudre*, his or mine; but when they happened, it seemed that everything was falling apart, that there was no hope.

I would say that Massimo, more than being a handsome young man, tall, athletic, with the broad shoulders of a swimmer and the hands of a rugby player (all sports he played with success, but not enough to move him to the national level, a source of anger and depression) was huge. He aroused something close to timidity in me when he stood up to leave at the end of the session, after a verbal battle. The attacks on me could be violent and contemptuous, when he felt he could not be understood, not loved, not wanted, treated like an old rag, even if nothing in my behavior or my words toward him could make him think that. But then there was always something that, little by little, he managed to find inside me, and he pulled it out with impertinence, almost as though to say: *You see? What did I tell you? You can't stand me, we are not the same thing, it's all a fraud, you want to send me away!*

In a dream, Massimo represented me as an overstuffed glutton in a restaurant by the sea, accompanied by a woman who was rather attractive but a little overweight. In his associations, the woman is my patient who has the session immediately prior to his (not Paola), and who he imagines is very seductive; doubtless I "let everything pass" with her, while with him I am inflexible. This is his fantasy. I am such a glutton in the dream that, when I get up from the table, the change of position makes me burp so violently that not only does everyone turn around, but the building in which the restaurant is located vibrates to the point of being uprooted from the ground. In actuality, in the previous session, I had felt exhausted by his attacks on me for some wrongdoing that I had committed. I had gone to the bathroom almost to liberate myself from this feeling and had inadvertently burped slightly, which, however, set me right again. In subsequent sessions, he effectively did nothing other than to surface and call to my attention all the intonations in my speech that allowed a certain light irritation to leak out, of which I became aware only thanks to him.

In the transference, Massimo felt harshly treated, even though there was no trace of that at first glance. He began to juxtapose me with his mother, to call me "Mrs. Grim," as he and his sister had called their mother because she was always rough in her manners. When he injured his knee as a child, there was "an energetic rubbing with alcohol," after which he was simply sent away again, "never with an affectionate gesture." With Giulia, his sister – needless to say – things were different. Their mother would still take care of the basics without sentimentality, but from a mile away, one could see that she admired her daughter much more than her son, even though she used to say that he was "a big boy" who "would go far in life." In reality, he began analysis because he felt blocked in his studies, he had violent and continual quarrels with his family, and his relationship with his girlfriend was of the "on and off" type; he could not keep her because he did not feel loved, yet he could not even begin to think of letting her go her own way because he felt "stuck to her like glue."

34

The siblings had been treated like twins, but they were not. In Massimo's third month of life, his mother became pregnant with Giulia. Not only in the narration of what had been recounted to him and that formed part of the "family culture," but also in bodily sensations, in what Klein calls *memories in feeling* (1956), Massimo reported in the transference the insult of having to pass from a state of total narcissistic investment on the mother's part to a sharp interruption of this "special attention." His detection of a variation, even a minimal one, of attention, or of a different tone of voice in me, re-enacted *in toto* this situation of immediate, unmotivated dethronement.

In that violent intrusion into my session with Paola, in mistaking the day of his appointment, Massimo had reproduced his sense of someone else being preferred to him. His unconscious had selected – with care, one might say – the other actors he might bring into the scene: the analysand Paola (his sister Giulia), and the mother-analyst locked in an intimate relationship that excluded him. Vain were his attempts to undermine that awful fusion in which the mother, throwing him out, had installed his sister in his place. *It's me, Massimo Stampeder. I was here first!* he seemed to shout into the intercom, because that place *had been* his. The 'fear of breakdown,' acted out in order to confront something that in reality *had happened,* is fundamental for understanding this order of phenomena described by Winnicott (1963). Because of this, Massimo had come early, on the wrong day: to present me with his central problem, the drama of his life, the crack in his existence. On that 'stage with many entrances,' to paraphrase Laplanche and Pontalis (1968), which is the primal scene, the arrangements among the characters are varied: Paola and I are Giulia and the mother, who enjoy each other and exclude him; Paola is the usurper of his place; and it is Giulia who has come to distract the mother from her total narcissistic investment, which he enjoyed in a fusional regressive fantasy. But Paola and I, in the *intimate room*, are also Massimo himself and his mother, *fused into togetherness.* And onto the stage of that scene he hurled the *presentation* of the traumatic agent as well, the agent by which he was attacked and from which he has never recovered; that is, Massimo himself has become the traumatic agent in order to control it.

The twin ship that was offered in the mother's narrative ("I've always treated you equally, like twins") was both an attempt to make amends and inadequate, given that there were two children to bring up, who were as demanding as they were idealized. To Massimo's mind this was a "fraud." It was a fraud because there shouldn't have been any equality, no distributive justice, given that *what he had was taken away from him,* and who would ever compensate him for this? It wasn't even recognized, so he could forget any hope of getting a compensation.[9]

I am putting into the form of a narrative tale what was actually, over the course of the analysis, interpreted to him in the transference. Indeed, I could say that interpretation was the discovery of this reality, or rather a *creation together with the patient,* of a psychic reality that triggered the appearance of *memories in feelings* (Klein, 1957), buried beneath the surface of existence.

Giulia and Massimo were beautiful children and then beautiful adolescents, in everyone's eyes: full of health, athletic, but Giulia – who participated in all the same sports that Massimo did – had that special touch, that higher level of class, in the opinion of their mother (who did not withhold severe judgments and was not given to faking appreciation). These special traits were seen as missing in Massimo, even though he was very competent; they were what rendered Giulia's dance one of fluid harmony, made her skiing descents a snowy lacework, her arm strokes in the pool "silken like those of a nymph," her tennis games a graceful and precise ballet. Both of them were first-class athletes, and their mother was a "bundle of muscles even at sixty years of age"; she had been a freestyle champion who had reached national levels. Their father had played for some time in the B series of the soccer national championships and in reality, he had always lived like someone confined in "series B." Massimo himself had not been capable of establishing himself in any sport, even in the ones at which he had succeeded; the expectations were too high and unreachable, and besides his efforts were continually undermined by comparison with his usurper. Massimo truly felt like a failure, rejected, like the uninvited guest at a gala dinner. And wasn't this already present from the beginning, with that loud, inappropriate ringing of the bell that had caused him to be sent away like a beaten dog? Wasn't this a transference before the transference?

Further reflections from behind the scenes, and some conclusions

I maintain the following: that the analyst can be a sort of "healthy carrier" – if he succeeds in remaining such – of a transference that, in the course of the day but also of the week, the month, and so on, flows over him like a rolling, winding river. The analyst offers support, of course; he is the shore of the river, the one who finds in each of his patients a specific variation that has to do with the patient's internal world. These are the "secret passages" between the analysand's unconscious and that of the analyst which Bolognini has written about, sometimes poetically, and also that "unthought represented," which Bolognini addresses in his paper 'Notes from the Deep' (2009). But this transference, for which the analyst is the shore or the riverbank, is also impregnated by the subsequent transference. In other words, the transference with the first patient inevitably, to a certain extent, gives form to, or influences the transference with the subsequent one.

It seems to me there is some meaningful analogy with what Freud essentially asked himself in his revolutionary essay, 'Inhibitions, Symptoms, and Anxiety' (1925), which changed the theory and technique of psychoanalysis much more radically than we realize.

How is it possible that the ego, not yet formed, may *register* the experiences that it was not capable of registering because the appropriate apparatus to register them had not yet been formed? Those experiences *deform* the ego, which must still be shaped, and nonetheless give it an imprinting, an unmistakable modelling. Winnicott, in 'Ego Distortion in Terms of True and False Self' (1960) gave his answer to this paradox.

Ultimately, we in the same sphere of phenomena that Freud describes in intrapsychic terms, in terms of relationships among the psychic demands that influence each other before they are able to shape themselves and that are deformed as a consequence. And we speak of the same phenomena, paradoxical ones, in intersubjective, interpersonal terms. By we, I mean that contemporary generation of psychoanalysts who are basically connected to Ferenczi, Bion, especially Winnicott, and to Balint and Loewald, and that entire psychoanalytic tradition that at the time made up the "silent revolution" (Ogden, 1992). This includes the way in which the analyst cares for the patient, thinking of him jointly though not symmetrically, as a *subject of analysis*, to paraphrase Ogden (1994).

Presentation and representation meet and face each other at different places and times – associated, aligned, it might be said – by the analyst's presence. The analyst functions as an intermediary who needs a certain lapse of time so that what irrupts unknowingly may be represented in the unfolding of the transference, in the construction of the psychoanalytic relationship. There, it can be noticed, understood, and perhaps interpreted (Winnicott, 1967). Certainly, we cannot free ourselves from this paradox of *two differ-ent forms of unconscious communication,* of two different methods of unconscious work. I am speaking in this case, for example, of a pure coincidence, because what is impressive is this simultaneous impact of the same core element, but in different forms and different areas, spatially and temporally.

"Psyche is extended; knows nothing about it," one of Freud's (1938, p. 300) last statements, and perhaps keeps together this para-dox without thought of resolving it.

What I have intended to discuss above may appear trivial. It is, at any rate, very personal, because it pertains to a challenging question that in my psychoanalytic practice I pose myself all the time, and to which I have been able to give only partial answers.

With the previous example, I tried to offer a preliminary answer to this interrogative: What happens in the space between one ses-sion and the next, when a patient goes away and we analysts, still saturated by what has happened, at times tired or confused or unsat-isfied, or perhaps satisfied with our involvement, give ourselves a moment of respite? What happens in the course of an analytic day, from the analyst's point of view, and how do these happenings influ-ence our capacity to listen? This aspect is scarcely discussed in the literature, as far as I know. Perhaps only Meltzer (1967), has given it some treatment, emphasizing the recursive nature of certain phe-nomena in the psychoanalytic process.

What I would like to underline here, on the other hand, has to do with the corruptions, contaminations, and failures that link one session with another, just as the analyst's mood, his personal wor-ries about health and family, necessarily influence his conduct. I am interested in how these factors predispose one to the appearance of *a transference before transference.* In the course of a day, the analyst finds himself in the middle of a flood of unconsciousness, including his own. At times, they offer a key to understanding the patient, but at other times they massively impede, to the point that various elements cannot be discerned. Besides reverie, besides the *suspension of memory and desire,* this is a position to aim at, but one that is difficult to reach.

So where does this unelaborated, residual material go, the material that, despite our efforts, continues to take up temporary residence in the analyst's consulting room? In part it is expelled, evaporated away

38

with the opening of the windows, but of course, being psychic phenomena, traces remain in the psyche. It is incredible to think "how much unconscious" may pass between the bodies of the analyst and the analysand, how much of an outpouring from one to the other may occur, and how little we are able to say about this very consistent part of unconscious communication.

In recent work, I included an examination of this aspect along with what Winnicott calls the *in-dwelling* of the psyche in the soma. I presented three clinical examples: an autistic child whom I supervised with Frances Tustin about 30 years ago, who became pale, lifeless, and distracted in a particular session because of the traumatic, temporary separation from her mother; an adolescent who had a violent and distressing, persecutory 'dysmorphic' experience with a depersonalizing quality; and a little girl, seen diagnostically, who felt that half of her body, the right side, was slightly but distressingly different. More recently, Lemma (2010) has focused on the importance of the body in psychoanalysis.

Alternatively, one might say that the theory I use has dark areas that do not allow me to really see "that thing there." I use this expression, borrowing it from my analyst, because he used it in a session that impressed me a lot. It was in the second or third year of my analysis when he chose to point out to me an accumulation of "unconscious things" that, if he had started to enumerate, would have been placed into the logical containers of the conscious mind, perhaps a bit obsessively (and I must recognize that I was a little bit obsessive), when they were instead things that should be left in their unconscious state. I must say that this expression gave me a strong feeling in analysis not only of the presence of my unconscious, but also of how my analyst perceived it, and how he was inviting me to see it. He invited me to see it myself – from *his* point of view, that is, being next to me. The *psychoanalytic relationship, the presentation of the unconscious* in the "here and now" of the session, the *unconscious in action* and its interpretation in action, and the *therapeutic alliance* were all together as one in that moment. They were narrated, sewn together with that expression that alluded to something we had encountered days, weeks, months, perhaps years earlier – a subject of my internal world, but not yet *recognized* with that Gestalt immediacy.

When I ran into a phrase of Winnicott's some years later (perhaps after my second analysis had terminated), it seemed to me that the area of experiential phenomena in the session was the same. Winnicott referred to something similar when he wrote of having found, "together with the patient, a satisfactory definition of his true self," which was precisely that which my analyst suggested to me and which both of us immediately grasped, because we both understood that what was "unspeakable" referred to a great many things. Perhaps one could also find what Winnicott, too, had wanted to capture, and what Bion wanted to describe when he used the term and the concept of *consensuality, conviviality,* to which many other analysts have alluded with equal profundity. Here one's thoughts cannot but go to the origins, that is, to the discussion of the "oceanic feeling" Freud [1936] spoke of Romain Roland.

The concept of the unconscious – the laws of its operation within the individual and in relationship with the other – survives and continues to be the supporting axis that distinguishes psychoanalysis from every other theory of human behavior. And we psychoanalysts should continue to look at its methods of operation, the laws that govern it, at condensation and displacement, and the two principal access routes by which it arrives and communicates with us: the *dream* and the *transference*. These are the two royal roads; they continually intersect and are in fact indistinguishable. The dream is also, by definition, transference – a continual transfer of representations and meanings from one layer to another in the mind of the dreamer, and of the analyst who listens to the dream as it is narrated and associates to it, an ongoing translation seeking representations and meanings. Transference is a dream, an oneiric staging, that chooses and deals with its characters, its figures, in the same way that dreaming furnishes the dream, just as playing needs personification in play.

Dreaming and playing as *psychic experiences* are thus interconnected as forms of unconscious manifestation, which at times we almost lose sight of, as though they were different activities, in the same way that transference is nothing other than a dream played out in the space of the analytic consulting room. It is also role playing, dreamed in the presence of the analyst. Incessant unconscious activity is always its origin, and the continual *cracking up* of the work of the unconscious, its *dissemination* (Bollas), is its surging wellspring. However, 150 years after the birth of psychoanalysis, the unconscious is what paradoxically weighs us down in our relationships with patients, because it seeps between us and them, and thus undermines the possibility of our being able to listen, to understand. It enriches us, because it makes us more capable of being able to 'know,' and yet at first it must obscure.

Notes

1 My translation from Italian.
2 The name is a fictitious one, chosen to evoke the feelings induced by his real name.
3 "Beaten dog" is an idiomatic Italian expression to convey the feelings of a frustrated, humiliated person who was unable to react. In this case, I made a slip of tongue and used "wolf" instead of "dog," for reasons that will be made clear later.
4 As a child psychoanalyst, I must refer here to the controversy between Melanie Klein and Anna Freud, and to Klein's (1957) cutting statement that, "Miss Freud says there is no transference in child analysis simply because she doesn't know how to see it." Anna Freud (1931) replied calmly and authoritatively, warning against the traps of a wild transference interpretation with children if it is made in overtly symbolic terms, far from their experience; however, with the distance of years (1965), once she, too, had accepted the existence of transference in child analysis, she stated "I am not convinced" that this transference is identical to what is seen with adults (Di Renzo, 2008). On denying the existence of what one doesn't manage to see, one could think of what Tom Main (1989) stated, that is, that the psychotic is he who cannot find anyone willing to accept his craziness.
5 My translation from Italian.
6 My own translation from the Italian edition.
7 I am referring to the line of thought that spans in particular the later Freud, and that culminates in his famous aphorism that preceding every other form of relationship children like expressing an object-relation by an identification: "I am the object." "Having" is the later relationship of the two. After loss of the object it relapses into "being." Example: the breast. "The breast is a part of me, I am the breast." Only later: "I have it" – that is, "I am not it" (Freud, 1938, p. 299).
8 Giovanna Goretti (2001) wrote exhaustively and persuasively about the development of the concept of projective identification, attributing to it, however, the primacy that I maintain may be pertinent to the mechanism of primary identification. Following the development of Winnicott's thought, I believe projective identification is secondary to a rupture of that primary tie that many authors have described (Winnicott, M. Balint, E. Balint, Little) in terms of sensual coexistence (primary love, fusionality, the basic unit), that is mobilized not to 'simply communicate' but in order to reconstitute (badly) that lost

unity. It is in analysis that this visualization is important, because it puts into play the functioning and quality of the analyst and his capacity to recognize what belongs to him (Winnicott, 1947).

9 The topics that are touched on here were part of Massimo's narration and the analyst's verbal interpretation, which included as well, at a certain point, a reconstructive proposal about this initial episode that only in retrospect could be understood and perhaps interpreted.

References

Balint, M. (1968). *The Basic Fault: Therapeutic Aspects of Regression.* London: Tavistock.

Bollas, C. (1987). *The Shadow of the Object. Psychoanalysis of Unthought Known.* London: Free Association Books.

Bollas, C. (1989). *Forces of destiny. Psychoanalysis and human idiom.* London: Free Association Books.

_____ (1995). *Cracking Up: The Work of Unconscious Experience.* New York: Hill and Wang.

Bolognini, S. (2008). *Secret Passages: The Theory and Technique of Interpsychic Relations.* London: Routledge.

_____ (2009). Notes from the Deep. EPF Bulletin, n. 63, 45–64.

Bonaminio, V. (2004). La persona dell'analista. In: *Forme dell'interpretare. Nuove Prospettive Nella Teoria e Nella Clinica Psicoanalitica. [Forms of Interpreting. New Conceptual Perspectives in Clinical Psychoanalysis.]* Edited by P. Fabozzi. Milano: Angeli, 2004.

Britton, R. & Steiner, J. (1994). Interpretation: Selected fact or overvalued idea. *Int. J. Psychoanal.,* 75:1069–1078.

Di Renzo, M. (2008). "Stare ad aspettare senza impazienza l'evoluzione naturale del transfert, che sorge dalla crescente fiducia del paziente nella tecnica e nella situazione psicoanalitica" Considerazioni sul transfert nella psicoanalisi con i bambini. *Riv. di Psicoanalisi.,* 54:2008.

Fabozzi, P. (2002). Libere associazionei, spazio potenzale e forme evocative. *Riv. di Psicoanalisi.,* 48:437–446.

Freud, A. (1931). *Introduction to Psychoanalysis for Teachers.* Engl. Four lectures in Writings, vol. 1 Translation. London: Allen & Unwin.

_____ (1965). *Normality and pathology in childhood.* The Hogarth Press and the Institute of Psychoanalysis.

Ferro, A. (1996). *In the Analyst's Consulting Room.* Engl. Transl.: London: Routledge, 2002.

_____ (1999). *Psychoanalysis as Therapy and Story Telling.* Engl. Transl.: London: Routledge, 2006.

Freud, S. (1905). Jokes and their relation to the unconscious. *S.E.*, 8.

———— (1915). The unconscious. *S.E.*, 14.

———— (1925). Inhibition, symptom and anxiety. *S.E.*, 20.

———— (1938). Findings, ideas, problems. *S.E.*, 22.

Giannakoulas, A. (1996). *L'interpretazione e le sue vicissitudini. La tecnica in questione. Quaderni di psicoterapia infantile.* Rome: Borla, 1988.

Goretti, G. (2001). The myth and the history of some psychoanalytic concept: Thoughts inspired by reading pf Orange et al. working intersubjectively. *Int. J. Psycho-Anal.*, 82(6):1205–1223.

Heimann, P. (1949/1950). On countertransference. In: *About Children and Children No Longer (1989).* London: Routledge.

———— (1956). Dynamics of transference interpretation. *Int. J. Psycho-Anal.*, 37:303–310.

Klein, M. (1957). *Symposium in child analysis in Love, Guilt and Reparation and other works 1921-1945.* London: Karnac Books and The Institute of Psychoanalysis.

———— (1957). *Envy and Gratitude and Other Works.* London: Hogarth, 1975.

Kohut, H. (1971). *The Analysis of the Self.* Chicago: The University of Chicago Press.

Laplanche, J. & Pontalis, J. B. (1968). *The Language of Psycho-Analysis.* Translated by Donald Nicholson-Smith. London: The International Psycho-Analytical Library, 1973.

Lemma, A. (2010). *Under the Skin: A Psychoanalytic Study of Body Modification.* London: Routledge.

Little, M. (1951). Countertransference and the patient response to it. *Int. J. Psycho-Anal*, 32:32–40.

Main, T. (ed.) (1989). *The Ailment and Other Psychoanalytic Essays.* London: Free Association Books.

Marion, P. (2010). Il tempo della Nachträglichkeit. *Riv. di Psicoanalisi.*, 56(2):297–318.

Meltzer, D. (1967). *The Psychoanalytic Process.* London: Heinemann.

———— (1978). *The Kleinian Development.* London: Clunie Press.

Ogden, T. (1992). The dialectically constituted/decentred subject of psychoanalysis, II: The contributions of Klein and Winnicott. *Int. J. Psycho- Anal.*, 73:613–626.

Ogden, T. (1994). *Subjects of Analysis.* London, Karnac.

Racker, H. (1968). *Transference and Countertransference.* London: The Hogarth Press and the Institute of Psychoanalysis.

Resnik, S. (2006). *Biographies de l'Inconscient. Préface Par R. Kaës.* Paris: Dunod.

Rosenfeld, H. R. (1987). *Impasse and Interpretation. Therapeutic and Anti-Therapeutic Factors in the Psychoanalytic Treatment of Psychotic, Borderline and Neurotic Patients.* Hove and New York: Brunner and Routledge.

Smith, H. F. (2000). Countertransference, conflictual listening and analytic object relationship. *J. Am. Psycho-Anal. Assn.*, 48:95–128.

Tustin, F. (1981). *Autistic States in Children.* London: Routledge & Kegan Paul.

Winnicott, D. W. (1947). Hate in the countertransference. In: *Collected Papers. Through Paediatrics to Psychoanalysis.* London: Tavistock.

_____ (1956). Clinical varieties of transference. In: *Through Paediatrics to Psycho-Analysis. Collected papers.* London: Hogarth, 1958.

_____ (1957). Nothing at the centre. In: *Psycho-Analytic Explorations.* Edited by C. Winnicott, R. Shepherd, M. Davis. London: Karnac, 1989.

_____ (1960). Ego distortion in terms of true and false self. In: *The Maturational Processes and the Facilitating Environment.* London: Hogarth, 1965.

_____ (1963). Fear of Breakdown. In: *Psycho-Analytic Explorations.* Edited by C. Winnicott, R. Shepherd, M. Davis. London: Karnac, 1989.

_____ (1967). Mirror role of the mother and family in child development. In: *Playing and Reality.* London: Tavistock, 1971.

Wright, K. (1991). *Vision and Separation: Between Mother and Baby.* New York: Aronson.

2

CLINICAL WINNICOTT
Traveling a Revolutionary Road

The development of Winnicott's thinking over the course of his career, reflected in his extensive *oeuvre*, demonstrates an extraordinary internal coherence. As he makes clear in *Playing and Reality*, even though he cannot assume that others are following the way his ideas developed, "there has been a sequence, and the order that there may be in the sequence belongs to the evolution of my work" (1968b, p. 86).

In this chapter, I will focus my remarks on a few aspects of that thinking, namely, what I define as 'the clinical Winnicott.' These areas permit us to consider specifically his clinical contributions, usually neglected and not sufficiently valued next to his important work on the psychoanalytic theory of development (Abram, 1996) or his monumental and highly influential theory of transitional space.

My conviction is that Winnicott's clinical thinking and practice form the basis upon which the author constructed his theory of infant development in relation to the environment, as well as his important contributions on the birth and development of the self and the transitional area. I am referring here to what I consider a sort of *generative core* in Winnicott's ideas, a crucial object in his clinical thinking, which has been disentangled and becomes understandable only later. We can consider his 1945 paper 'Primitive Emotional Development' a sort of implicit master plan from which his areas of thought departed and then developed, a point of view which Ogden (2001) references.

The concept of *transitional space* is revolutionary not only for the broadening of clinical psychoanalysis that it created, but also because Winnicott invented it as a concept, with the aim of locating objects that, in the theory of his time, did not exist, because there was no space in which to position or see them. These objects were what Winnicott saw and interpreted, but which other analysts not equipped with his theory could not fully appreciate.

Towards the end of his work – as shown in the epigraph – Winnicott became aware of his own participation in the origins of the so-called British Independent Group (Kohon, 1992; Giannakoulas, 2010), which formed a strong branch of British psychoanalysis. This group had taken the best of the extraordinary Kleinian revolution of the 1940s, then placed the patient in the foreground, emphasizing his intrapsychic needs and self-state.

In a note on the first page of Chapter 3 in *Human Nature* (1988), Winnicott – jotting down an idea to be developed, almost like a hermetic verse in a Montale poem – wrote: "*Note for revision:* psychoanalysis starts with the patient + → develop theme to unconscious cooperation process, growth and use of intimacy, self-revelation, surprise" (p. 88). Each of these terms would merit a separate examination since they were already beginning to describe an area of clinical conceptualization quite different from the psychoanalysis of the time.

In actuality, for Winnicott, the patient was the point of psychoanalytic departure: analysis was a practical task; if there was no patient, there was no analysis. Then there was that '+,' which irrefutably expressed all that came afterward – not the drives, the relationships, the fantasies, but instead the unconscious cooperation, the growth, and use of intimacy. *Had we ever heard this language, before Winnicott?* It is from this perspective that we can position Winnicott in the belief that, through the intermediary of the transference, psychoanalysis is essentially *a relationship between two persons.*

What the depressed patient requires of his analyst: Winnicott's use of the concept of depression

While acknowledging the influence of Klein, a distinctive Winnicottian stamp is evident in the argumentative style of his early writing – a highly individual and personal tone in his choice of words that quickly renders his discussion of depression different from that of Klein's. Simultaneously, one can find another distinctive thread in his reflections on depression, one that overlaps and is interwoven with the first, but must be kept conceptually apart in order for us to fully grasp its meaning, namely, Winnicott's direct focus on *the essence of the psychoanalytic relationship,* i.e., the intimate structure of that relationship and even its textural patterns. This can seem surprising and disorienting due to an incongruity with the context of the work in which it was placed.

Winnicott wrote:

> The depressed patient requires of his analyst the understanding that the analyst's work is to some extent his effort to cope with his own (the analyst's) depression, or shall I say guilt and grief resultant from the destructive elements in his own (the analyst's) love.
>
> (1945, p. 138)

This dense observation concentrates multiple lines of thinking that are only explicitly articulated later. What leaps out are the close ties Winnicott establishes between psychoanalytic work and the analyst's personal work. He highlights his effort to cope with his own depression. Between this job and the task of analyzing lies the analyst's answer to the patient's request.[1]

According to Winnicott, analysis is possible only if the analyst is capable of working out his own depression in the course of his relationship with the patient. He must work toward resolution of his own psychic challenges in order to create a place inside himself from which to receive the patient's experience. The analysis starts with the patient, but paradoxically it is the analyst who has to create a place inside himself to allow the analysis to start. This also means that, in the presence of the patient, the analyst must revivify that dead internal object that is the 'depressed mother' in order to experience the patient's internal mother-object.

Depression in terms of the introjection of an internal dead object, the depressed mother, is an original conception of Winnicott's distinctively different from those of Freud and Klein – to whom, however, he makes reference. He fully developed the concept later, starting from his essay on 'Reparation in Respect of Mother's Organized Maternal Defense Against Depression' (1948), and in greater detail in 'Communicating and Not Communicating Leading to a Study of Certain Opposites' (1963a). "The analyst's response," wrote Winnicott, "makes the difference from the outset in the way that the patient's depression develops, transforms and is worked through."

This implicit intuition emerged more strongly and found its full expression in the paper 'The Use of an Object' (1969), where Winnicott suggested that it is the reality of the analyst which makes the difference, i.e., his being an 'objective object' that survives the patient's attacks, not merely being the receptacle of the patent's attacks via projective identification. The analyst's response – his striving to be real and alive for the patient – gives a unique imprint, also technically, to the analysis of depression.

Winnicott's concept of depression in his theory of the false self

In his 1948 paper 'Reparation in Respect of Mother's Organized Defense Against Depression,' Winnicott described the 'false reparation' that we find in clinical practice: *false* because it is not specifically tied to the patient's guilt, but refers to another subject. This concept gave rise to his clinical discoveries on dissociation in connection with the false self (1960).

At the outset of the 1948 paper, Winnicott observed that "this false reparation appears through the patient's identification with the mother, and the dominating factor is not the patient's own guilt but the mother's organized defense against depression and unconscious guilt." Further on, he notes: "The depression of the child can be the mother's depression in reflection. The child uses the mother's depression as an escape from his or her own; this provides a false restitution and reparation in relation to the mother, and this hampers the development of a personal restitution capacity" (pp. 91–93).

With these considerations, he was beginning to describe the psychic work done on behalf of the other from within the self, carried out through the process of identification. The scale of this work varies widely, until gradually it comes to include occupation of the self by the other.

Toward a new meaning of the work of interpretation

In a surprising paper of 1959, uncannily entitled 'Nothing at the Centre' Winnicott transmitted a vivid image of his clinical methods – his way of fantasizing about and elaborating the clinical material:

The striking thing was what happened when I made a certain interpretation … I interpreted that if nothing was happening for her to react to, she came to the centre of herself where she knows that there is nothing. I said this nothingness at the centre is her tremendous hunger ... As soon as the trend of my interpretation became clear to her ... she fell dead asleep and stayed asleep for about twenty minutes. When she began to waken and to become impatient with having been to sleep and missing the hour, I began again on interpretation, whereupon she went suddenly into a new sleep and stayed like it until the end of the hour. When she wakened, she said: "I have been glued to the coach." This patient often goes to sleep ... This time the sleep had a new quality ... I assumed that the sleep represented a particular kind of resistance to the interpretation. The essence of interpretation was that there is a dissociated self which is nothing; it is nothing but a void ... This is the first time that she and I in the course of four years analysis have found together a satisfactory statement of her true self and at the same time of her appetite. (p. 50)

This passage offers an example *in vivo* of the oscillation between the patient's communication and non-communication in the here and now of the session. It also illustrates the analyst's capacity to let himself go, to tolerate giving himself up to this wave-like movement, without forcing the patient to communicate – and at the same time maintaining his position as the other.

In doing psycho-analysis I aim at:

Keeping alive;
Keeping well;
Keeping awake.
I aim at being myself and behaving myself.
(1962, p. 166)

Here, in a paper whose classically technical title is 'The Aims of Psycho-analytical Treatment,' the author begins quite provocatively. He talks of himself and makes reference to what is *not* so technical, but on the contrary very personal: i.e., the basic matrix of 'staying' with the patient in the session.

Interestingly, Bion's (1967) well-known recommendation to the analyst to "suspend memory and desire" was, like Winnicott's, anything but 'technical.' Like Winnicott, Bion emphasized not a strategy of technique, but a position for the analyst to aim for in the consulting room, in the here and now – a position that enabled him both to stay with himself and with the patient.

It is important to underline a notable distinction between Winnicott and Bion's position. Whereas Bion highlighted the analyst's mental functioning, it is the integrity of the analyst's psyche-soma to which Winnicott first calls our attention. The activity of thinking is evoked by Bion's image; even when the analyst suspends thinking. What we see when we read Bion is a thinking analyst. The analyst described by Winnicott, in contrast, is someone whom we see simply breathing. To Winnicott, the mind is an organized defense, a pseudo-integration that replaces and holds together a precarious psychosomatic integration; it protects the self from dis-integration, from fragmenting into pieces. Winnicott is speaking here of a live analyst capable of desiring what the analysand brings to the session and of remembering what he has brought in the past: an analyst with an emotional appetite for clinical material, and one who shows himself to be present – as we see his undated paper, 'A Point in Technique.'

Bion's primary focus, derived from the Kleinian tradition, is on the various parts of the personality and internal objects. Winnicott's attention, conversely, is directed mainly at the totality of the self and its oscillation from non-integration to integration and personaliza-tion. This difference in the vertices of observation is evidenced not only by the content of the two authors' reflections, but also by their grammatical choices, as in their contrasting uses of *what* and *who* in characterizing psychoanalytic discourse.

Container and *holding*, respectively, are other characteristic terms which encapsulate Bion and Winnicott's unique points of view. A *container* is a thing, an object that performs a function akin to encir-cling or gathering in. By contrast, *holding* refers to a bodily posture, and here again we see Winnicott's prevailing attention to the psy-chosomatic matrix. The dreaming function implied in Bion's won-derfully evocative description of maternal reverie refers to mental operations as thinking activities. What is generally, and in my view wrongly, considered to be the Winnicottian counterpart pertains more to the affective and bodily dimension – the "primary maternal preoccupation" (1956), which first of all evokes the mother's breath-ing as she watches over her sleeping child. Here we find another expression of Winnicott's prioritization of "keeping alive, keep-ing well, keeping awake." Thus, as indicated, *container* and *holding* describe different functions and processes.

Winnicott vs. Bion: Clinical approaches to interpretation

In his paper 'Differentiation of the Psychotic from the Non-psychotic Personalities' read before the British Psycho-Analytical Society on October 5, 1955, Wilfred Bion reported some clinical material with the comment – typically turning the usual perspective upside down – "it is a clinical experience based on these theories rather than the description of an experience on which the theories are based" (1957, p. 52).

Bion then proceeded to recount the initial part of the session, involving a patient who had arrived a quarter of an hour late, and spent some time turning from one side to another on the couch, trying to find a comfortable position.

> At length he said, "I don't suppose I shall do anything today. I ought to have rung up my mother." He paused and then said: "No, I thought it would be like this." A more prolonged pause followed, then: "Nothing but filthy things and smells," he said. "I think I've lost my sight." Some twenty-five minutes of our time had now passed, and at this point I made an interpretation, but before I repeat it I must discuss some previous material which will, I hope, make my intervention comprehensible.
>
> (1957, p. 53)

Approximately two pages later, after trying to link up the material presented to previous aspects of the patient's history (the hernia) and the psychoanalytic process with him, Bion made his point of view clear:

> "I ought to have rung up my mother" could mean that his failure to do so was being visited upon him by the punishment of not being able to do any analysis. It also meant that his mother would have known what to do about it, she could get associations out of him or interpretations out of me.
>
> (1957, p. 55).

This quotation, which I wish to develop, gives a good idea of Bion's way of working, of his ability to listen and how he placed himself within the psychoanalytic process with the patient, in line with Kleinian theory. Bion's reference to the mother is for him a reference to an internal object, persecutory on the one hand, and seen, on the other hand, as so omnipotent as to be able to 'get associations out' of the patient and interpretations out of him.

Let's assume that this is 'the real' interpretation Bion would have given the patient in those particular conditions; let's also assume that this interpretation reveals, in general, the way Bion made interpretations at least in this period of his clinical practice. It is a fiction, of course, but perhaps a useful one, because it allows us to compare this interpretation with Winnicott's way of interpreting. Also this is useful in order to discover similarities and differences among the two analysts and to better understand how they envisaged interpretation in the here-and-now of the session; in other words, what kind of implicit epistemology lay behind their work.

On October 7, 1955, two days after Bion's paper had been presented, Winnicott wrote to him: "Dear Bion, I find I want to write to you about your Wednesday paper. First, I would like to say that I think of you as the big man of the future in the British Psycho-Analytical Society" (1987, p. 89). The letter continues in such a way as to give us a vivid impression of the atmosphere of lively contrast present in those years within the British Psycho-Analytical Society. But it is not this aspect I was most interested in. At another point in the letter, Winnicott refers explicitly to the themes in Bion's paper:

> I feel very much in sympathy with your idea that your interpretation was probably the right one at the moment even if after it was given it immediately became inadequate or inaccurate.
>
> I would like to go a little further in expressing what I started to speak to you about when I took part in the discussion. It does seem to me that the material you reported cried out for an interpretation about communication.
>
> (1987, p. 91)

Winnicott makes an additional point, which allows us to get to the heart of his conception of the transference-countertransference relationship.

> I would say that if a patient of mine lay on the couch moving to and fro in the way your patient did and then said: "I ought to have telephoned my mother." I would know he was talking about communication and his incapacity for making communication. Should it interest you to know, I will say what I would have

interpreted: I would have said: "A mother properly oriented to her baby would know from your movements what you need. There would be a communication because of this knowledge, which belongs to her devotion and she would show that the communication had taken place. I am not sensitive enough or orientated in that way to be able to act well enough and therefore in this present analytic situation I fall into the category of the mother who failed to make communication possible. In the present relationship therefore, there is given a sample of the original failure from the environment which contributed to your difficulty in communication. Of course, you could always cry and so draw attention to need. In the same way you could telephone your mother and get a reply. But this represents a failure of the more subtle communication which is the only basis for communication that does not violate the fact of the essential isolation of each individual.

You will see that *from my point of view you were talking about the environment although you said were not going to do so* and you were indicating by this clinical material that this man has a relative lack of capacity for communicating because of some experience in which his mother or whoever was there failed in the original maternal task at the stage when the mother is closely identified with her baby, *i.e.* at the very beginning.

(1987, pp. 91–92, my italics)

I've quoted this passage in full for a variety of reasons, but primarily in order to show the natural, almost ingenious way (though so personal and involved) Winnicott deals with clinical questions. He was clearly more interested in this than in theoretical elaboration and systemization. The 'naturalness' combined with a sense of personal participation – so familiar to his readers – are even more evident in a letter such as this, in which Winnicott's sole concern is to communicate privately with Bion, to understand and make himself understood.

The subject of his letter becomes merged with the problem facing him and his interlocutor at that moment, the possibility of communication. The ability Winnicott has to transfer clinical experience with the patient onto paper – even when, paradoxically, as in this case, the patient is not his own – is a quality that Khan (1975) has already stressed and one that emerges even more clearly in the letters recently collected in one volume and translated into Italian.

There is a further reason why I have dwelt on this passage: it summarizes Winnicott's conception of the therapeutic relationship and the mutual position of the analyst and analysand in a clinical setting elaborated and developed in the course of a 40-year-long therapeutic practice. Clearly, Winnicott is summing up his position for someone already familiar with it, who is able to appreciate its consistency, together with its internal evolution.

For Winnicott, communication is always two-way, from the patient, be it adult or child, to the analyst and vice versa; it is the communication of experience which brings the *authenticity* of the relationship into play for both partners. But this often gives rise to the mistaken impression that Winnicott is an *interactionist*. Undoubtedly, in his conception of the individual's maturational processes, the actual concrete interaction between the mother (environment) and the infant is fundamental, just as in his conception of the transference-countertransference relationship, but in his view the *mode* of the mother-infant interaction is central to the transformative psychotherapeutic process. For Winnicott the communication must be authentic. And the authenticity of the communication is connected to the theme of the true and the false self. Winnicott refers to this in his letter:

> Incidentally I am very interested in your development of the theme of the neurotic part of the personality which, so to speak, brings the psychotic part to analysis, a theme (...) which I have referred to in the language of the false self hiding the true self and eventually allowing the true self to emerge for analysis.
>
> (1987, p. 93)

So here we have a basic problem: What do we expect to emerge during analysis? What are the goals of psychoanalytic treatment? The patient's inner world, his jumble of primitive fantasies, working through them by analyzing the transference until the depressive position has been reached or, in other words, a more integrated relationship with the object. For Winnicott, analysis is all this, but it is also more – there is the question of *communicating the true self.* The patient-and-the-analyst's possibility of making contact with the *private core* of the true self, which for Winnicott, was fundamentally incommunicable. As we can see, the description of this thing which is incommunicable can get complicated. The reader is challenged

54

to think in paradoxes. But for Winnicott, it was this experience of communicability and incommunicability which made an analysis true, or authentic, and he tended to focus our attention on this.

In an essay published in 1963, "Communicating and Not Communicating Leading to a Study of Certain Opposites," Winnicott met this problem head-on:

> I suggest that in health there is a core to the personality that corresponds to the true self of the split personality; I suggest that this core never communicates with the world of perceived objects, and that the individual person knows it must never be communicated with or influenced by external reality (...) Although healthy persons communicate and enjoy communicating, the other fact is equally true, that *each individual is an isolate, permanently noncommunicating, permanently unknown, in fact unfound.*
>
> (1963a)

In my opinion, here is a paradox which was extremely productive to Winnicott's thinking. In the mother–infant relationship, as in the relationship between analyst and analysand, he was attributing a fundamental role to the *other* in the development and maturation of the individual. The infant can only grow and develop in relation to the mother, and only if the mother, as the other, recognizes him as an individual. "For Winnicott the paradox of infant-mother relationship lay in that the environment (mother) makes the becoming self of the infant feasible" (Khan, 1975, p. xxxvii).

In the same way, the individual can know himself in analysis only through the analyst as the *other*. But if the *other* (the mother, the analyst) is capable, he/she enables the individual to recognize and get in touch with that "non-communicating central self, forever immune from the reality principle, and for ever silent. Here communication is not non-verbal; it is, like the music of the spheres, absolutely personal. It belongs to being alive. And in health, it is out of this that communication naturally arises" (1963a, p. 192).

Although considered by some to be too 'simple,' too 'environmentalist,' or 'interactionist,' it might appear here that Winnicott is giving quite the opposite impression; he seems almost mystical, metaphysical, and far removed from the concreteness of the clinical report. The truth is that few psychoanalysts shared Winnicott's overriding interest for the clinical dimension: he never strayed from the clinical data no matter how ingeniously he conceptualized them (Fromm & Smith, 1989). Winnicott was so interested in the clinical level that it seems to the reader his descriptions of the analyst-patient relationship *as* mother-infant relationship lose sight of the *metaphorical dimension.*

To go back to communication, the theme is complicated because Winnicott is challenging the reader to single out one particular aspect of the experience in the psychoanalytical relationship, as he tries to communicate in the letter to Bion.

Communicating and not-communicating

Winnicott himself admitted that in his line of argument regarding the communicating and non-communicating self "a complication arises" (1963a, p. 182) from the fact that the infant develops two kinds of relationships at the same time – that to the environment-mother and that to the object, which becomes the object-mother. This distinction is crucial for an understanding of his thoughts regarding the reciprocal position between patient and analyst in the clinical situation. "The environment-mother is human, and the object-mother is a thing, although it is also the mother or part of her" (1963a, pp. 182–183). This distinction is linked to the distinction between the 'subjective object' and the 'objectively perceived object,' as well as to the opposition between communicating and not-communicating: the latter, in turn, is divided into a simple not-communicating and an active or reactive not-communicating.

This knot of concepts is tied to his description of clinical phenomena in the analytic situation, which Winnicott saw basically as a *sui generis* reproduction of the mother-infant relationship, although according to his own theoretical description. I think it is useful to reformulate this concept in terms used by Christopher Bollas (1979). When referring to Winnicott's contribution to the parallel and comparative study of the mother-infant relationship and the psychoanalytic situation, Bollas proposed that the analytic ecology was an acting-out of what Freud repressed: the early object relation of mother and child.

But let us go back to the distinction between object-mother and environment-mother: according to Winnicott, when reproduced in the clinical situation, it marks the fundamental distinction between the analyst's contribution as an individual and the analyst's contribution in terms of holding by means of the analytic setting. Khan (1969) linked the holding function of the analytic setting to the patient's *being*: and the transference (the object relation) to the patient's *experiencing*. In fact, Winnicott said:

It is helpful to postulate the existence for the immature child of two mothers - shall I call them the object-mother and the environment-mother? I have no wish to invent names that become stuck and eventually develop a rigidity and an obstructive quality, but is seems possible to use these words, object-mother and environment-mother, in this context to describe the vast difference that there is for the infant between two aspects of infant-care: the mother as object, or owner of the part-object that may satisfy the infant's urgent needs; and the mother as the person who wards off the unpredictable and who actively provides care in handling and in general management. What the infant does at the height of id-tension and the use thus made of the object seems to me very different from the use the infant makes of the mother as part of the total environment. In this language it is the environment-mother that can be defined as affection and sensuous co-existence, while it is the object-mother who becomes the target of excited experience sustained by crude instinctual tension.

(1963b, pp. 75–76)

With respect to the patient, then, just like the mother with regard to her infant, the analyst is confronted with two rather different clinical phenomena; for the patient, he is two different things.

This is where Winnicott's theory about psychoanalytic technique becomes particularly explicit and original. The analytic situation is relatively unimportant when there is a structured ego, and the analyst takes the very first elements of infant care for granted; in other words, when the infant's experience with the environment-mother has been characterized by *predictability* and a settled *continuity of being*. The analytic situation or *ecology* (made up of space, time, and the presence of the analyst) actually becomes more important than the interpretation when the patient is in a deeply regressed state – by which we mean a return to total dependence, and to the early developmental processes (1956, p. 297 and *passim*).

These two different forms of analysis, which Winnicott identifies with two different psychopathologies, neurotic on the one hand and borderline, schizoid, or psychotic on the other hand – or rather, to two different moments that may occur in the same analysis – place the analyst in two positions: he is the *object* of the transference (the equivalent of the mother-object) and he is the *functor* of the analytic ecology, in other words, the environment-mother. The nature of the latter relationship lies at the basis of the *ego-relatedness* that Winnicott saw as a possible *matrix of the transference.*

Clearly then, this conceptual distinction risks being badly misconstrued if it is connected solely to Winnicott's theory of the child's development and maturational processes. I have tried to show instead that its main importance lies at the clinical level, and I have only just begun to explain the implication for technique and for patient-analyst interaction represented by Winnicott's model. A more systematic procedure would be necessary, which is impossible to realize in a general presentation of this nature. However, some progress might be made if we connect this clinical distinction to the theme of *communication* already mentioned earlier, and to that of *object status,* two angles which taken together enable us to see what happens in the clinical process according to Winnicott.

The *object,* from being at first a *subjective* phenomenon, gradually becomes an object *objectively perceived* (1963a, p. 180). There is the well-known statement by Winnicott that the infant experiencing omnipotence within the facilitating environment continually creates and re-creates the object until the process gradually becomes built-in and gathers a memory backing (1963a, p. 180). As this process of creating the object proceeds, the transformation or modification of the object from being subjective to objectively perceived is carried along, in Winnicott's opinion, more by dissatisfactions than satisfactions: "Instinct-gratification gives the infant a personal experience and *does but little to the position of the object*" (1963a, p. 181, my italics). Once again, this statement should be linked to the clinical situation in order to make it clear how ungratifying the analyst's position is with regard to the patient in Winnicott's theory – contrary to what many people think. This is because "the infant's experienced aggression, that which belongs to muscle erotism, to movement, and to irresistible forces meeting immovable objects, this aggression, and the ideas bound up with it, lends itself to the process of placing the object, to placing the object separate from the self, in so far as the self has begun to emerge as an entity" (1963a, p. 181). Before the state of *fusion* is achieved, one has to allow for the fact that the infant's behavior is reactive to failures in the facilitating environment or of the environment-mother. This may look like aggression but in fact it is the sign of the child's acute state of distress and suffering. Instead, when the infant achieves *fusion* the frustrating aspect of object behavior has value in educating the infant in respect of the existence of a non-me world. Adaptation failures on the part of the environment have value insofar as the infant *can hate the object*, that is to say, can retain the idea of the object as potentially satisfying, while recognizing its failure to behave satisfactorily (1963a, p. 81). It will be seen that in Winnicott's clinical theory, the analyst's recognition of environmental failure is inseparable from recognizing where it belongs in the infant's development, since this does not simply imply a clinical problem, but also a different *response*, or attitude, on the part of the analyst with regard to this failure inscribed upon the patient's self.

And for Winnicott, this is a question of *communication:* when the object is subjective, it is unnecessary for communication to be explicit; when the object is objectively perceived, communication is either explicit or dumb (1963a, p. 182). In a less serious illness of the neurotic type, an active non-communication (clinical withdrawal) must be expected in the analytic process, because of the fact that communication can so easily become linked with some degree of false or compliant object-relating; silent or secret communication with subjective objects, carrying a sense of the real, must periodically take over to restore balance (1963a, p. 184).

Winnicott points out that even in the clear-cut psychoneurotic case, where there is apparently no difficulty because the analytic communication takes place through verbalization, there is a risk that the analysis becomes an infinitely prolonged collusion of the analyst with the patient's negation of non-communication. In such cases, silence may be the most positive contribution the patient can make, and so the analyst is involved in a waiting-game.

More dangerous, however, is the state of affairs in an analysis in which the analyst is permitted by the patient to reach to the deepest layers of the analysand's personality because of his position as subjective object, or because of the dependence of the patient in the transference psychosis; here there is danger if the analyst interprets instead of waiting for the patient to creatively discover. It is only here, at the place when the analyst has not yet changed over from a subjective object to one that is objectively perceived, that psychoanalysis is dangerous, and the danger is one that can be avoided if we know how to behave ourselves. If we wait, we become objectively perceived in the patient's own time, but if we fail to behave in a way that is facilitating the patient's analytic process (which is the equivalent of the infant's and the child's maturational process), we suddenly become not-me for the patient, and then we know too much, and we are dangerous because we are too nearly in communication with the central still and silent spot of the patient's ego-organization (1963a, p. 189).

In my opinion, this passage illustrates very well the complex interweaving of clinical concepts I have referred to: the communication of the true and the false self in the psychoanalytic process, the passing from subjective object to objectively perceived object and the two types, or two different depths, of analysis, the second of which explicitly reproduces the infant's maturational process in its relationship with its mother.

The object: Two ways of relating to the object and the 'use' of an object

In fact, as Phillips has pointed out (1988, p. 87) for Winnicott the mother–infant relationship "was, quite literally, the source analogy in his work. His new ideas about early development and psychosis as an 'environmental deprivation disease' necessarily involved modifications of the classical psychoanalytic technique."

We are not interested here in examining the ways in which Winnicott departed from psychoanalytic procedure in purely technical terms. In order to appreciate his thinking with regard to technique, one must read his essay 'The Aims of Psycho-analytical Treatment' (1962, p. 166) remarkable for being rigorous, yet original and full of paradox: "I aim at being myself and behaving myself." And at the end he concluded:

In my opinion our aims in the practice of the standard technique are not altered if it happens that we interpret mental mechanisms which belong to the psychotic types of disorder and to primitive stages in the emotional stages of the individual.

(1962, p. 169)

He then added, with his characteristic love of paradox:

> If our aim continues to be to verbalize the nascent conscious in terms of the transference, then we are practicing analysis; if not, then we are analysts practicing something else that we deem to be appropriate to the occasion. And why not?
>
> (1962, p. 170)

Regarding the patient regressed to a state of infantile dependence, for whom the analysis can become dangerous if the analyst does not provide an adequate response, Winnicott said: "I have always felt that an important function of interpretation is the establishment of the *limits* of the analyst's understanding" (1963a, p. 189). And in another section of the same article:

> In our work, especially in working on the schizoid rather than the psycho-neurotic aspects of the personality, we do in fact wait, if we feel we know, until the patients tell us ... if we make the interpretation out of our own cleverness and experience, then the patient must refuse it or destroy it. An anorexia patient is teaching me the substance of what I am saying now as I write it down.
>
> (1963a, p. 182)

In a 1968 essay Winnicott proposed "a very simple statement about interpretation," that "the analyst *reflects back* what the patient has *communicated*" (1968a, p. 209, my italics). This technical position is echoed by statements he made to Giovacchini (1973, p. 36): "I interpret for two reasons: (1) in order to let the patient, know that I am alive, and (2) to let him know that I am not omnipotent, that I can make mistakes."

What emerges from these passages is Winnicott referring to the *change of position* with regard to the patient, particularly the patient who has regressed to a state of dependence. Has this theoretical and technical problem any relevance to what we call *countertransference?* It would be interesting to pursue this line of reasoning, but that would involve a careful examination of the various positions present in the literature, in order to place Winnicott in an adequate theoretical and conceptual space of his own. Here, it is important to point out that Winnicott is declaredly in favor of the term reverting to its original meaning, while still being fully aware of why this meaning has been extended. In Winnicott's opinion, "this would leave us free to discuss the many interesting things that analysts can do with psychotic patients who are temporarily regressed and dependent, for which we could use Margaret Little's term: *the analyst's total response to the patient's needs*" (1960, p. 164, my italics).

Winnicott's point of view regarding countertransference had already been expounded in a previous work of 1947 entitled, 'Hate in the Countertransference,' whose radical, self-revealing nature is already clear. He classified the countertransference phenomena as follows:

1. The countertransference as a disturbance factor in the relationship with the patient, a pathological obstruction to the analyst's possibility of understanding him;
2. The identifications and tendencies which provide the positive setting for analytic work and make it different in quality from that of any other analyst;
3. The countertransference which he calls truly objective, that is the analyst's love and hate in reaction to the actual behavior of the patient, based on objective observation. Winnicott is very clear on this point: in therapeutic work with psychotic patients (or with analysands in a state of deep regression), the analyst:

> Is in the position of the mother of an infant unborn or newly born ... The analyst must be prepared to bear strain without expecting the patient to know anything about what he is doing, perhaps over a long period of time. To do this, he must be easily aware of his own fear and hate (...) Eventually, he ought to be able to tell the patient what he has been through on the patient's behalf, but an analysis may never get as far as this.
>
> (1947, p. 198).

What were Winnicott's intentions in assuming such a radical position? The essay in question obviously has to be read in the light of the atmosphere of scientific debate and strong emotional tensions existing within the British Psycho-Analytical Society in the mid-40s. Without embarking upon a historical analysis; however, useful it might be to clarify many of the clinical and theoretical concepts we are still confronted with today, it is enough to bear in mind one central aspect: the clinical experiences of analysis with psychotic, borderline, and schizoid patients being carried out at the time by many analysts, from

Klein and her followers to Winnicott himself, Balint, Fairbairn, and so on, which posed urgent questions about what the patient transferred of his past onto the analyst, and how the analyst should respond (Phillips, 1988). The position of the Kleinians is well known. The analysis of psychotics, like the analysis of children, requires no particular modification of the classical technique. Winnicott's response is to see the problem from another point of view: "In the analysis of psychotics (...) quite a different type and degree of strain is taken by the analyst" (1947, p. 197). This is a clear statement of the type of participation Winnicott is alluding to on the analyst's side, during the therapeutic process with patients who are psychotic or have regressed to a state of primary dependence. He continues:

> There is a vast difference between those patients who have had satisfactory early experiences *which can be discovered in the transference,* and those whose very early experiences have been so deficient or distorted that the analyst has to be the first in the patient's life to supply certain environmental essentials.
>
> (1947, p. 198, my italics)

I have already clarified how I think Winnicott intended the term 'environment': it is equivalent to 'the other,' that unavoidable *human* psychological factor that describes the primary form of psychic life, the factor which 'at the origin' (and in regression) is inextricably tied to the very fact of existing, of being. Therefore, it does not seem necessary to dwell on the fact that Winnicott definitely did *not* see the analyst's therapeutic function as a *corrective emotional experience.* I think it is more important to stress that Winnicott alludes, here as elsewhere, to a *qualitative differentiation of the transference* at the clinical level. Perhaps it would be more true to say that Winnicott seemed to limit the transference to the *repetition* of those phenomena and relationships that have been *experienced at least once.* Therefore, Winnicott's idea of transference as a clinical concept excluded that whole area of primary phenomena, which some patients may never have experienced, and which, in a sense, await the opportunity presented by analysis – and the analyst's willingness to accept the burden – in order to find room to grow for the first time:

> For the neurotic the couch and warmth and comfort can be *symbolical* of the mother's love; for the psychotic it would be more

true to say that these things *are* the analyst's physical expression of love. The couch *is* the analyst's lap or womb, and the warmth *is* the warmth of the analyst's body.

(1947, p. 199)

But why did Winnicott speak of *hate* in the countertransference? The fascinating example he gave to illustrate his point is the story of the adoptive child who tests out the new family environment he has found through aggressive behavior, looking for proof of his guardians' ability to hate him: he can only believe in being loved after reaching being hated. In the same way, "in certain stages of certain analyses the analyst's hate is actually sought by the patient, and what is then needed is hate that is objective. If the patient seeks objective or justified hate he must be able to reach it, else he cannot feel he can reach objective love" (1947, p. 199).

As we have mentioned above, one important factor determining Winnicott's special interest in the theme of hate was the nature of the scientific debate going on in the British Psycho-Analytical Society in the mid-40s. Winnicott felt he needed to follow his own course, by taking the perspective adopted by Klein and turning it upside down. As Phillips (1988) has pointed out, whereas Klein had based her theory on the infant's innate destructiveness towards his mother, Winnicott proposed the opposite: "I suggest that the mother hates the baby before the baby hates the mother, and before the baby can know his mother hates him" (1947, p. 200).

It would be interesting to take this diametrical conceptual divergence as a starting point and make a comparative study of Klein and Winnicott's thinking. But this would be the subject of a separate paper.

I suggest, however, that it is crucial to point out that Winnicott refers to hate in order to emphasize the necessity for *authentic feelings*, both on the mother and the analyst's part, and for their presence to be authentic in order for the relationship to be recognized as a true relationship:

A mother has to be able to tolerate hating her baby without doing anything about it (...) The most remarkable thing about a mother is her ability to be hurt so much by her baby (by his ruthless love for her) and hate so much without paying the child out, and her ability to wait for rewards that may or may not come at a later date.

(1947, p. 202)

Similarly,

> if the analyst is going to have crude feelings imputed to him, he
> is best forewarned and so forearmed, for he must tolerate being
> placed in that position. Above all he must not deny hate that
> really exists in himself. Hate *that is justified* in the present setting
> has to be sorted out and kept in storage and available for eventual
> interpretation.
>
> (1947, p. 196)

The last sentence clearly indicates the psychoanalytic function
of the analyst's inner recognition of the authenticity and reality of
his own feelings regarding the patient. In these terms, therefore,
we could examine what so-called transference-countertransference
dynamics are for Winnicott. When the patient is in a deeply regressed
state, the transference takes another form, which can be defined
in terms of "psychotic transference": but for Winnicott it is still a
primitive *present communication* from the patient to the analyst, a
communication that has not yet adopted the 'idiom of transference,'
to use Khan's expression. Correspondingly, for the countertransference, too, besides this disturbing aspect, and the positive identifications and tendencies it brings to the psychoanalytic work, the
secret lies in reaching its core, its authentically objective nature: the
analyst's feelings "in reaction to the actual personality and behavior
of the patient, based on objective observation" (1947, p. 195). In this
sense, the concept of countertransference becomes, for Winnicott,
what we have seen him refer to as *"the analyst's total response to the
patient's needs."*

According to my interpretation of Winnicott, the problem of rede-
fining the conventional concepts of transference-countertransference
is further clarified in another of his papers, 'On Transference' (1956).
Here, too, Winnicott distinguishes between two different forms of
analysis:

> Whereas in the transference neurosis the past comes into the con-
> sulting-room, in this work it is more true to say that the present
> goes back into the past, and *is* the past. Thus the analyst finds
> himself confronted with the patient's primary process in the set-
> ting in which it had its original validity.
>
> (1956, pp. 387)

By means of a 'good enough adaptation' by the analyst (providing the primary 'environment'), a basic attitude which cannot be defined as countertransference without distorting Winnicott's thinking on the subject, a phenomenon takes place at deeper levels of analysis which needs to be recognized and identified: "The patient makes use of the analyst's failures" (1956, p. 298). They are used as past failures in the environment, which the patient can perceive and encompass, and be angry about: "The analyst needs to be able to make use of his failures in terms of their meaning for the patient, and he must if possible account for each failure even if this means a study of unconscious countertransference" (1956, p. 298).

He continues by saying that what would be called resistance in work with neurotic patients in this type of analytic work always indicates that the analyst has made a mistake, and the analyst can do the most important work only by using his own mistakes: "The part that enables the patient to become angry for the first time about the details of failure of adaptation that (at the time when they happened) produced disruption. It is this part of the work that frees the patient from dependence on the analyst" (1956, p. 299).

There follows a statement which is directly relevant to our discussion: "In this way the negative transference of 'neurotic' analysis is replaced by objective anger about the analyst's failures" (1956, p. 299). So transference is replaced by an objective feeling on the patient's part about the analyst, just as the countertransference is replaced by the core of objective feelings the analyst has about the patient. This work is exactly, Winnicott explains, because the analyst must be sensitive to the patient's needs and must wish to provide a setting that caters for these needs. Surprisingly enough, he adds, "The analyst is not, after all, the patient's natural mother" (1956, p. 299).

The number of writings made available after Winnicott's death gives an idea of the disordered creativity of Winnicott, of his need to write and communicate his own clinical experiences, of his capacity to capture them in the *écriture*. This need to communicate is evident in his collection of letters titled *The Spontaneous Gesture* (1987). In reading his letters one meets a Winnicott who, after a scientific meeting at the Institute of Psycho-Analysis, or after having read an article or a paper on a professional journal or newspaper, puts pen to paper and starts writing to Bion, Segal, Meltzer, and so on. This need for communication with others, which shows what I would call the paradox of Winnicott as a person, was apparently in contradiction to a statement such as: "Each individual is an isolate, permanently non-communicating, permanently unknown, in fact unfound" (1963a, p. 192). Such a statement would hardly be compatible and consistent with those who consider Winnicott a theorist who supported *tout court* object relations theory, at least in its contemporary version as a theory of interpersonal relations.

In the mother-infant relationship, as in the relationship between analyst and analysand, Winnicott attributed a fundamental role to the other in the development and maturation of the individual. The infant could only grow and develop in relation to the mother if the mother recognized him as an individual. As Khan put it: "For Winnicott the paradox of infant-mother relationship lays in that the environment (the mother) makes the becoming self of the infant feasible" (Khan, 1975, p. xxxvii).

In the same way the individual can know himself in analysis only through the analyst as *other*. But, at the same time, if the analyst is capable, he/she enables the patient to recognize and get in touch with the "non-communicating central self, for ever immune from the reality principle, and for ever silent. Here communication is not non-verbal; it is, like the music of the spheres, absolutely personal. It belongs to being alive. And in health, it is out of this that communication naturally arises" (Winnicott, 1963a, p. 192).

The difference between regression and withdrawal

There are additional elements of particular interest in the passage quoted earlier from 'Nothing at the Centre' concerning both interpretation and the issue of the manic defense.

"I interpreted that if nothing was happening for her to react to, then she came to the centre of herself where she knows that there is nothing" (1959, p. 50). Here Winnicott's interpretation is precise and clear-cut, without presence, and the space created in which interpretation can happen functions as the 'transitional' element. Furthermore, the interpretation contains two significant elements.

First, there is analysis of her defense: "if nothing was happening for her to react to." The Winnicottian concept of reacting to environmental impingement is present in the background, but this passage also uses clinical evidence to portray a bit of theory *in vivo*; second, there is a courageous, direct statement about a 'void' within the patient: 'at the centre' there is 'nothing.' Paradoxically, this provides the patient with a sense of self that is somehow 'full' in that it transmits something important; that is, because she and the analyst have "found together a satisfactory statement of her true self and at the same time of her appetite" (1959, p. 50). The statement is satisfactory because it has satisfied the patient's appetite, filling her up. The internal void can begin its transformation into a presence through being experienced rather than denied via a manic defense. The statement is also satisfactory because it satisfies the appetite of Winnicott as analyst – that is, his desire to provide the analysand with a meaning that makes sense.

What analyst and patient 'found together' (1959) came alive in the analyst's interpretation. What developed was a shared "illusory experience" (1951, p. 3), which at the same time was private and individual to the analysand. As Winnicott described in his 1959 paper, it is in the sleep into which the patient falls – which "had a new quality" and "represented a particular kind of resistance to the interpretation" – that it was possible to identify the private side of the void denied by the manic defense. In this clinical situation, sleep in the session became a form of clinical withdrawal, a sort of pathological independence. Through the relationship with the analyst and his capacity to understand and tolerate this sleeping– without immediately interpreting it as an attack or withdrawal from the work – it became a regression to dependence.

Winnicott elaborated on this theme in 'Notes on Withdrawal and Regression' (1965):

> The correct word for the Wednesday session was withdrawal ... With this patient it is extremely important that I understand the difference between regression and withdrawal. Clinically the two states are practically the same thing. It will be seen, however, that there is an extreme difference between the two. In regression there is dependence, and in withdrawal there is pathological independence ... I have learned at the school of this analysis that withdrawal is something that I do well to allow. (p. 149)

In 'On Transference' (1956), Winnicott took up similar themes:

> That which would be called resistance in work with neurotic patients always indicates that *the analyst has made a mistake,* or in some detail has behaved badly; in fact, the resistance remains until

the analyst has found out the mistake and has tried to account for it, and has used it … It is here that we can see the sense in the dictum that every failed analysis is a failure not of the patient but of the analyst … The analyst [must] … look for his own mistakes whenever resistances appear.

(1956, p. 388, italics in original)

Going back to the distinction between withdrawal and regression, Winnicott differentiated between these two phenomena by focusing on the analyst's function and his capacity to tolerate the patient's resistance, which corresponded to a failure on the analyst's part. In broader terms, the analyst's mistake might be seen as a failure of the primary holding environment.

What is crucial here is the distinction between *object-mother* and *environment-mother* (1963b, pp. 75–76). This is important not only in terms of the theory of infant development, but primarily for its technical implications. In particular, the object-mother and the environment-mother are related to the Winnicottian concepts of *subjective object* or *objective object*, introduced in 'Hate in the Countertransference' (1947); these concepts are further developed in 'The Use of an Object' (1969), which I will discuss later.

The following comments are particularly illuminating from a technical point of view:

I would say that *in the withdrawn state a patient is holding the self* and that if immediately the withdrawn state appears *the analyst can hold the patient,* then what would otherwise have been a withdrawal state becomes a regression. The advantage of a *regression* is that it carries with it the opportunity for correction of inadequate adaptation-to-need in the past history of the patient … By contrast the *withdrawn* state is not profitable and when the patient recovers from a withdrawn state he or she is not changed.

(1954, p. 261, italics in original)

A 'very simple statement about interpretation'

The interpretation of the 1959 paper is now more clear: The state of sleep indicated the moment in which withdrawal turned into regression. In the clinical situation, there was a patient who sleeps and an analyst, Winnicott, who 'dreamed' an interpretation. We are here facing a generative paradox, according to which an individual phenomenon, defensive withdrawal, is transformed into a state defined by the analyst who participates in it, while the patient is regressed and dependent.

The psychoanalytic situation is a paradoxical place in which the intrapsychic relationship between sleep, on the one hand, and 'the-dream-as-guardian-of-the-sleep' on the other, evolves into an intersubjective relationship, in which a part of the total operation is fulfilled by each participant. The new quality of this sleep – an insight that transforms withdrawal into regression – had previously been 'mused' by Winnicott, starting from the time of the patient's comment about having been 'glued to the couch' (1959). Like dreaming, musing is rooted in somatic sensations, in experiencing them, i.e., Winnicott's unique attention to the 'psychosomatic matrix.'

Winnicott muses and re-dreams about much more in relation to his patient's feeling of being glued to the couch. Through his consideration of her sensation as a "particular kind of resistance to the interpretation," it is possible for us to grasp his conception of psychoanalytic interpretation, which he elaborates as follows: "I have always felt that an important function of the interpretation is the establishment of the limits of the analyst's understanding" (1963b, p. 189). The limits of the analyst's incomplete understanding – so incomplete as to generate "a particular kind of resistance" – become, in that precise moment, the somatic limits for the patient, in her feeling "glued to the couch." What she found was the boundary of her manic omnipotence.

Whenever Winnicott proposed an interpretation to the patient, he seemed aware that this proposal's central aspect was not the disclosure of an unconscious fantasy, secluded and in some way fixed within the patient, but a statement conveying an outlook on the patient's self, an amplification of the emotional and relational meaning in the here and now – which, in turn, sent the analyst back into a process of reflection and semantic circularity (Bonaminio, 1993). This is clearly portrayed in 'Interpretation in Psychoanalysis' (1968a).

> The purpose of interpretation must include a feeling that the analyst has that a communication has been made which needs acknowledgement … Giving an interpretation back gives the patient [an] opportunity to correct the misunderstandings. (pp. 208–209)

In the same paper, Winnicott surprises us by saying: "This very simple statement about interpretation may be important by the very fact that it is simple ... The principle that I am enunciating at this moment is that the analyst reflects back what the patient has communicated" (1968a, pp. 208–209). In the expression *reflects back*, the paradox of the discovery of the self through the other finds its virtual point of refraction in an interpretation that "must include a feeling that the analyst has that a communication has been made which needs acknowledgement" (p. 208).

In his delineation of the cross-dialectics within the consulting room, what comes to mind is his paper on the mother's 'mirror role' (1967). "What does the baby see when he or she looks at the mother's face? What the baby sees is himself or herself. In other words the mother is looking at the baby and what she looks like is related to what she sees there" (p. 131).

In Winnicott's reference to "the mother's role of giving back to the baby the baby's own self" (p. 138), his use of *giving back* is very similar to that of his *reflecting back* to the patient. Thus, the statement about the mother's role of giving back can be viewed as constituting the matrix with which to 'metaphorize' the entire analytic relationship and the function of interpretation.

The author continued:

This glimpse of the baby's and the child's seeing the self in the mother's face, and afterwards in the mirror, gives a way of looking at analysis and at the psychotherapeutic task. Psychotherapy is not making clever and apt interpretations; by and large it is a long-term giving the patient back what the patient brings.

(1967, pp. 137–138)

It is not only the dialectical interplay between self and other that Winnicott elucidates through reference to the analyst's function of reflecting. We can here discern the explication of a detailed clinical theory that illuminates the function of interpretation in the analysis with the patient described in 'Nothing at the Centre':

The patient can be giving the analyst a sample of the truth; that is to say of something that is absolutely true for the patient, and ... when the analyst gives this back, the interpretation is received by the patient who has already emerged to some extent from this limited area or dissociated condition.

(1968a, p. 209)

Here, Winnicott's concept of pathological dissociation is brought into the very intimate texture of the analytic relationship; from being a fact of the single patient, it becomes a fact of the analytic relationship of both analyst and patient; nevertheless, in that very moment, the patient "has already emerged to some extent from this limited area or dissociated condition" (1968a, p. 209).

I see here a generative Winnicottian version of Freud's (1933) famous statement, "where Id was, there ego shall be" (p. 80).

Winnicott's future developments in psychoanalysis

Winnicott's paper, 'The Use of an Object' (1969) begins provocatively and revolutionarily as follows: "I propose to put forward for discussion the idea of the use of the object. The allied subject of relating to object seems to me to have had our full attention" (p. 711). Here Winnicott makes clear the distinction between *subjective object* and *objective object*. He was introducing a distinction scarcely mentioned in the work of other authors. In a paper originally presented in 1968b entitled 'The Use of an Object and Relating through Identifications,' he wrote:

> What I have to say in this present chapter is extremely simple ... It is only in recent years that I have become able to wait and wait for the natural evolution of the transference arising out of the patient's growing trust in the psychoanalytic technique and setting, and to avoid breaking up this natural process by making interpretations ... It appalls me to think how much deep change I have prevented or delayed in patients *in a certain classification category* by my personal need to interpret. If only we can wait, the patient arrives at understanding creatively and with immense joy, and I now enjoy this joy more than I used to enjoy the sense of having been clever.
>
> (1968b, p. 86, italics in original)

Each sentence from this quotation could be discussed in depth. I will highlight only the following points:

• Winnicott makes a clear-cut and clinically useful distinction between interpreting, which is a particular form of the analyst's inner psychic activity, and making an interpretation, i.e., the verbal interpretive comment conveyed to the analysand.

- Crucial to the success of treatment is the analyst's capacity to wait for the natural evolution of the transference, which can arise only out of the analysand's trust in the psychoanalytic technique and setting.
- Winnicott warns that an interpretation can potentially interrupt a natural process, which means that it can be experienced by the patient as traumatic if the analyst lacks sensitivity (to be able to accurately determine what to interpret), tactfulness (to know how to interpret), or timing (to know when to interpret).
- Winnicott's comment about "how much deep change" can be "prevented or delayed" by the analyst's "personal need to interpret" – i.e., his own narcissism – must not pass unnoticed.

Later, a ground-breaking statement:

> I think I interpret mainly to let the patient know the limits of my understanding. The principle is that it is the patient and only the patient who has the answers.
>
> (1968, p. 86)

Winnicott used interpretation not to uphold the analyst's pretense of omnipotently knowing everything about the patient's unconscious feelings, drives, and desires. But to do the opposite, to recognize the limits of his understanding and present himself to the patient as a real object which can be used for the patient's benefit.

Some authors believe that the core problem dealt with in this paper is the introjection of a surviving object together with the non-surviving object. In my view, this aspect comes after a more important step. Winnicott was trying to expand a view of the subject *vis-à-vis* the object, along a trajectory which was initiated when he described, as early as 1942, the subjective meaning of the period of hesitation. The object here is not only the internal object created as a result of infant/patient projections, but a real object – real not in the sense of external.

The object being real is determined by its capacity to survive attacks. Surviving the attack does not mean simply surviving, but also implies that the object may be wounded from this attack, but it can recover. This dynamic returns us to the infant/patient in analysis and the sense that the object who survives is real, hard, tough, and capable of standing up, that it is something against which his (the infant/patient's) omnipotence breaks and falls.

73

I have tried to show in this chapter that, contrary to common belief, it is not Winnicott's theory of infant development which influenced his clinical work, but, vice versa, his psychoanalytic work with adults which served as a lens through which he was able to understand early development.

Note

1 Although from a different perspective, Ogden (2001) was the first to underline this incredibly Winnicottian statement.

References

Abram, J. (1996). *The Language of Winnicott: A Dictionary of Winnicott's Use of Words*. London: Karnac.

Bion, W. R. (1957). Differentiation of the psychotic from the non-psychotic personalities. *Int. J. Psychoanal.*, 38:266–275.

_____ (1967). Notes on memory and desire. In: *Melanie Klein Today*, Vol. 2. Edited by E. B. Spillius. London: Routledge, 1988.

Bollas, C. (1979). The transformational object. *Int. J. Psycho-Anal.*, 60:97–107.

Bonamino, V. (1991). D. W. Winnicott and the position of the analyst and the analysand in the psychoanalytic situation. *Riv. di Psicoanalisi.*, XXXVII:626–666.

_____ (1993). Del non interpretare: alcuni spunti per una rivisitazione del contributo di M. Balint e due frammenti clinici. *Riv. di Psicoanalisi.*, 39:453–477.

Freud, S. (1933). New introductory lectures on psycho-analysis. *S. E.*, 22.

Fromm, M. G. & Smith, B. L. (eds.) (1989). *The Facilitating Environment: Clinical Applications of Winnicott's Theory*. Madison, CT: International Universities Press.

Giannakoulas, A. (2010). *La tradizione psicoanalitica britannica indipendente*. Rome: Borla.

Giovacchini, P. L. ed. (1973). *Tactics and techniques in psycho-analytic psycho-therapy*. London: Hogarth.

Khan, M. M. R. (1969). Vicissitudes of being, knowing and experiencing in the therapeutic situation. In: *The privacy of the self (1974)*. London: The Hogarth Press.

_____ (1975). *Introduction to: D. W. Winnicott, Collected Papers. Through Pediatrics to Psychoanalysis (1958). London: Karnac. Reprint of the original edition*, London: Tavistock Publications.

Kohon, G. (1992). *The British School of Psychoanalysis: The Independent Tradition*. London: Free Association Books.

Ogden, T. (2001). Reading Winnicott. In: *Conversations at the Frontier of Dreaming*. London: Routledge, 2018.

Phillips, A. (1988). *Winnicott*. Harmondsworth: Penguin, 2007.

Winnicott, D. W. (1945). Primitive emotional development. *Int. J. Psychoanal.*, 26:137–143.

_____ (1947). Hate in the countertransference. In: *Through Paediatrics to Psycho-Analysis*. London: Hogarth/Inst. of Psychoanalysis, 1975, pp. 194–203.

_____ (1948). Reparation in respect of mothers' organized defense against depression. In: *Through Paediatrics to Psycho-Analysis*. London: Hogarth/Inst. of Psychoanalysis, 1975, pp. 91–96.

_____ (1951). Transitional objects and transitional phenomena. In: *Playing and Reality*. London: Tavistock, 1971, pp. 255–261.

_____ (1954). Withdrawal and regression. In: *Through Paediatrics to Psycho-Analysis*. London: Hogarth/Inst. of Psychoanalysis, 1975, pp. 255–261.

_____ (1956). On transference. *Int. J. Psychoanal.*, 37:386–388.

_____ (1959). Nothing at the centre. In *Psycho-Analytic Explorations*. Edited by C. Winnicott, R. Shepherd, & M. Davis. London: Karnac, 1989, pp. 49–52.

_____ (1960). Ego distortion in terms of true and false self. In: *The Maturational Processes and the Facilitating Environment: Studies in the Theory of Emotional Development*. London: Hogarth/Inst. of Psychoanalysis, 1965, pp. 140–152.

_____ (1962). The aims of psycho-analytical treatment. In: *The Maturational Processes and the Facilitating Environment: Studies in the Theory of Emotional Development*. London: Hogarth/Inst. of Psychoanalysis, 1965, pp. 166–170.

_____ (1963a). Communicating and not communicating leading to a study of certain opposites. In: *The Maturational Processes and the Facilitating Environment: Studies in the Theory of Emotional Development*. London: Hogarth/Inst. of Psychoanalysis, 1965, pp. 179–192.

_____ (1963b). The development of the capacity for concern. In: *The Maturational Processes and the Facilitating Environment: Studies in the Theory of Emotional Development*. London: Hogarth/Inst. of Psychoanalysis, 1965, pp. 73–82.

_____ (1965). Notes on withdrawal and regression. In: *Psycho-Analytic Explorations*. Edited by D. W. Winnicott, C. Winnicott, R. Shepherd, & M. Davis. Cambridge, MA: Harvard University Press, 1989, pp. 149–151.

_____ (1967). Mirror role of mother and family in child development. In: *Playing and Reality*. London: Tavistock, 1971, pp. 111–118.

_____ (1968a). Interpretation in psycho-analysis. In: *Psycho-Analytic Explorations*. Edited by C. Winnicott, R. Shepherd, & M. Davis. London: Karnac, 1989, pp. 207–212.

_____ (1968b). The use of an object and relating through identifications. In: *Playing and Reality*. London: Tavistock, 1971, pp. 86–94.

_____ (1969). The use of an object. *Int. J. Psychoanal.*, 50:711–716.

_____ (1987). *The Spontaneous Gesture: Selected Letters of D. W. Winnicott*. Edited by F. R. Rodman. Cambridge, MA: Harvard University Press.

_____ (1988). *Human Nature*. New York: Schocken Press.

_____ (undated). A point in technique. In: *Psycho-Analytic Explorations*. Edited by C. Winnicott, R. Shepherd, & M. Davis. London: Karnac, 1989, pp. 26–27.

A TASK WHICH CAN NEVER BE ACCOMPLISHED

Dealing with Mother's Mood – Winnicott's Clinical Understanding of Psychic Work Carried Out for the [M]Other

By Vincenzo Bonaminio and Mariassunta Di Renzo

As happens with many other concepts that Winnicott dealt with in the course of his work, when one sets about examining his view of *depression,* one notices that almost all his writings give reflections that pertain to it, and that his interest in this subject is present almost without interruption from the beginning through to the end. It seems almost as though, depending on the point at which the detailed examination of his arguments begins, the author, from time to time, may not have been interested in anything if not depression, or dissociation, or feelings of boredom and manic defense, or the facilitating environment, or transitional objects and phenomena, or authenticity/falsity of the self, or subjective and objective objects – and all this from the very beginning.

The risk of viewing his writing this way can of course be of decontextualizing the work – extracting it by force, so to speak, from the torrent of clinical and theoretical debate in which he was fully immersed, and which he confronted at the beginning of the 1930s, in that special environment – if not a completely unique one – that began to evolve into the British Psychoanalytical Society.

In speaking of depression and of attention to depressive phenomena as one of Winnicott's initial interests, which then continually accompanied him through all his work – though intermittently – one cannot fail to take into account Melanie Klein (1935; 1940). Her work forcefully brings to the forefront of clinical attention and psychoanalytic practice a quantitative leap in the acquisition of anxiety and of the depressive position at the level of development, and of the personality's depressive organization as a psychopathological configuration.

Nevertheless, while recognizing the affinity of Winnicott's initial interest in depression and depressive feelings with Klein's pioneering work of the previous decade – whose influence he acknowledged and utilized extensively – one cannot fail to notice in the words, in the argumentative style with which he confronts his subject in his early writings, a distinctive stamp, a personal flavor in his choice of terms and adjectives that render his treatment of depression already distinguishable, *ab initio,* from that of Klein.

Naturally, we are referring here not only to depression in and of itself, a topic to which Winnicott introduces important and subtle clinical and conceptual distinctions that we will examine. We are also referring to the full range of feelings and moods that directly or indirectly – either by overlapping or in contrast, either by origin or in later development – have to do with depression.

Even in only glancing at the chronological list of his writings, one notices that Winnicott's essays on depression carry a particular imprint that distinguishes them from Kleinian ones: we are referring to 'The Manic Defense' (1935), 'Reparation in the Function of the Organized Maternal Defense Against Depression' (1948), 'Withdrawal and Regression' (1954a), 'The Depressive Position in Primitive Emotional Development' (1954b), 'The Capacity to Be Alone' (1958), 'The Development of the Capacity for Concern' (1963a), 'Communicating and Not Communicating Leading to a Study of Certain Opposites (1963b), and 'The Value of Depression' (1964).

But it is also his not-strictly-orthodox writings on depression that contain occasional but striking observations on depressive feelings – those of sadness, or, by contrast, of the manic defensive reaction. One unexpectedly finds these observations in his essay on 'Ocular Psychoneuroses of Childhood,' for example, in which Winnicott (1944) observes – one could say with great self-assurance – that:

> In children as in adults, depression can be recognized as a mood, and clinically it appears very commonly in its form of common

anxious restlessness, or a denial of depression by forced activity and liveliness. Along with this, as in depression phases in adults, one can see self-destructive actions, deliberate or accidental, and also hypochondriacal worry over the body or parts of the body. Far from being a rare illness, depression is a very common state in children as well as in adults, and is not even necessarily abnormal; hypochondriacal worry joins up with normal concern.

(1975, p. 87)

Considering this series of essays on depression and associated feelings permits us to highlight and examine one of the important threads running through Winnicott's work, which views depression not only as a serious psychopathological problem in adults and children – requiring the analyst's special attention in recognition and in clinical technique – but also as a phenomenon indicative of psychic health, promoting growth and psychological integration. Simultaneously, however, another important and original thread in Winnicott's reflection on depression can be singled out, one that overlaps and is interwoven with the first, but that must be kept conceptually distinct in order for us to fully grasp its intrinsic meaning.

We refer to that clinical approach to depression that Winnicott, from the beginning, brings to a consideration of this theme *inside the heart of the psychoanalytic relationship itself*. And he does this immediately, early on, in 'Primitive Emotional Development' (1945).

Winnicott's observation – which we quote in what follows, in order to allude to this second thread in his work about the meaning of depression, at least partially – can seem surprising and disorienting due to a certain incongruity with the context of the work in which it is placed. That is, it can seem so unless one considers it a current observation in contemporary psychoanalysis – which in many ways it is, specifically as a forerunner – that belongs to that particular clinical psychoanalysis that aims directly at the core of the relationship between patient and analyst, that takes apart its structure and even its textural patterns.

By contrast, we are in reality dealing with an observation that dates back precisely to 1945, and that appears almost abruptly not only in the aforementioned essay, but also abruptly appears, one could say, in the wider context of his work, constituting in a certain sense an unexpected anticipation of a distinctive development in his thought on the subject of depression: a development that we will try to track in this paper, distinguishing various interconnected components. Thus, he writes:

> The depressed patient requires of his analyst the understanding that the analyst's work is to some extent his effort to cope with his own (the analyst's) depression, or shall I say guilt and grief resultant from the destructive elements in his own (the analyst's) love. (p. 138)

This extremely dense observation, almost an undissolved coagulation of previous clinical experiences (and probably also personal ones) and reflections on these, concentrates a multiplicity of lines of development that are only later articulated. These reflections will gradually gather steam, so to speak, though laboriously and not always with clarity. But an element immediately leaps to our attention as revolutionary, almost radical, in the clinical psychoanalytic practice of that time, causing one to reasonably question whether Winnicott was as fully aware as he was, in contrast, most definitely aware of the disorganizing impact for the clinical theory of his time (both Kleinian and Anna Freudian) of his bold statement, "There is no such thing as a baby..." (Winnicott, 1948). What literally leaps out before our eyes, then, is the close ties that Winnicott establishes between psychoanalytic work and the work of the analyst as his particular effort to cope with his own depression, and between these two jobs *and* the analyst's answer to the patient's request.

Here in this passage, the description of the analytic relationship is, so to speak, turned upside down, or, to paraphrase Marx, it is repositioned with its 'feet on the ground.' The description is rotated by 180 degrees with respect to the conventional one, previously taken for granted: the analysis is possible only if the analyst is capable of working out his own depression, his own mourning, in the course of his relationship with the patient. He must work out his own depression in order to create a place inside himself from which to receive the patient's experience of depression. In our opinion, this mourning that the analyst must be able to carry out inside himself, in order to enter into contact with the patient and respond to his request, also means for the analyst to *revivify that dead internal object* that is the analyst's 'depressed mother,' in order to live the depression of the patient's internal mother-object.

In reality, literally, in the passage just cited, Winnicott doesn't explicitly speak either about the analyst elaborating his own mother's depression, or of receiving the patient's depressed mother inside himself. Depression in terms of introjection of an internal dead object, the depressed mother, implicitly present in this writing, is an original conception of Winnicott's distinctively different from Freud and Klein, to whom, however, he makes reference. But it is a particular concept of his that only later will he fully develop, as we will see, starting from his essay on 'Reparation in the Function of the Organized Maternal Defense Against Depression' (1948), and that will reach an even more profound description in 'Communicating and Not Communicating Leading to a Study of Certain Opposites' (1962). Here in the 1945 essay, we can grasp only its germinative nucleus.

In fact, it is only by considering these two elements in the subtext of this sentence that it is possible to understand the meaning that is otherwise obscure. Ogden (2001), too, poses himself the problem of rendering this sentence of Winnicott's comprehensible, but he proposes a different solution from the one that traces the origins of what will be the future development of his conception. Ogden writes:

> In the space of a single sentence, Winnicott suggests (by means of his *use of the idea*, rather than through his explication of it) that depression is a manifestation of the patient's taking on as his own (in fantasy, taking into himself) the mother's depression (or that of other loved objects), with the unconscious aim of relieving her of her depression. What is astounding is that this conception of the patient's depression is presented not through a direct statement, but by means of a sentence that is virtually incomprehensible unless the reader takes the initiative of doing the work of creating/discovering the conception *of the intergenerational origins and dynamic structure of depression.* (p. 303, *my italics*)

If the path to understanding this sentence of Winnicott's is different because it is based on the creative inference of the reader, and not on the later resignification of subsequent developments of his contribution, the conclusions are nonetheless the same:

> Only if the analyst is able to contain/live with the experience of the (internal object) mother's depression (as distinct from his own depression) will the analyst be able to experience the patient's pathological effort to relieve the mother's psychological pain (now

felt to be located in the analyst) by introjecting it into the patient's self as a noxious foreign body. (p. 304)

Winnicott, then, is interested from the beginning in understanding the forms in which depression appears in the patient, within the interior of the clinical psychoanalytic arrangement, in which declining moods, feelings, and defenses against them manifest themselves, and in what way the analyst can confront them, in what way he must take on the charge of the analyst's specifically transformative task.

The analyst's *response* says Winnicott, from the outset, makes the difference in the way the patient's depression develops, transforms itself, and is worked through. His striving *to be real and alive for the patient,* gives a unique imprint to the analysis of depression and dissociation (with schizoid patients) and feelings connected with or ascribed to boredom, apathy, a sense of futility, of freezing up and paralysis – this last an aspect that we will explore in depth later on.

How an alive analyst can confront depression, the sense of boredom, and dissociation

In relatively recent years, much has been written and a good deal of attention drawn to the importance of the *realness* of the analyst, i.e., his capacity for *spontaneity, freedom,* and *aliveness* in responding to the analysand on the basis of his own experience in the psychoanalytic situation, in such a way that he is not shackled by stereotypical attitudes in the observance of analytic neutrality (Ogden, 1999, p. 129).

Over a period of around 40 years, Winnicott's famous, and by now overquoted, statement – "In doing psychoanalysis I aim at: keeping alive, keeping well and keeping awake. I aim at being myself and behaving myself" (1962, p. 166) – may legitimately be regarded as the source of the all-important emphasis placed on the analyst's *keeping alive* in the course of the session. What was Winnicott referring to? What clinical situations did he have in mind in making this arresting statement, assuming we don't pass it off as an offhand declaration of principle? In other words, what interferences and what defenses and resistances had cropped up, and what petrified language had taken root in his experience, in the relations between analyst and patient that stopped the analyst from being himself, from keeping awake and generally keeping himself alive? These qualities cannot be taken for granted. It is the result (if a result there be) of a continuous process of elaboration, characterized moment by moment by what Smith (2000) defined as *conflictual listening,* in emphasizing "an ongoing conflictual responsiveness in the analyst that contains, like the momentary states, not only affective signals but all the components of conflict" (p. 107).

In other words, Winnicott is obviously referring to the *work* done by the analyst:

> I would rather be remembered as maintaining that in between the patient and the analyst is the analyst's professional attitude, his technique, *the work he does with his mind.* Now I say this without fear because I am not an intellectual and in fact I personally do my work very much from the body-ego, so to speak. But I think of myself in my analytic work working with an easy but conscious mental effort.
>
> (1960, p. 161, italics in original)

Here Winnicott is calling attention to the distance and diversity of positions between the two partners of the analytic couple in session: one of them enters into analysis mainly because he is ill and expects to be cured; while the other one, the analyst, is supposed to be in a position to cure him.

In this keeping alive for the patient, we maintain – as we have earlier (Bonaminio & Di Renzo, 2000) – that there is a discernible *benign aspect* of the 'psychic work for the other' done on the part of the analyst, which provides the title and focus for our paper.

Generally speaking, the essentialness of the *other* – as we have identified and discussed in another article (Bonaminio & Di Renzo, 2003) – its unavoidability for the mind of the subject, the paradox of the fact that the relationship with the *other* makes it possible to become oneself, i.e., an individual – all this implies not only the contribution of the *other* to the formation of the individual self, but also the contribution to the *other* on the part of the individual self.

Naturally, as analysts, we are used to considering this latter aspect from the countertransference register, in the widest acceptance of the term. Particularly in certain phases of the analysis or with certain difficult patients, i.e., when the patient has clinically regressed to functioning at primitive levels, but with a highly sophisticated defensive organization, the analyst's psychic work becomes relatively speaking the *only* mental activity available, a sort of loan from the analyst to the analysand. The patient uses this for a given period, a shorter or a longer one, as he goes through the process of ego integration.

Bion's (1959) notion that the analyst (mother) keeps alive, and can somehow call into life aspects of the analysand (infant) – projected aspects of the self – through the successful containment of projected identifications, is one way of describing this process (Ogden, 1999).

In Winnicott's (1955a; 1956b) terms, the analyst's "psyche-soma" integrity, his capacity to respond to the patient's needs, performs the function of *holding*: i.e., he supports and holds together the dissociated and regressed parts of the patient, always aware that he is a subjective object for him, and possesses "some of the characteristics of a transitional phenomenon," but is "all the time maneuvering into the position of standard analysis" (1962, p. 166), and – paraphrasing Winnicott, in anticipation of our argument that follows – this coincides with the moment when the analysand "can *start on* his own life" (1948, p. 92) and can have the "feeling of existing in his or her own right" (1962, p. 168).

It is significant that in his discussion of the analyst's role vis-à-vis the patient's in his above-mentioned paper, Winnicott make precise reference to the fact that this role must vary in accordance with the patient's diagnosis (1960a, p. 162). Of the two types of diagnosis he refers to, the "antisocial tendency" and the "borderline patient," and the latter is undoubtedly the most interesting for our discussion:

> The analyst will need to be able to play the part of mother to the patient's infant. This means giving ego-support in a big way. The analyst will need to remain orientated to external reality while in fact being identified with the patient, even *merged in* with the patient.
>
> (1960a, p. 163, italics added)

"Identified with the patient" and even "merged in with the patient" are – in our view – two of the ways in which Winnicott describes, within the countertransference register, the "analyst's work for the patient."

In schizoid pathology, the process may be described from a different but converging point of view. The *extraneousness of the self to itself* on the part of the schizoid patient (his 'manic defense') is proposed again *in toto* in the total transference as a clinical fact of the

84

psychoanalytic relationship. The work of the analyst's countertransference consists of that part of his emotions and personal thoughts that make him progressively available, from pre-consciousness to awareness, including an awareness of something around the patient, something that alludes to the dissociated self that the patient knows nothing about ('denial of reality'), including 'suspended animation' as a clinical characteristic (Winnicott, 1935). The sense of boredom and helplessness the analyst may experience while listening to the petrified narrations of the schizoid patient are, in countertransference terms, the something around the patient that has to do with the part of the dissociated self that is extraneous to the patient, and naturally to the analyst as well.

The ongoing transformations occurring in analysis can be visualized along a continuum in process, basically characterized in any given segment by the *offer*, the *loan* of functions from the analyst's mind to the patient, and, in the segment that follows, by the progressive emergence of the self-analytic element *inside* the patient.

The analyst's work for the patient

The first signs of an emerging capacity to have an overall view of the state of the self can be traced in a dream in the intermediate phase of Paolo's analysis. He was a man in his early 30s who had asked for psychoanalytic help two years earlier, complaining of the sensation that he had "never done anything solid or meaningful." He was also very disturbed about his incapacity to get "an overall view of himself and his life, his past and future prospects." He felt "a sense of precariousness and insecurity" in all areas of his life: marriage, work, and relationships with friends.

Paolo had entered treatment expecting analysis to be "like a mirror where he could see and find himself, so he could feel he really existed." He saw it as an "attempt to get his life back and have a space of his own," and "to kindle the spark that would set alight something living inside." This expectation was soon revealed in the transference, in the early phase of the analysis, in sharp and intense contrast to an inner relationship with an opaque, nonresponsive primary object, completely lacking in vitality. As it later became possible to reconstruct, this was the precipitate in the ego of his early traumatic experience of his mother's serious and prolonged depression following the sudden death of his father when Paolo was two and a half years old. This condition, in turn, seemed to have amplified his mother's (presumable) postpartum depression in the first months of his life, giving it further significance for the child in retrospect, in terms of cumulative trauma.

This is his dream:

> I dreamed I was going to look at my beehives. One stood in the shade of a walnut tree, where it seemed to me it couldn't develop properly, and that it should be placed in the sunshine because it was spring. The other hive was placed in the sun, but the top of the hive was open, so it couldn't offer the bees any warmth or protection. The honeycomb frame was set horizontally instead of vertically, and the bees were fighting for their lives.

The walnut tree in the dream was the one at which his grandmother would leave him as a child, while she was working on the farm. She was the one who had to take care of him because of his mother's depression. The bees, in which he had recently begun to take a great interest, whenever he returned to his home village on weekends, appear here in a dream for the first time, not just as scant references in his narrations. This indicates the beginning of an osmosis and reciprocal animation between the internal world and the external world. In terms of our argument, it signals a progressive abandoning of the suspended animation that characterizes manic defense.

The narration of this dream to the analyst would appear to constitute the first time the analysand was capable of representing the dilemma that characterized the previous phase of the analysis, up to that moment: either he was entrusting himself to a relationship of dependence, with all the risks and catastrophic anxieties that involved (the open bee hive, the horizontal honeycomb – i.e., the child lying in his mother's arms, like the patient lying on the analyst's couch); or else he was maintaining a precarious narcissistic equilibrium while continuing to support himself on his own, as he had always tried to do, by leaning on a false self that allowed him a pseudo-independence and a pseudo-maturity (the closed beehive in the shade, the vertical honeycomb – i.e., a narcissistic defense of the autistic, self-sufficient shell, or, in other words, a psychic retreat as a sort of entombment in which he was identified with the dead mother).

This was also the first time that a *whole experience of self* was dream-able, i.e., symbolisable, and contained in a single 'psychic scene,' though still lacking integration of the partial, split-off aspects of the self. It included aspects of the relationship that until now could be expressed only through *enactment*, and which, as such and still only partially, formed the patient's total experience of *self* at that moment.

With the symbolization generated by this dream, a metaphori-cal dimension connected to the world and the life of bees could now be more fully formed within the psychoanalytic relationship. Here not only the analysand, but also the analyst could draw from a sort of mine of images, as though from a source of imagination. This allowed her, the analyst, to communicate to the patient some-thing around his self, which could be infused with meaning, at the same time that she articulated the countertransference and made it dynamic, freeing it from the paralysis that had so consistently char-acterized it.

In other words, the analyst could set out from the symbolization of the dream and imagine that, in the transference, she represented something like the walnut tree for the patient, the covering and pro-tecting shade, which will now open the way to life and growth. Or she may be like the spring sunshine that enabled all this to happen, though risking impingement on a vulnerable, newborn self as he regressively entrusted himself to her. All these are images from the transference relationship which could now be communicated back to the patient in words. This type of psychic work, the elaboration occurring at this level, starts to take on characteristics of mutuality and reciprocity – even though, of course, this does not imply sym-metry of the contributions of the two parties to the psychoanalytic process.

But what was going on *before* this symbolization gradually took shape and turned the work of the psychoanalytic couple into a job for two? The silence that Paolo sometimes used to hide behind at the beginning of sessions (especially Monday sessions), that made a soporific impression on the analyst – as though her mind were fog-ging up – was now configured as protection from direct contact, as though the patient had brought along a mask, gloves, and fumiga-tor to lull his bee-like emotions to sleep, lest they buzz around in the relationship and attack, sting, and overwhelm him. But *before*, given the absence of a shared representation, the emotional states of the countertransference, and, more precisely, the physical sensations aroused in it, could not be returned to the patient. Somehow they did not even seem usable for analytic work, since they appeared to be only the analyst's sensations, her own internal difficulty in listening to the patient.

When these states started to get the upper hand, the only possible way the analyst could find to represent them was the feeling of being overwhelmed: her problem was survival, struggling to exist. Even when these states could gradually begin to be linked to the patient's emotional states enacted during the session, they could not be spoken about or communicated since they occurred only in the form of the internal – prevalently bodily – states of the analyst: torpor, sleepiness, paresthesia of the lower limbs, numbness in the forearm, sensations of physical inconsistency, as though the body were about to dissolve in the welter of Paolo's *impersonal* communications, and above all in his prolonged, recurrent, tomb-like silences. Or else there were sensations of psychomotor restlessness, such as slight agitation, itching, stomach gurgling – on the whole a disturbing emphasis of internal sensations of the body at moments when Paolo was engulfed in the particularly intense emotional states that erupted during his communications in session.

This is the countertransference *work* to which we are referring. And rather 'dirty work' it is, through which the analyst has to endure the primitive states of his/her psyche-soma condition and then go on to work them out, thereby offering the patient a bit of his/her own mental functioning. This makes it possible for the psychoanalytic relationship – though not the patient himself, at this point – to make use of the analyst's mental functioning, to be grounded in it in view of work that is more shareable, and is thus more sophisticated in terms of symbolization.

In the context of our argument, Paolo's dream may also be seen as the representation of a total vision of the oscillations that characterized the course of the previous phase, and that now, in retrospect, have become more comprehensible.

It became evident in this early phase that Paolo tended to lock himself up in long silences as he lay motionless and practically devitalized on the couch. This resulted in the creation of an unbridgeable distance, a loss of contact, and a gulf between patient and analyst, and at the very time when a more spontaneous and intense emotional communication had opened up in the relationship – a situation that had led the analyst to expect construction and growth of the relationship. Her disappointment was accompanied by depressive feelings and sensations of impotence and paralysis. This was a reactivation in the analytic scenario of a specific emotional sensation: the mother's depression, mirrored in Paolo's infantile depression.

In the course of the psychoanalytic process, it became clear that Paolo's withdrawal was not configured solely as an expression of the compulsion to repeat the disinvestment of an object experienced as capable of disappointing, abandoning, and disappearing, in his bid to get control of the traumatic situation. Simultaneously, it was also configured as an unconscious identification with the depressed mother who had been transformed from the source of her child's vitality into a colorless figure, unreachable and inaccessible. This identification, however, appeared to allow and even guarantee Paolo union with his mother (Green, 1980), and at the same time was configured as a de-animated, devitalized psychic retreat (in the dream, the closed beehive in the shade), as a protection from the relationship with a mother who was not only *alive*, but *much too present,* and an excessive source of stimuli and projections – a mother unable to fulfil her proper function of containment, regulation, and elaboration of her own emotional states as well as those of her child (the open beehive exposed to intense heat and light).

To further elaborate our initial argument, we might say that, on the basis of the countertransference sensations encountered in Paolo's analysis were essential for survival in the face of the patient's tomb-like silence; but it was equally essential not to be *too* alive or *too* awake, so as not to expose him to a vitality that he was in no condition to withstand.

In the dream of the two beehives, the hopelessness, the impossibility is clearly brought forward as a dilemma. But because of the very fact that it was represented in these terms, the situation had already become less impossible.

Deep down in the lower levels of the analytic scenario, something happened, work has been done, and from down there, i.e., from the analyst's bodily sensations – as she laboriously acquires meaning inside herself, thus performing a function on behalf of the patient – the work has moved upward, into the upper levels. The mists have evaporated, the haze is lifting, and this has made it possible to discern something that gives meaning to what happened before.

References

Bion, W. R. (1959). *Attacks on linking. Second Thoughts.* London: Heinemann

Bonaminio, V., & Di Renzo, M. (2000). La comprensione clinica di winnicott del "lavoro psichico svolto per l'altro": "far fronte all'umore della madre." Relazione presentata al II Congresso Internazionale, "Winnicott nel 2000." Milano, Italy, 16–19, November 2000.

_____ (2003). L'imprescindibilità dell'altro. *Un percorso nel pensiero clinico di Winnicott sul sé e l'altro, e il lavoro di controtransfert dell'analista nella situazione psicoanalitica.* Interazioni, 2-2003/20:62–73.

Green, A. (1980). The dead mother. In: *On Private Madness.* London: The Hogarth Press and The Institute of Psychoanalysis. Original publication: La mère morte. In: *Narcissisme de vie, narcissisme de mort.* Paris: Editions de Minuit.

Klein, M. (1935). A contribution to the theory of intellectual inhibition. In: *The Writings of Melanie Klein: Volume I.* London: Karnac Books, 1992.

_____ (1940). Mourning and its relation to manic-depressive states. In: *The Writings of Melanie Klein: Volume I.* London: Karnac Books, 1992.

Ogden, T. H. (1999). Analysing forms of aliveness and deadness of the transference-countertransference. In: *The Dead Mother. The Work of André Green.* Edited by G. Kohon. London and New York: Routledge. Originally published in *Int. J. Psycho-Anal.*, 1995, 76: 695–709.

_____ (2001). Reading Winnicott. In: *Conversations at the Frontiers of Dream.* London: Routledge, 2018

Smith, H. F. (2000). Countertransference, conflictual listening. And analytic object relationship. *J. Am. Psycho-Anal. Assn.*, 48:95–128.

Winnicott, D. W. (1935). The manic defense. In: *Collected Papers: Through Pediatrics to Psychoanalysis* (1958). London: Tavistock Publications.

_____ (1944). Ocular psychoneuroses of childhood. In *The Collected Works of D. W. Winnicott: Volume 2, 1939–1945.* Edited by Lesley Caldwell & Helen Taylor Robinson. Oxford: Oxford Press, 2017.

_____ (1948). Reparation in the function of the organized maternal defense against depression. In: *Collected Papers: Through Pediatrics to Psychoanalysis (1958).* London: Tavistock Publications.

_____ (1954a). Withdrawal and regression. In *The Collected Works of D.W. Winnicott: Volume 4, 1955–1955.* Oxford: Oxford Press, 2017.

_____ (1954b). The depressive position in normal emotional development. In: *The Collected Works of D.W. Winnicott: Volume 4, 1955–1955.* Oxford: Oxford Press, 2017.

_____ (1956). Primary maternal preoccupation. In: *Collected Papers: Through Pediatrics to Psychoanalysis (1958)*. London: Tavistock Publications.

_____ (1958). The capacity to be alone. In: *The Maturational Processes and the Facilitating Environment (1965)*. London: The Hogarth Press and The Institute of Psychoanalysis.

_____ (1960). Ego Distortion in Terms of True and False Self. In: *The Maturational Processes and the Facilitating Environment (1965)*. London: The Hogarth Press and The Institute of Psychoanalysis.

_____ (1962). The aims of psycho-analytical treatment. In: *The Maturational Processes and the Facilitating Environment (1965)*. London: The Hogarth Press and The Institute of Psychoanalysis.

_____ (1963a). The development of the capacity for concern. In: *The Maturational Processes and the Facilitating Environment (1965)*. London: The Hogarth Press and The Institute of Psychoanalysis.

_____ (1963b). Communicating and not communicating leading to a study of certain opposites. In: *The Maturational Processes and the Facilitating Environment (1965)*. London: The Hogarth Press and The Institute of Psychoanalysis.

_____ (1964). The value of depression. In: *Home Is Where We Start from*. Harmondsworth: Penguin, 1990.

4

THE ANALYST OSCILLATING BETWEEN INTERPRETING AND NOT INTERPRETING

Defense Is an Attempt to Deny Inner Reality; It Is an Escape to External Reality and an Attempt to Maintain Suspended Animation

We shall shortly give fuller attention to the essential meaning that should be attributed, in our opinion, to *denial* of inner reality. But this is a good place to draw attention to the fact that it is to Khan that we owe the extension of Winnicott's concept of manic defense, linking it to the psychodynamic of the psychic state that compels a person to be boring in analysis (Khan, 1978, p. 2):

> The boring patient is trying to maintain omnipotent control over his inner reality [manic defense] by obsessional over-control of language and material. His narrative is a petrified space where nothing can happen (…) The patient who compels boring narrative on us is not letting language and metaphor elaborate or change his experience. He creates a space of discourse where both he and the analyst are paralyzed by the technique of the narrative as well as its monotonous and repetitive contents. (p. 3)

If the analyst has "to learn to tolerate this counterfeit discourse in order to help the patient," (ibid.) we may well ask ourselves if his efforts at confronting the patient's state of depression and psychic deadness with aliveness do not really constitute the analyst's specific work for the patient, which we have examined above and discussed in some detail.

Our argument is that, at the basis of various forms of denial of inner reality and suspended animation, and their various degrees of intensity where manic defense appears in the analysis, there is a *primary identification* (in terms of primary defensive mechanism) with a depressed object that is 'psychologically dead for the child,' and, in any event, not a source of vitality for the subject. Later on we shall naturally make more extensive reference to Green's (1980) classic work on the dead mother complex. Here, however, we wish to emphasize that we believe our connecting this identification with a dead primary object – i.e., an object that does not provide aliveness for the child – and with the concept of manic defense, and also with the concept of *psychic work done for the other,* may well be an integration with the work of Green; and we believe it constitutes our use of it within the wider framework of clinical research in the Winnicottian tradition.

We have already illustrated this configuration with the case of Paolo, above all focused it in the context of the analyst's work on behalf of the patient, in an attempt to confront, give meaning to, and elaborate the feelings of boredom and psychic death that arose in the clinical setting due to the patient's petrified narrative and tomb-like silences. We shall now go on to condense a fragment of the psychoanalytic treatment of a child of six, Alessandro. During the period under consideration, the child produced a series of drawings whose intensely figurative power lent itself admirably to a description of the other side we referred to, within the clinical relationship: i.e., the psychic work that the subject (not yet a subject, but on the way *to becoming a subject*) performs *for* the *other* – that is, for the depressed mother.

The child who fell in a ravine, alone, in the cold and dark

What follows is a fragment of clinical material concerning a supervision which was covered more extensively in a previous paper (Bonaminio, 1999).[1]

Alessandro was in his third year of therapy, begun at the age of three owing to a borderline developmental disorder with consistent psychotic risk and an autistic-like defense organization. During the period we are examining, the child produced a series of games with animals, as well as drawings that continually represented, with significant variations, 'a child falling into a hole.' Almost intentionally, he seemed to want to tell his own story of a catastrophe, his own psychological catastrophe. But most of all, it seemed that this psychological catastrophe, intuited from the very beginning of the analysis and steadily, laboriously reconstructed as the analytic work progressed, could now be represented by the child in the first person, and at the same time distanced in the second occurrence of the *après coup* (*Nachträglichkeit*).

The emerging representation of himself as 'a child *precipitating down*[2] into a void' is the precipitate of a more cohesive sense of self. On more secure and solid ground, the child looks at himself: the child who fell into the void. However, that self is no longer his whole self, but a part of his self: *a generative dissociation* within the self has occurred, and this permits recovery of what was not representable before. Only later, after a month had gone by since the series of drawings we mentioned were produced, and during a game based on the same theme, the therapist felt she was prepared, also on the basis of supervision, to offer the child this reconstructive interpretation of his personal story. To her surprise, Alessandro's reaction was "But it *wasn't* like that!" – thereby showing he had understood and that he was able to process, by means of a *negation*, the communication about himself from his therapist – and, as in a series of concentric circles, from the supervision as well, which contained the relationship between therapist and supervisor that in turn contained the child's relationship with his therapist.

This generative dissociation, this division into two basic structures, a 'simple' and a 'complex' self – which Bollas (1990) assigned the characteristic of *experiencing self* in the dream, and the 'organizing intelligence,' which elaborates the dream environment and gives it meaning, and which Fonagy and Target (1996) describe from the child's developmental point of view as the development of the self-reflective capacity – is precisely what we referred to earlier in this paper. It is a crucial moment in developmental transition from which to watch and understand the child's experience of psychological catastrophe, despair, loss, and mourning – in a word, the entire developmentally differentiated range of depressive feelings.

The notion of basic dissociation of the personality is implicit in the manic defense concept, as originally described by Winnicott (1935) i.e., *denial* (Freud's *Verleugnung*) of inner reality, and particularly of the sensations related to depression and suspended animation. It is an issue Winnicott was to develop 10 years later (1945) in the context of integration and non-integration, which was to lead him to make a definitive formulation of dissociation of inner reality in his paper (1960), 'Ego Distortion in Terms of True and False Self' (Khan, 1975).

Along this line of clinical research, Winnicott insisted on *basic dissociation* in personality. It is dissociation, not repression or splitting – both of which imply an ego to do the work – that fore-closes the child's further development if the integration (facilitated by the environment) cannot be made or is blocked: "Only after integration - Winnicott writes (1955) - can the child start to have a self" (Phillips, 1988).

What we are proposing is to consider the manic defense, with its underlying mechanism, as the psychic hinge that generates this developmental dissociation. On the one hand, it liberates the subject from disintegration and psychotic fragmentation, as well as from auto-sensual autistic protections,[3] while on the other hand, in subsequent mental development, it introduces the issue of split-off, dissociated parts of the self, displaced somewhere (or possibly 'nowhere') – parts with which contact must be resumed in order to integrate them into the self.

This 'reflective function of the self,' the 'organizing intelligence' gives meaning to the representation and is brought out in the draw-ings that Alessandro did during this period of his treatment. Namely, this occurs with the appearance in one of the drawings (Figure 4.1a and b) – with a clear Oedipal connotation – of a character: the incredibly expressive mouse he drew in the corner of the sheet of paper, which is watching the entire scene, in which an iron cat-child is being intruded upon by a couple of adults.

To highlight this generative dimension of dissociation when it is linked to primary depression and manic defense, and later with 'reparation with respect to the mother's organized defense against depression,' we shall show in the following series of drawings how the 'Oedipal statute' that the child was able to reach alongside the consolidation of the self-reflective function opened up the way for the construction of a representation that has to do with a more primitive event – i.e., the psychological catastrophe, the 'original breakdown,' the 'fall into the void' – but also the contact with mother's depression.

95

4.1a

4.1b

4.2a

At first with hesitant strokes, then with more determination, Alessandro began to draw a mountain slope (Figure 4.2a). On top of the mountain, he drew a poodle looking toward the right of the page. On the left, he drew something that remained incomplete and unidentified. The therapist said it looks like a cat's head, but Alessandro had gone on to draw a dachshund on the left, looking in the opposite direction to the poodle. He said they are both *strays,* then added a smiling sun. Next, he started coloring in everything, including the vague form still only half-filled with grey. The therapist commented that the two dogs were not walking in the same direction. "Then the poodle falls …" Alessandro said, pointing to the mountain. "It's a ravine …"

He immediately asked for another sheet of paper in order to draw the following scene, as in a comic strip where the succession of frames narrates the story (Figure 4.2b).

The poodle fell *headlong down* into the ravine – i.e., the *break-up* occurred. On the right, Alessandro pointed to where the dog fell and firmly added a vertical cliff wall on the left to depict a *horrific space* where there was no hope of a foothold. "But how could this happen?" asked the therapist. "He fell down. He didn't see the

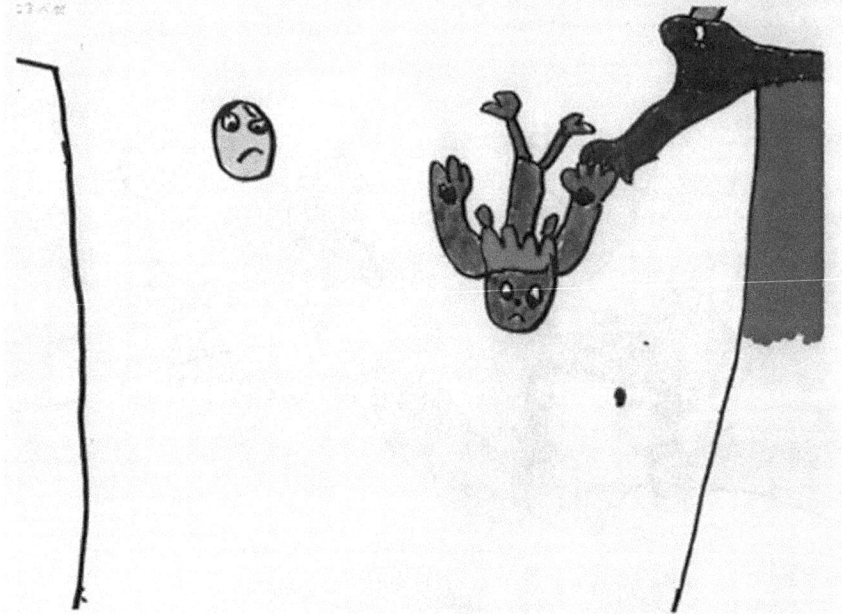

4.2b

precipice ..." the child replied. "Isn't there anyone there to help him?" Alessandro filled in the other dog and said: "He tried to hold him, but it was no good ..." Then he drew stones falling and a sad-looking sun, in contrast to the smiling sun in the first picture.

Next, he asked for another sheet to draw the sad dachshund walking away (Figure 4.2c), and a little later added a tear coming out of its eye.

The therapist asked if the dachshund was going to look for help. "No, there's no one there," Alessandro answered. "But what about the poor poodle down there? He must be terrified," the therapist said.

On another sheet, Alessandro drew the poodle after the fall (Figure 4.2d). He said: "He was alone. It was all cold and dark; he was very frightened and hurt badly." The therapist commented: "It must have been a dreadful experience for the poor poodle when the dachshund wasn't able to save him. He fell into the void, down into the ravine, and now he is frightened; he feels lonely and abandoned. Perhaps he hid in that dark cave, waiting for someone to come and save him from dying." Alessandro answered: "There's no one there," and then he drew a bone and some water and a fire near the dog.

In the first frame of this representation, the retrospectively idealized primary relationship is emphasized by the happy feeling

4.2c

4.2d

expressed in the yellow of the sun. Here, too, an apparently peripheral detail, added later, colors the entire scene with emotion, while
the *mood change* toward depression will be expressed in the next
drawing, by the change in the face of the sun – a 'reflective self'
who observes and participates emotionally in the scene, at the same
time bearing the signs of *identification* with mother's depression, as
we shall see further on.

But this first frame already contains elements that foresee the
breakdown: the incomplete figure drawn *between* the two main
characters seems to allude to the separating, intrusive *traumatic agent*
that looms closer and closer. The moment of break-up, the intolerable separation from the primary relationship with the object, as in
an expressionist painting, finds its focus of attraction in the dog's
look of terror as it falls into a bottomless void, observed with a
desperate awareness. The dog falls intact, *without breaking;* it is not
threatened with fragmentation. Only some small pieces (the two
stones breaking off the sheer face of the mountain) are lost during
the fall. Maintenance of bodily integrity alludes to the protection
guaranteed by an autistic–like defense, which preserves the self from
fragmentation (Winnicott, 1967, p. 1974; Tustin, 1981). But this puts
the *capacity for thinking* at risk. The red cap on the dog's head seems
to represent his mind, which risks flying away under the pressure of
the fall into the chasm; yet it still sits squarely, *indwelt* on the dog's
head. As in a *'michelangelesque'* detail, except reversed, the mother
and child's hands (the paws of the two dogs, the one standing on the
edge and the other falling) strain to touch each other. But the reach
is in vain; break-up is inevitable.

In the final drawing, we find the poodle looking sad and depressed.
A line has been drawn around him, partly filled in with black. The
bottom of the precipice is a sort of black hole, where we see the dog –
cold and lonely, injured and dying; but it is also a place of survival
with respect to denied existence. It is the place of basic dissociation
of the self, the place of autistic defense, a double shell colored in
with the black of depression and death. Outside the autistic shell are
the bone, the meagre oral survival, then a blazing fire, graphically
similar to the transfiguration of the sun after the fall, all that remains
of the light and heat – as a symptom of hope of what was retained by
the autistic–like defense, and which, as the experience of an object
that has been present, seems, at a psychopathological level, to guarantee the child prevention of more serious psychotic damage – just

as the red cap-mind, still firmly indwelt on his head, will ensure communication.

We have deliberately passed over any reference to the third frame (Figure 4.2c) in the sequence because discussing it last allows us to comment on the representation of the depressed mother and contact with her. The other dog has remained on the edge of the precipice, staring, lost and sad, into the void. The teardrop of suffering and depression welling from its eye was added later. Significant similarities between mother and child (the dog falling and the dog up on the edge of the ravine) appear in this sequence: in looking at the two drawings (Figure 4.2c and d) with one superimposed on the other, we notice identical positions and postures, as well as the use of the same colors.

In this process of primary identification with the mother – she, too, lonely and depressed, like her child – it is possible to make out the original basis, the identification precipitate of the psychic, relational mechanism which will later become what Winnicott (1948) describes as "the [child's] reparation in respect to the mother's organized defense against depression."

A task which can never be accomplished: Confronting the mother's mood

Actually, the concept that Winnicott expressed in his 1948 paper refers to the false reparation that we find in clinical practice: *false* because it is not specifically tied to the patient's guilt, but refers to *another*. Although this theory, a radical one compared to the Kleinian ideas of the time, gives rise to his clinical discoveries on dissociation in connection with the *false self* we believe, as we have pointed out on other occasions, that the relevance of the central core of the configuration as described by Winnicott is far more comprehensive. It can explain, heuristically, more primitive and precocious psychopathological and clinical phenomena in the structure of the self, along a continuum (but with more significant qualitative differences) with the further developed schizoid phenomena with which Winnicott's concept was initially associated.

At the outset of his 1948 paper, Winnicott observed that "this false reparation appears through the patient's identification with the mother, and the dominating factor is not the patient's own guilt but the mother's organized defense against depression and unconscious guilt." Further on, he says: "The depression of the child can be the mother's depression in reflection. The child uses the mother's depression as an escape from his or her own; this provides a false restitution and reparation in relation to the mother, and this hampers the development of a personal restitution capacity." And later: "It will be seen that these children in extreme cases have *a task which can never be accomplished* [italics added]. Their task is first *to deal with mother's mood* [italics added]. If they succeed in the immediate task, they do no more than succeed in creating an atmosphere in which they can *start on their own lives* [italics in original]" (1948, pp. 91–93).

When Winnicott puts forward considerations like these, he is beginning to describe the psychic work done on behalf of the other within the self through identification. The scale of this work varies widely, until it comes to include occupation of the self by the other.[4]

As we have mentioned, the presence in the self of this depressed object is dealt with in Green's paper on 'The Dead Mother' (1980). Starting out by considering the problem of mourning and loss, Green goes on to make it clear that he intends to describe the clinical configuration of "an imago which has been constituted in the child's mind, following maternal depression, brutally transforming a living object, which was a source of vitality for the child, into a distant figure (...) [The] 'dead mother' ... is a mother who remains alive, but who is, so to speak, psychically 'dead' in the eyes of the young child in her care" (1980, p. 142).

Even though Green does not specifically quote Winnicott's paper on 'Reparation in the Function of the Organized Maternal Defense Against Depression,' he explicitly declares that Winnicott's contributions (as well as Kohut's, Abraham and Torok's, and Rosolato's) are the source of his reflection on this theme. It is precisely the primary identification with the dead object (i.e., identification with the *hole left* by the decathexis) that lies at the center of his analysis.

This mirroring identification, Green continues, is almost obligatory once the reactions of complementarity (artificial cheerfulness, agitation, etc.) have broken down. This reactive symmetry is the only medium available to establish union with the mother via a sympathetic process. It is *not in fact an authentic reparation*, but *mimicry* aimed at possessing the object – since it is no longer possible to possess the object in another way – by becoming not only *like* the object, but *the object itself*. Identification occurs without the ego being aware of it and against its will, hence its *alienating* character (1980, pp. 276, my italics).[5]

We have dealt more extensively with this identification, which Green calls alienating, in previous works on child analysis defining it as "ego-alien" in developing a concept expressed by Winnicott during a later period, in his 1969 paper on 'Mother's Madness Appearing in the Clinical Material as an Ego-Alien Factor.' However much this identification may be out of tune with the individual's own peculiarities, it is not directed toward growth, but toward psychic survival. It turns up, like a cyst, in the child's internal world, as a 'foreign body' that he must get around, must isolate (via a dissociation mechanism), but must also annex (in identification elements); on the one hand, he guarantees for himself, albeit in a 'compliant' way (false self), the love of the primary object, and on the other hand, he protects and 'secretly' hangs on to the existence of the potential true self.

In a recent essay by Bollas (1999) — which, significantly, was written for the collection of papers devoted to Green's work on 'The Dead Mother' (Kohon, 1999) — we found a further definition of this internal object: as an *interject*, not an *introject*. The *intrusion*, the *presence* of the other's unconscious core, the *impingement* and the primary defense against it, is the principal mechanism of these psychopathological configurations, and not the child's projective identification of parts of the self onto the object.

This is the point of view Winnicott took in an unpublished paper (1967), when he conceptualized autism as "a highly sophisticated defense organisation," characterized by invulnerability as an extreme defense against primary depression and primitive agonies (Winnicott, 1967, pp. 220–222), resulting from, *inter alia*, the impossibility of confronting the "mother's unconscious (repressed) hate of the child." Significantly, he had already dealt with this subject in 'Hate in the Countertransference' (Winnicott, 1947).

What Winnicott defines in this paper as the constant effort of the autistic child "to arrive at the starting point" – i.e., to "counteract the parents' unconscious wish (covered by reactive formation) that the child should be dead," which "hampers the development of a personal capacity" – is very similar to the impossible task of the depressed child in *dealing with mother's mood* – which we have seen in 'Reparation in the Function of the Organized Maternal Defense Against Depression' – in order to be able to create an atmosphere in which he can start on his own life.

That this configuration of close interrelationship between the maternal mood and the child's self-states constitutes the dominant characteristic that, to significantly different degrees, cuts across various forms of early psychopathology (from autism to depression and schizoid states), and can represent itself *in toto* in the clinical varieties of the transference (Winnicott, 1956, is demonstrated by a further clinical observation that Winnicott advances in his essay on 'Communicating and Not Communicating Leading to a Study of Certain Opposites.' Here he speaks of the *idea of being alive,* which involves at least two opposites: on one hand, "the condition of death as in the manic defense," and on the other, "a simple absence of vivaciousness." Thus, he writes:

> *In certain cases,* however, the mother's central internal object is dead at the critical time in her child's early infancy, and her mood is one of depression. Here the infant has to fit in with a role of *dead* object, or else has to be lively to counteract the mother's preconception with the idea of the child's deadness. Here the opposite to the liveliness of the infant is *an anti-life factor* derived from the mother's depression. The task of the infant in such a case is to be alive and to look alive and to communicate being alive....The aliveness of the child whose mother is depressed is a communication of a reassuring nature, and it is unnatural and an intolerable handicap to the immature ego in its function of integrating and generally maturing according to inherited process.
>
> (1963, pp. 191–192)

So it is from this point of view, the psychic work done for the other, that we propose manic defense as a 'more developed' organization, in comparison to the autistic defense, which, however, reveals traces of the same situation – i.e., attempts to face up to the unconscious and unelaborated psychic reality of the object: the mother's unconscious hate, the mother's madness and depression.

In the case of the mother's depression, the internal mechanism of managing unthinkable anxiety takes the form of identification with the dead object, as we have seen – i.e., the object who is psychically not alive for the child (Green, 1980) and who blocks the authentic and personal experience of depression, guilt, and reparation.

With his outburst "but it wasn't like that" – which Alessandro turns on the therapist when she maps out for him a reconstructive interpretation of his own personal history in the course of playing, along the same lines as his drawings – the patient is indicating a crystallization, we think, of this very mechanism. Negation protects the child from contact with the unthinkable that has now become representable: the depressed, sad mother with whom he identifies, and whose guilt must be repaired by trying to accomplish an impossible task, since recognizing it implies proposing again the traumatic separation from the primary, fusional, idealized object.

But in the "it wasn't" (which, like the manic defense, is an attempt to negate psychic internal reality), we also have the function of negation (Freud's *Verneinung*) as a judgment mechanism – one that, in the course of negation, actually recognizes and places an inevitable internal reality. According to Laplanche and Pontalis (1967), this judgment mechanism indicates the moment when an idea begins to arise.

Notes

1 Our thanks to the child's psychotherapist, Dr. Ursula Post of Rome, who was in supervision with V.B. for kindly allowing me the use of the raw clinical material of a fragment of her treatment with this boy, in order for me to elaborate it in the context of this paper.
2 That is, falling down.
3 The expression *auto-sensual autistic protections* refers specifically to Tustin's clinical conceptualizations (1981).
4 "The child as 'therapy' of the post-traumatic manic defense of the parents" is the subject of a paper by Giannakoulas (1992), in which the author, in the tradition of Winnicott and Khan, stresses that "by taking care of the most seriously damaged aspects of the parents and their deep depression, [the child] becomes guardian and protector of their hidden selves."
5 This quotation from Green is the authors' translation into English from the Italian edition.

References

Abraham, N. & Torok, M. (1978). *L'écorce et le noyau*. Paris: Aubier-Flammarion.

Bollas, C. (1990). Origins of therapeutic alliance. Paper presented at *The Week-End Conference for English-speaking Members of European Societies*. London, 12–14 October, 1990 Also in *The Mystery of Things*. London: Routledge, 1999.

_____ (1999). Dead mother, dead child. In: *The Dead Mother. The Work of André Green*. Edited by G. Kohon. London and New York: Routledge. Also in: C. Bollas, *The Mystery of Things* (1999). London and New York: Routledge.

Bonaminio, V. (1999). Depressione primaria, difesa maniacale e "riparazione in funzione della difesa materna." In: Il piacere offuscato. Lutto, depressione, disperazione nell'infanzia e nell'adolescenza. A. Racalbuto & E. Ferruzza, eds. Rome: Borla, 1999.

Fonagy, P. & Target, M. (1996). Playing with reality. *Int. J. Psycho-Anal.*, 77:217–233.

Giannakoulas, A. (1992). Il bambino come "terapia" della difesa maniacale post-traumatica. *Interazioni*, N. 0:25–35.

Green, A. (1980). The dead mother. In: *On Private Madness*. London: The Hogarth Press and The Institute of Psychoanalysis. Original publication: La mère morte. In: *Narcissisme de vie, narcissisme de mort*. Paris: Editions de Minuit.

Khan, M. M. R. (1975). *Introduction to the New Edition of "Through Pediatrics to Psychoanalysis" (1958)*. London: Karnac.

_____ (1978), *Introduction to: D. W. Winnicott, Holding and Interpretation. Fragment of an Analysis (1972)*. London: Karnac,1989.

Kohon, G. (ed.) (1999). *The Dead Mother. The Work of André Green*. London: Routledge.

Kohut, H. (1971). *The Analysis of the Self*. Chicago: The University of Chicago Press.

Laplanche, J. & Pontalis, J.-B. (1967). *The Language of Psycho-Analysis*. London: Hogarth Press, 1973.

Phillips, A. (1988). *Winnicott*. Harmondsworth: Penguin, 2007.

Tustin, F. (1981). *Autistic States in Children*. London: Routledge & Kegan Paul.

Winnicott, D. W. (1935). The manic defense. In: *Collected Papers: Through Paediatrics to Psychoanalysis (1958)*. London: Tavistock Publications.

_____ (1945). Primitive emotional development. In: *Collected Papers: Through Pediatrics to Psychoanalysis (1958)*. London: Tavistock Publications.

_____ (1947). Hate in the countertransference. In: *Through Paediatrics to Psycho-Analysis. London: Hogarth/Inst. of Psychoanalysis*, 1975, pp. 194–203.

_____ (1948). Reparation in the function of the organized maternal defense against depression. In: *Collected Papers: Through Paediatrics to Psychoanalysis (1958)*. London: Tavistock Publications.

_____ (1956). Clinical varieties of transference. In: *Through Paediatrics to Psycho-Analysis. Collected Papers*. London: Hogarth, 1958.

_____ (1960). Ego distortion in terms of true and false self. In: *Through Paediatrics to Psycho-Analysis. Collected Papers*. London: Hogarth, 1958.

_____ (1963). Communicating and not communicating leading to a study of certain opposites. In: *The Maturational Processes and the Facilitating Environment: Studies in the Theory of Emotional Development*. London: Hogarth/Inst. of Psychoanalysis, 1965, pp. 179–192.

_____ (1967). Mirror role of the mother and family in child development. In: *Playing and Reality*. London: Tavistock, 1971.

5

THE PERSON OF THE ANALYST

Introduction: The author's position

The following is a deliberately declarative statement: *for me psychoanalysis exists mainly as a clinical, therapeutic enterprise to try to help the suffering patient.* Theory is important – clinical work without a theoretical framework is inconceivable – but for me, as a practicing analyst, the clinical dimension comes first.

I have deliberately used the expression, 'the theory of psychoanalytic technique,' because it is a subject which has a noble tradition in psychoanalysis, distinct from simply 'technique,' which may fall into the realm of practical problem solving of an impasse or a way of conveying to the patient what the analyst thinks *sic et simpliciter.*

But why do I consider approaching this theme hazardous? Can you imagine an Italian-speaking analyst who does not speak nor comprehend a single word of the German language; that is, the language of 18th and 19th century *Kultur,* i.e., the philosophy which grounds modern and postmodern thinking, the language of psychoanalysis and Freud, accepting the challenge of speaking about interpretation? (*Deutung* in Freud's original.) And discussing it in a way which cannot be but imprecise, because in some respects this is a language which Freud invented?

Let me make a naïve parallel: even though opera, because it is created out of music, is universal and understandable by people who are cultivated in it, and even though German opera has nothing to envy in Italian melodrama, I think that for Italian-speaking people, opera is understood in a different way. It is something that runs in their veins. Italian children, because of the melodramatic and passionate attitudes of their mothers and fathers understand it in a manner different from any other people in the world.

Psychoanalysis has a very complicated problem, because it has been popularized in a language which deeply alters the original German, that is, in English, and has undergone a determinization of what Freud implied when he invented a language for his new science. One of the terms which has been most altered is certainly the central concept of psychoanalysis – I would dare say – that of *Deutung*, translated in English as "interpretation," which only by approximation covers the many nuances and meanings Freud intended. My suspicion is that many of the subjective meanings implied in this term – and, accordingly, in the practice of *Deuten*, i.e., interpreting – have got lost. Freud himself seemed to be unsatisfied with the term – so let's imagine how he would have felt about its translation!

"'Interpret!' A nasty word! I dislike the sound of it; it robs me of all certainty. If everything depends on my interpretation who can guarantee that I interpret right? So, after all, everything is left to my caprice."

Then he makes a theoretical objection:

> Just a moment! Things are not quite as bad as that … Why do you choose to except your own mental processes from the rule of law which you recognize in other people's? When you have attained some degree of self-discipline and have certain knowledge at your disposal, your interpretations will be independent of your personal characteristics and will hit the mark. I am not saying that the analyst's personality is a matter of indifference for this portion of his task. A kind of sharpness of hearing for what is unconscious and repressed, which is not possessed equally by everyone, has a part to play. And here, above all, we are brought to the analyst's obligation to make himself capable, by a deep-going analysis of his own, of the unprejudiced reception of the analytic material. Something, it is true, still remains over: something comparable to the 'personal equation' in astronomical observations. This individual factor will always play a larger part in psycho-analysis than elsewhere.
>
> (Freud, 1926, pp. 218–219).

Moreover, it is in these very same pages that Freud describes interpretation in terms of a work consisting in 'guessing with tact' in the 'right moment' what is concealed beyond disguises and allusions in the clinical material. By underlining this, Freud makes the whole question of *Deutung* more complex.

It is for this reason that by implying in my title the idea of interpretation as an oscillating movement in the analyst's attitude, I also implied the central question of the three W's, i.e., what, why, and when to interpret. Even though I have made clear in the above pages that my interest is mainly clinical, I am fully aware that there is a lot of theory in my assertions. Let me mention to begin with a sentence by Winnicott which is a sort of leitmotif in my practice and in my theoretical assumptions as well. Winnicott introduces a distinction which is hardly found in other authors. In 'The Use of an Object and Relating through Identifications' (1969) he wrote:

> What I have to say in this present chapter is extremely simple. Although it comes out of my psychoanalytical experience I would not say that it could have come out of my psychoanalytical experience of two decades ago, because I would not then have had the technique to make possible the transference movements that I wish to describe. For instance, it is only in recent years that I have become able to wait and wait for the natural evolution of the transference arising out of the patient's growing trust in the psychoanalytic technique and setting, and to avoid breaking up this natural process by making interpretations. It will be noticed that I am talking about the making of interpretations and not about interpretations as such. It appalls me to think how much deep change I have prevented or delayed in patients in a certain classification category by my personal need to interpret. If only we can wait, the patient arrives at understanding creatively and with immense joy, and now I enjoy this joy more than I used to enjoy the sense of having been clever. (pp. 86–87)

Each sentence from this passage could be discussed in depth for the purposes of this chapter.

- To begin with, his clear-cut distinction between interpreting, which is peculiar to the analyst's inner psychic activity, and making an interpretation, i.e., the verbal interpretive comment.
- The analyst's capacity to wait for the natural evolution of the transference, which can only arise out of the analysand's trust on psychoanalytic technique and setting.

109

- It is only for brevity's sake that I do not analyze here the deep meanings implied in the last part of the above sentence, i.e., about the analysand's trust in the psychoanalytic technique and setting.
- The conception that an interpretation may have the power of breaking up a natural process, which means that interpretation can be also traumatic for the patient if the analyst lacks sensitivity (what to interpret), tactfulness (how to interpret), and timing (when to interpret).
- Finally, it cannot pass unmentioned the recognition about "how much deep change can be prevented or delayed in some patients by the analyst's personal need to interpret": i.e., his own narcissism.

It is in this very same page that, a few lines below, we read what I think can be considered a revolutionary statement which changes the very essence of 'interpreting.'

> I think I interpret mainly to let the patient know the limits of my understanding. The principle is that it is the patient and only the patient who has the answers. We may or may not enable him or her to encompass what is known or become aware of it with acceptance. (p. 87)

In Winnicott's thinking *Deutung* should be separate from the analyst's fantasy of omnipotence and omniscience, and recognize the limits of his understanding, in order that he can be a real, usable object for the patient.

Deutung and interpretation seem to me to stand like two cowboys facing one other, ready to draw their pistols to first kill or wound the other! *Deutung* stands as an activity, a mental activity which underlines the subjectivity of the analyst; while interpretation – at least in some of its extreme meanings – has acquired the disguise of objectivity.

I leave apart the many other terms which have undergone the same alteration of meaning, and the increasing literature about this topic (Laplanche & Pontalis, 1967; Bettelheim, 1983). Laplanche and Pontalis in particular have given an unparalleled account of the spectrum of subtleties which the term *Deutung* possesses. In my view interpretation overlaps almost entirely with hermeneutics, which has an authoritative and noble tradition in psychoanalysis, regardless of whether one agrees or not with this current of thought.

So, let me clarify, on what side of the two cowboys I stand. I will use the word interpretation throughout this paper exclusively to mean the subjective activity of the analyst … and the patient.

Some conceptual issues

In order to facilitate the comparison between different points of view among us, and to promote discussion, I have decided to present three different fragments of analytic work from approximately the same span of time. My aim with these passages is to be coherent with my title, i.e., to present the analyst oscillating between interpreting and not interpreting.

I will try to show how this oscillation has different gradients. I consider that it is a function of the analyst's countertransference – which is influenced and affected by his own feelings, and by 'the here and now situation' between the two participants in the analytic dyad. Moreover – it goes without saying – this oscillation is influenced by the nature of the patient's transference as well. The oscillation covers an ample spectrum characterized by a discrete continuity from 'proper' interpretation (the verbal interpretation of the analyst in response to a verbal or non-verbal communication of the patient); to comments and or confrontations which try to organize what the patient has brought in his narrative (including being silent); to the activity of non-interpreting, which I believe is an important part of the analyst's interpreting. I mean by this that not-interpreting should have the same status as a verbal interpretation, and the same function to promote or not the patient's therapeutic change.

Khan (1969) clarified beautifully what I mean by not-interpreting:

> The act of interpreting should include also the analyst's reticence – that is, his not-interpreting, as Winnicott (1954) and Balint (1968), among others, have stressed in recent years. In the area of analytic work where the setting is facilitating holding and being, it is essentially not interpreting that is the analyst's contribution. To the question of what is not interpreted, the answer is ambiguous. What one can identify is that the act of not-interpreting is not a simple passive act. It is the result of that precedes it, in which a patient's resistance deriving from his ego-pathology, interfering with his own authentic experiencing of his being in the analytic setting has been mitigated. (p. 205)

I do hope I have made clear enough, up to now, what my intention is. To do this I will dare, at first, to present a fragment where my long internally elaborated interpretation resulted in approaching the patient's anxiety the wrong way, and led to an acting-out. I sustain that the patient's acting-out was the direct result of my not having understood the patient, and more importantly of having used a language which was semantically incomprehensible for her state of being in that moment. We could also discuss if the American term 'enactment' is more useful or not in this context, in so far as it emphasizes the unconscious participation of the two parties, analyst and the analysand (Jacobs, 1991).

Interestingly enough, this wrong interpretation – of which I was aware a moment after I uttered it – had a useful therapeutic effect, because it allowed me to understand better where I had failed and to take the chance to interpret this. I am referring here, even though in a different context, to Glover's concept of "the therapeutic effect of wrong interpretation" (1931), but mainly to a view that implies that the patient and analyst, particularly in certain moments of the analysis, are in the same area of experience.

Ferro (1992) would describe this as a "bi-personal field." Bolognini (2011) conceptualizes this as a secret passage between the analyst and the patient, something which the two partners become aware of after it has been acted out, i.e., *Nachträglichkeit*.

My way of conceptualizing this is in Winnicottian terms: the analyst in that moment is for the patient a subjective object, and if he does not take this into account and interprets in a timed but not-good-enough way – resulting in becoming an objective object too suddenly – a disruption of a continuity of being occurs as well as a disruption of the sensual coexistence between the patient and the analyst. It is here, after the disruption and not before, that projective identification may allow for the patient to regain the lost experience of fusion with the analyst, what Little (1986) called the "basic unity which guarantees psychic life."

Of course, a good-enough, well-timed interpretation can be so only if it takes into consideration where the self of the patient is in relation to the analyst, and how much he can tolerate a discrete objective aspect of the analyst. The analyst's sensitivity to dosing the verbal aspect of an interpretation is related in terms of timing to promoting psychic change for that specific sample of experience that the analysand and correspondingly the analyst is living.

Clinical presentations: When, what, and where to interpret

Before proceeding to the three examples one question has to be asked: How does an interpretation arise in the analyst? I have given some clues in the previous lines, and, for the interested reader, I also discuss this theme in Chapter 4.

So, is it possible for the analyst to choose, in the midst of the torrent of the analyst–analysand relationship, i.e., is it literally possible to have the time to make a choice about what is the more appropriate interpretation in the moment? I do not think so. Interpretation, as any other psychic event in the session, is a compromise formation (Smith, 2000) which puts together different elements from different sources.

This must give interpretation a lighter, postmodern meaning, which considers it not as the revealing to the patient of his inner unconscious fantasy that the analyst can grasp and explain to him, but a progressive approximation to the inner state of the patient. In this sense, it is much more important that the analyst has the capacity to listen to the patient's response to his interpretation than the content of interpretation itself, what Faimberg called 'listening to listening' (1981). As I have tried to show above, Winnicott was pioneering with this kind of view, and it seems to me that his ideas have not yet been fully absorbed in the mainstream of psychoanalytic tradition. Bearing this in mind, how can we consider 'objectifying' Winnicott's position, when at the beginning of 'Fragment of an Analysis' (1986) (also known as 'Holding and Interpretation') he comments before formulating an interpretation: 'Various interpretations were possible here and I chose the following …' (p. 21)

In my view Winnicott is using a fiction in order to show how complex are the patient's unconscious productions and the varieties of possible meaning, and how the analyst 'has to believe' that the interpretation he formulates derives from a choice of possible other interpretations. Only after *Nachträglichkeit*, i.e., when the analyst can reflect on what has gone on in the session, can he consider different, sometimes divergent ways of understanding the patient, and then in later sessions, when it is appropriate, perhaps offer a different interpretation. We know Britton and Steiner (1994) have touched upon the same problem by introducing Bion's idea of 'selected facts.' In my view, however, their position is less radical than Winnicott's because it tends to restore objectivity to the analyst's interpretation even though within a range of selected facts.

Winnicott's ideas about what is in his view interpretation is clearly stated in his posthumous *Psychoanalytic Explorations,* which contains, in Chapter 32, an unpublished paper, as complex as it is precious. I will use some of his considerations contained in 'Interpretation in Psychoanalysis' (1968) to enrich the background in which the interpretation to the patient who was felt to have "nothing at the centre" is proposed by Winnicott. I'm referring here to the three-and-half-page paper whose uncanny title is 'Nothing at the Centre' (1959): this is one of those fragmentary papers which transmits to us a vivid picture of the way Winnicott worked, particularly how he would fantasize about and elaborate clinical material:

> On the occasion of this particular hour that I am referring to the patient was in her usual state of manic defense in which all goes well, and everyone likes her, but both she and I knew that this was precarious and just behind it all was something else.
>
> The striking thing was what happened when I made a certain interpretation. It was she who pointed out that her happiness was due to the fact that some things had been happening to her but that she was the same underneath. I interpreted that if nothing was happening for her to react to then she came to the centre of herself where she knows that there is nothing. I said this nothingness at the centre is her tremendous hunger. The hole in the middle which is herself is a hunger for everything and belongs to the whole of her life and includes the emptiness before impregnation as well as sexual and oral desire. As soon as the trend of my interpretation became clear to her, and the interpretation was not altogether new, she fell dead asleep and stayed asleep for about twenty minutes. When she began to awaken and became impatient with having been to sleep and missed the hour, I began again on interpretation, whereupon she suddenly went into a new sleep and stayed that way until the end of the hour. When she awoke she said: "I have been glued to the couch (...)."
>
> This patient often goes to sleep (...) This time the sleep had a new quality, I thought, one which she describes as being glued to the coach. I assumed that the sleep represented a particular kind of resistance to my interpretation. The essence of the interpretation was that there is a dissociated self which is nothing; it is

nothing but a void, it is only emptiness and when this emptiness comes alive, she is nothing but one huge hunger. This is the first time that she and I in the course of four years of analysis have found together a satisfactory statement of her true self and at the same time of her appetite. (p. 50)

What I would call a 'semantic circularity' of interpretation, is clearly stated by Winnicott. Here, the accent is put on 'communicating and not communicating.'

"The purpose of interpretation must include a feeling that the analyst has that a communication has been made which needs acknowledgement," Winnicott wrote in his 'Interpretation in Psychoanalysis' (1968). And just few lines later: "Giving an interpretation back gives the patient opportunity to correct the misunderstandings." But it is later on that Winnicott astonishes us with his disarming simplicity: "This very simple statement about interpretation may be important by the very fact that it is simple ..." And at the same time, he astonishes us with his clinical depth: "The principle that I am enunciating at this moment is that the analyst reflects back what the patient has communicated" (pp. 208–209).

In the expression "reflects back" the paradox of the individual who discovers the self through the other clinically finds its virtual point of refraction in the interpretation that "must include a feeling that the analyst has that a communication has been made which needs acknowledgement." In delineating these cross dialectics within the consulting room, what comes to mind is the paper on the 'Mirror Role of the Mother' (Winnicott, 1967) included in *Playing and Reality* (1971).

"What does the baby see when he or she looks at the mother's face?" Winnicott wondered in this paper. "What the baby sees is himself or herself." In other words the mother is looking at the baby and what she looks like is related to what she sees there (p. 131). This referring to – as he writes – "the mother's role of giving back to the baby the baby's own self" (p. 138), this 'giving back,' is very similar to that 'reflecting back' mentioned in the paper about the patient with 'nothing at the centre' and constitutes the matrix which can 'metaphorize' the analytic relationship and the function of interpretation:

This glimpse of the baby's and the child's seeing the self in the mother's face, and afterwards in the mirror, gives a way of looking at analysis and at the psychotherapeutic task. Psychotherapy is not making clever and apt interpretations; by and large it is a long-term giving the patient back what the patient brings [so] the patient will find his or her own self, and will be able to exist and feel real.

(Winnicott, 1967, pp. 137–138).

But it is not only the dialectic interplay between the self and the other that the paper on interpretation elucidates through that reference to the function of the analyst "reflecting back to the patient what the patient communicated to him." In the lines following this statement it is possible to read a detailed clinical theory which enlightens, for the aims of my intervention, the functioning of the interpretation with the patient who had 'nothing at the centre.'

To conclude let us follow Winnicott's argumentation in the 1968 paper as if it had been written to better understand what happens in that specific clinical situation illustrated in the 1959 paper:

In the limited area of today's transference, the patient has an accurate knowledge of a detail or of a set of details. It is as if there is a dissociation belonging to the place that the analysis has reached today (...) from this limited position the patient can be giving the analyst a sample of the truth; that is to say of something that is absolutely true for the patient, and that when the analyst gives this back, the interpretation is received by the patient who has already emerged to some extent from this limited area or dissociated condition.

(1968, p. 209)

This is an example of a 'wrong interpretation' which gives, however, the opportunity to the analyst to understand from the patient's response where he failed, and therefore where the original caring environment failed (Winnicott, 1956).

Gina started therapy when she was 35 years old. She came to me after having been "tossed around from one therapist to another." She said during our first telephone conversation, "They all either don't have time or don't have room for me ... I have had several contacts over the phone but I hope I can at least meet you to see what you are like." Already, during this first contact, I realized she mispronounced almost all the surnames of the analysts she had been in contact with. My surname was also mispronounced. Later, in the therapy, I gave a meaning to the phonetic approximation: what I thought was a clouded, precarious, superficial representation of the object, perceived on the edge or the boundary of a line beyond which the object itself could dissolve or disappear.

The borderline personality features of this patient became apparent during our first sessions. Following these, I proposed to commence therapy with three sessions a week. Later developments brought to the surface – so to speak – different facets of these features, which could be described as a 'multitude of selves' seeking cohesion and coherence which had never come about during her emotional development. In this brief study I will present only those useful and explanatory elements needed in this context.

After an initial period of satisfaction, having been "accepted" by me, the transference and counter-transference relationship was marked by the patient's sharp and recurring feeling of exclusion and refusal, and her intense sensibility to the practically imperceptible variations in my disposition towards her. Gina's personal history was mottled by memories of painful and traumatic experiences: the reclaiming and elaboration of these memories came about in a discontinuous manner, alongside the discontinuity of her experience of being.

My initial difficulty in tuning into her communications was that my attempts at understanding were immediately perceived by Gina as a rejection. In fact, the subtle 'suspicion' with which I initially handled her intentions of "becoming a psychotherapist" determined the first fracture in the transference-countertransference relationship. The elaboration of and recuperation from this fracture repeatedly took up our time in the therapeutic field. The suspicion also became a strong feature of her attitude towards an object she "could not trust": an attitude which contributed to relentless feelings of exclusion.

She had "gone and found herself a husband in Belgium": meaning they had met in the country which she had gone to for work in one of her typical, heat-of-the-moment decisions (yet another aspect of her many fragmentary and unfinished life experiences). She met an attractive young Belgian ("penniless, just like me"), they got married, against her mother's will, when she was already pregnant. About 18 months into their marriage, which was already creaking since their return to Italy, her husband – who had found himself

117

a position working for an embassy – left her and their daughter, Sabina.

Sabina became a key figure in the therapy. The patient focused on her child her attempts to restore her child-like self. She gave her a positive environment, different from her own but constantly threatened by precariousness and ruptures. Sabina also represented that part of herself which I, as an analyst, "should know about."

The very elements making up the therapeutic setting (the scheduled sessions, the weekly interruptions, etc.) were considered an imposition. Her sensitivity to my moods, which I have already referred to, became overwhelming because I felt as though they tended to undermine my own personal space. My countertransference was put to a hard test. On the other hand, the patient perceived each and every of my "inflections" in the relationship as a barrier I intended to build "against" her. This was apparent, for instance, following a session in which she felt I had been "nasty" to her (the child-like language she used at that time); or following interruptions, such as weekends or winter or Easter holidays which she felt were "stupid," "foolish," only for my "fucking convenience." Gina touched upon the founding elements of my being with her and which she did not wish to discuss or have interpreted because, actually, the holidays and the interruptions were only mine, not hers, and not related to her needs. I should have taken this into account when voicing my comments and in my way of offering interpretations. During these attacks I felt pursued and angry.

On one occasion, during the second year of therapy, I felt as if I were being unjustly and unreasonably reproached. I pondered at length as to whether I should offer an interpreting comment or to suspend any interpretation. I decided I should offer an interpreting comment. I remember taking great care in choosing precisely the most appropriate words, but these turned out to be completely inadequate. I thought I was being gentle with the patient without realizing that my acting out was just around the corner. I braced myself and said that it seemed as though she "was doing everything she could to be irritating, to make me feel how irritated she was feeling because of me."

After a frosty silence, loaded with tension, Gina suddenly stood up and walked angrily towards the door, crying and muttering words I couldn't understand. She left, slamming the door behind her. Everything took place so fast I had no time to say anything or even realize what had happened. Obviously afterwards, when I was alone in the room, having been left there mid-session – my own violent emotions were apparent – I understood the meaning of the acting-out during, caused by what had happened between us.

Five minutes later, still within the session time, I heard a knock at the door. When I opened the door, Gina was standing there. She said she had been "nasty to me." She asked me if I could be so "kind" as to take her back. Once she was back on the couch, we talked about the fact that she was absolutely sure – and at a non-metaphoric level of her experience – that she had heard me say she was irritating, that I couldn't stand her and that I wished to get rid of her. She had actually to expel herself from the session so as to maintain the image of a "kind" therapist who could think about her when she wasn't there, that's to say once the "irritating" Gina had been dispatched.

During this phase, Gina found interpretations expressing a metaphoric relationship intolerable, because they went beyond the level of concrete life experience in which she was capable of living. However, clarifications regarding her feelings seemed to get through to her, because they pinpointed, named, and separated the confusing factors in her mind, whilst guaranteeing proximity and solidarity.

Faced with the analyst's words – which the therapist understands but she as yet could not, Gina felt she "couldn't take it." She felt that because of her own failing, she was being barred from a relational world which the therapist's words referred to. At this level, the interpretation became excluding and, as such, against her. This was yet another aspect of the perception of something intentionally negative being done to her, which I have already referred to.

On a more general note, I feel that interpretations expressing metaphorical relations are inevitably complicated from a semantic point of view. Although they refer to mechanisms of unconscious communication (in this specific example, reversal), they have to rely on an appreciation of a certain complexity simply because they describe a personal experience. *De facto,* these interpretations mortify the patient, and make the patient feel excluded, because their nature implies the presence of two separate minds, two interlocutors, which in the patient's experience sometimes do not exist.

An example of the analyst's necessity of not-interpreting while oscillating between the two poles: the patient signals to the analyst his/her wish of not receiving an interpretation which hinders her process.

In this example the patient shows the analyst how interpretation can "steal" her capacity for doing or thinking, which contributed to her fear of not being capable. In relation to this, please consider Winnicott's point about how interpretation can prevent or delay change (1969).

The very first stages in the analysis of Viviana, a 43-year-old woman with definite (though carefully disguised) intelligence and sensibility, were characterized by constant declarations of her insuperable difficulty in speaking, in getting involved in the therapy, in allowing a more intimate form of communication. These self-complaints introduced the theme of self-devaluation and the representation of herself as inadequate, unsuitable, and clumsy into the analytical scene right from the beginning. Meanwhile, in another place, inaccessible to this analysis, she preserved an idealized image of herself as someone with a wealth of emotional sensitivity capable of involvement with the object by permeating it.

Her complaints, however, were also the amplified expression of her disappointment towards me during sessions – a kind of transference inside the relationship with the analyst – inherent in the actual act of having had to choose me. The patient had been sent to me by an older, more experienced colleague, whom she had seen during a public lecture, and whom she had contacted, though just by telephone, after a lengthy lapse in time during which she had fantasized an intense, ideal analytical relationship with him.

Over the course of her first telephone call to me, the patient had with great sensitivity noticed my hesitancy in fixing an appointment for a preliminary interview. In actual fact, at that moment it was not at all clear to me what availability I had, nor could I foresee how much time would elapse before beginning. Actually, I must have been correspondingly sensitive, because right from the first call (which I had considered just a vague probe made by the patient) I was aware of my own inexplicable strand of discomfort as to the length of time needed. However, during the first encounter, arranged by two more telephone calls, I became more and more convinced that I could go ahead with the analysis, which, in any case, would begin before an even further delay owing to holidays. Only after several months of analysis did I realize how long I had held the patient in a state of expectancy with regard to her needs. Though it was beyond my intentions I had 'parked' her. I realized how this particular disposition, my initial emotional attitude, a vague and uncertain state of mind, brought plenty of grist to her feeling of being a misfit, clumsy, and incapable of attaining any real involvement with me.

Thus the gap felt by the patient when she compared me with that ideal analysis, conducted by that marvelous analyst, was amplified. But rather than discuss this aspect of her need to jealously guard inside herself an ideal caring relationship, I would like to shift our attention to the aspect that I had intended to illustrate. This concerns the internal problems the patient had to solve so as to be able to accept me as her analytical partner and what she would have liked my specific contribution to be.

It was half-way through the week, after two almost totally silent sessions during which, feeling myself to be in a scarcely evocative relational state, I had been trying hard to get my inner bearings, and attempting to attach a more specific meaning to the patient's silence. I had volunteered some comments on the present situation, linking them up with the themes already mentioned above. My intention was to facilitate communication by signaling to the patient where I was and that I might be able to comprehend where she was.

After a long silence Viviana said in a subdued voice that a little time before she'd had a dream but had not told me about it (dreams, for the patient, constitute a 'good analytical product' which reduces the awkwardness of having to converse and talk about herself). Yet another long silence ensued, and I began to fear that perhaps from now on I would be deprived of this source of communication as well.

In previous months I had felt that dreams served the function of indicators bordering a path over an area of land where one has difficulty getting one's bearings. On the other hand, I was aware that any delicate pressing of the patient to relate her dream could have the effect of shutting her off still further, as she may have felt encroached on. Then, almost as a continuation of a stream of inner thoughts, I heard her narration of the dream:

> I had to go somewhere else from my workplace, but I did not know how to go about it. So I lingered for a while to see what could be done. A colleague of mine was going in the same direction, but I was undecided as to whether to ask him or not ... then I asked him timidly ... He was going by bicycle and told me to bring a mountain bike ... The scene changed and we met up on a very busy road full of lorries and trucks ... it seemed like a motorway, but it was

121

inside Rome. I followed him but we had to shout at each other to make ourselves heard over the roar of the traffic. He was kind and every now and then looked over his shoulder to check that I was following. At a certain point he was on the other side of the road ahead of me. He gestured every now and then without losing his patience, he warned me to be careful of the flow of traffic, indicating that a van was now approaching, now a car. I knew what I wanted to do ... make a U-turn, but I stalled every time. I couldn't manage to get any further. I felt clumsy and incapable.

The patient thus raised the curtain on a scene which was certainly part of a broader course of action, and which described incisively, and with increased significance, the dynamics of the analytical relationship. But it was this single scene that she now invited the analyst to observe. The expectation was that what he had been unable to see in his mental preoccupation with the two-body relationship should not escape him further.

First the patient described the passages from an individual condition, "I had to move elsewhere ... I dallied a little ... I was undecided ... I asked him timidly," then moved to the interaction of the analytic pair. Here the analyst–colleague, in responding to the patient, suggests taking the same road together by means of a two-wheeled vehicle, a bicycle. The use of a bicycle underlines the analyst's request for a muscular effort which might frustrate those very primary needs of getting 'a lift.' The only association to the dream – the mountain bike and its heavy duty function – seems to lead precisely in this direction. So, this 'impingement to the functioning' (Winnicott, 1960) that the patient appeared to perceive the analyst imposing on her takes on a more specific meaning as the dream scene gradually unfolds (and the analysis proceeds). At this stage, the analyst was conceived as a reasonably adequate and sensitive collaborator, who could signal his presence to the patient and guide her through the maze of (inner) traffic and background noise by means of verbal communication (interpretation). However, the therapist seems to have a mental map of her route, an internal model which is all oriented in terms of two-people or bi-personal field relationships. This point of view cannot take notice of an individual act which concerns the patient alone, defined as a risk that she alone must run, in her own way.

This means that the analyst had not succeeded in suspending his presence, as it were, by creating that vacuum, or, if one prefers, that negative capability (Keats, 1817), which would have allowed the patient to be alone in the presence of another (Winnicott, 1958), in order to devise or create her own modality (the U-turn) for choosing or not choosing her analyst, and thus creating her very own, true analysis.

The relevance of the analyst's negative contribution to the creation, maintenance, and growth of the analytical relationship, in other words, the importance of this not-interpreting, seems to me clearly emphasized in the dream. The analyst's mental map, drawn up on a two-person axis, impedes individual creation by blocking it and putting something else in its place, thus organizing the patient's illness and leading to her feeling "clumsy and incapable."

This is indeed a product of the two-person relationship, not in the sense of an iatrogenic illness but as a way of communicating by means of the negotiation of something. In this specific instance the conflict between dependence and independence, the opposition between child and adult parts, her image of herself as clumsy, disabled, and incapable, counterpoised by an ideal self-image as whole and functioning efficiently. This is partly taken away from her (extractive introjection that Bollas (1987) refers to) by the analyst–parent who has no need for a mountain bike, which is perceived as yet another support, a mortifying prosthesis.

I certainly do not wish to suggest – almost in contradiction to what I wrote in the opening passages – that a therapeutic model structured along the lines of an analytic pair tends to organize the patient's illness, and that this result should be avoided. But I do hold that we should at one and the same time contemplate another scene where the analyst's presence as partner may hinder the patient from creating anything individual.

All this can obviously only occur within a relationship. In this sense I believe I can define not-interpreting, in the best technical way possible, as the analyst's virtual position within an order in which we assume an asymmetrical contribution of two partners, that indeed it should be the patient leading the way and the analyst riding behind, and perhaps occasionally comments on the scenery.

An example of the analyst's anxiously oscillating in the countertransference, aiming at finding the right balance between interpreting and not-interpreting and – if interpreting – what and when: a case of taking a risk.

When Marco, six and a half years old, came into the consultation room on a Tuesday, accompanied by the day hospital assistant of the department where I received him for psychotherapy three times a week, I immediately noticed a different behavior from the behavior I had been taking for granted over the past months. Generally he rushed to the table where the box of toys awaited him and started elaborating a very simple play which in my notes at the time I had described as 'animating with puppets.' But it didn't used to be this way. I had never before seen a patient of latency age so blocked in his movements and language. It took at least three to four months of waiting and cautious verbal interventions to get the child to abandon, very slowly, a blocked mode which could last the whole session, and with tiny movements, approach the toys to touch them, then handle them and start animating them. A few interpretations of his fear of entering into contact with Vincenzo, some rare facilitating and encouraging comments, a great deal of patience, lots of waiting: these were the ingredients of what I considered to be a small therapeutic success. But on this day he seemed to have regressed to his previous blocked state.

What in God's name is happening to Marco today? I asked myself, stunned, almost irritated, above all unprepared in seeing him this way, motionless on the doorstep of the room, after I have said "Hello!" with my usual friendliness.

I waited a few seconds, tried to catch something: I thought, *it can't be anything to do with the Monday session during which, after the long weekend, Marco often hesitates.* I quickly thought back to what had happened the day before. *A great session!* I thought. I had actually been surprised by the speed at which Marco had approached his toys and started playing with them. *So what happened? What did I do?* I asked myself anxiously. *Why has he regressed so rapidly?*

Months and months spent in the cardinal virtue of patience – a virtue which Eleonora Fe d'Ostiani (a fervently Catholic but also extraordinary secular child therapist and one of my first analytic supervisors) called the analyst's negative capability – seemed to have been destroyed. I tried an encouragement, my tone slightly manic: "Come on, Marco, Vincenzo is here, let us play, like yesterday ..." I realized I had hardly ever used the plural "us" with this child. While the boy overcame his inhibition, I had always respected his spontaneity. Using the plural would have felt like exploiting, cheating, taking over his spontaneity.

Now I realized my mistake may have made things worse. But I wasn't sure. I became confused. I felt an anxiety taking over that I realized I must control. My worry seemed excessive.

I thought, *Give him some time.* But my anxiety did not relent. I was tempted to approach him, push him along, be more affectionate. I can't deny also feeling very irritated by the way the session might unfold and how much work appeared to have been lost.

I reviewed the previous session in my mind, but this, in itself, distracted me from the here and now, and I became preoccupied with the idea that Marco had noticed I was no longer paying attention to him. I noticed his body stiffening. Slowly, he brought his hand to his penis and pinched the tip of it, maybe the foreskin, through his trousers. This seemed to reassure him. But not me. I saw an old gesture: the pinching his penis was an obvious sign of the child closing himself inward.

Then I remembered what I thought had been a trivial detail from the previous session. About 15 minutes into the Monday session, while Marco was already playing with his toys, there was a noise in the corridor. The child didn't seem to notice, whereas I listened more carefully. A little later, it became clear someone was agitated in the corridor. It was only after the door to our room was noisily hit from the outside, so much so that it seemed to swell, that I realized someone, or some boys were fighting. The noise went away quickly, and I thought to myself, *it hasn't got anything to do with us. We are safe in here.* However, re-thinking the episode made me view it in a different light, as a 'narrow escape,' and I realized I had no idea of what Marco thought of it.

I understood that I had been concentrating on my own situation – *"su lo mio particulare"* – to put it in Dante's words, but had not paid attention to the way the child had lived through the episode. There was an obvious omission in my behavior from the day before. Only now I wondered, *is there time to repair the situation … but what if I am wrong? What if I say something about yesterday and yesterday is not the problem? Will I risk losing the child even more, cause an even deeper regression?* I felt as if I were on the edge of a cliff, and furthermore, that I was there alone. This whole imaginative elaboration, as Winnicott would say, of what might have happened, seemed only to have concerned me, and had nothing to do with the child.

I decide to risk it. I said to him, as if I were only now making the discovery:

Ah! I've got it! You are still frightened by the big bang against the door yesterday. It sounded like a clap of thunder, a loud and

125

frightening noise. And Vincenzo didn't even say anything about it ... he left you alone ... you didn't understand what was happening whereas maybe I did understand ... so why didn't I say anything? Darn it! Vincenzo sometimes forgets to say things ... Ok I'll explain it to you now ... Marco wants to know, right? ... Vincenzo instead was too busy trying to understand what was going on and left Marco alone with his fear about what had happened, and he didn't understand. "It wasn't anything serious," that's what I should have told you! It was just an upset child who didn't want to go to the doctor, maybe he was frightened about his doctor's check-up and wanted to run away and bumped into the door and made that really loud noise. Vincenzo was worried for that child when he heard those sounds but when he understood what was happening, he stopped worrying and when the child bumped against the door, Vincenzo's fear was already over. But Marco's fear wasn't and Vincenzo didn't say anything and Marco felt alone with his fear and couldn't understand what was happening.

Whatever happened, right or wrong, imaginative elaboration or countertransference delirium, this rather long – but also very 'loving' – comment, seemed to have a magic effect. A few seconds after I finished talking, the 'pinch' was released. A few more seconds passed, and then, without saying a word, Marco walked towards the table and began playing with the box of toys, as if the session had begun there and then.

The child started playing with the puppets, bringing them to life, 'animating' them, and I thought I had brought back to life the child, so to speak, who had been paralyzed by that loud noise. My imaginative elaboration now allowed me understand something more about the reasons behind the inhibition of this child. He had, after all, been sent to be diagnosed and then directed towards psychotherapy because of an unusual inhibition.

I had 'failed' – as Winnicott (1956) would have said – in the very same way in which his primary environment had failed. I now understood that too much was expected of this child: the fact that he was a peaceful boy who "just sat there," had allowed the environment around him, to some extent, to take for granted his apparently proper way of functioning. "He doesn't act out, he keeps quiet and calm; wherever you put him there he stays," his parents had said to me. But this meant that no one ever explained more than was required, more than the bare minimum, just as I myself had done the day before.

My clinical examples are, of course, only short vignettes, which omit lots of important details that might have given more sense to the entire psychoanalytic process and, consequently, given more evidence about the choices available to the analyst and how we might understand their outcomes. However, as Winnicott said: "I ask you to trust that what I have written is as close as possible to how the psychoanalytic process was going on."

The person of the analyst: Interpreting, not interpreting, and countertransference[1]

The purpose of this chapter is to present some personal reflections on the notion of *the person of the analyst* in contemporary psychoanalytic thinking, a topic which has long been of interest to me (Bonaminio, 1997). It is worth specifying that the expression *contemporary psychoanalytic thinking* encompasses such an extended number of contributions, points of view, and reflections, that it is not possible to be totally exhaustive. I have more modestly crafted a personal contribution inspired by European thinking, and specifically from Italy (although over time I have given close attention to American psychoanalytic thought on these themes). My references to the literature cannot but be *selected,* and as a result, they are limited to a subset of the many authors who have written on the themes discussed here.

I think we all agree that, at a certain level, the expression *the person of the analyst* refers to the influence of the analyst's person on the psychoanalytic process and its therapeutic or anti-therapeutic effect – a factor present in Freud's mind from the beginning (as early as 1910, and later, as is well known, in his 1937 paper). Nonetheless, at a deeper level, we may see that this expression actually contains layers of meaning, incorporating the history of psychoanalytic thinking and its impact on technique, and in fact has an intrinsically dialectical character.

The expression *the person of the analyst* immediately presents us with a question: is there always and inevitably a *person* behind the analyst? Is the analyst supposed to be able to limit as much as possible the infiltration of personal factors into his analytic attitude and functions? Or is there a total and inevitable overlapping between

127

the person and the analyst? Or are the two terms so conceptually different, and positioned at such different levels of abstraction and clinical meaning, that it may be misleading even to consider them in the same breath?

These are only a few related questions that touch on a large territory. Rather than developing a comprehensive list of subtopics, I have in this paper a more limited aim: I propose to approach this theme along two different lines of thinking that are distinct yet in my view intertwined. These two lines are *clinical narration* and *the analyst's interpretations*. To begin with, I will consider each at a descriptive level.

Clinical narration

Clinical narration is the only means of communication that we possess as analysts conveying information to other analysts. Every piece of clinical narrative writing reflects the way the analyst has *experienced* the clinical encounter with his analysand. We recall, for example, Freud's well-known account of Katharina in his *Studies on Hysteria* (Breuer & Freud, 1892–1895):

> In the summer vacation of the year 189★ I made an excursion into the Hohen Tauern so that for a while I might forget medicine and more particularly the neuroses. I had almost succeeded in this when one day I turned aside from the main road to climb a mountain which lay somewhat apart and which was renowned for its view and for its well-run refuge hut. I reached the top after a strenuous climb, and, feeling refreshed and rested, was sitting deep in contemplation of the charm of the distant prospect. I was so lost in thought that at first I did not connect it with myself when these words reached my ears: "Are you a doctor, sir?" But the question was addressed to me, and by the rather sulky-looking girl of perhaps eighteen who had served my meal and had been spoken of by the landlady as Katharina. To judge by her dress and bearing, she could not be a servant, but must no doubt be a daughter or relative of the landlady's. Coming to myself, I replied: "Yes, I am a doctor: but how did you know that?" (p. 125)

That is how it begins, like a piece of fiction: Freud's writing transforms his experience of the moment. Of course, his talent for writing and narration is unsurpassed in the field. And yet we know that the clinical experience of the relationship between two people talking in a room can be communicated and *transformed* only through narration and writing. Bion (1967b) observed: "I do not regard any narrative purporting to be a fact … as worth consideration as a 'factual account' of what happened" (p. 1).

When I write a clinical report, or when I present my clinical work to colleagues, I do not intend to speak about myself, wishing instead to focus on the object of my presentation and to preserve my own privacy, my own personal feelings. I can do this, however, only up to a certain point. If I wish to communicate something then I must inevitably reveal something about myself, i.e., about my personal, idiomatic way of encountering the patient. Furthermore I select some facts from the patient's discourse, "hearing voices" (Smith, 2000), so to speak, from inside myself. My clinical narration speaks about myself; it reveals the other, and through the other reveals us to ourselves.

From this point of view, the situation of talking or writing on a specific clinical subject is not all that different from the situation in which the analyst finds himself while at work: seated more or less comfortably in an armchair near the analysand, who is stretched out on the couch. The analyst listens to what the patient is talking about at that particular moment, but he also listens to the patient's silences. The analyst finds himself transported to the times and places where his analysand's narration invites him to go, and he meets the analysand's objects. But he also encounters objects of his own, evoked by the analysand, and at the same time he is listening to his own thoughts, experiencing and mentally recording the emotions stirred within him, allowing himself to be carried away by his own intimate associations as they distance him and distract him from the patient.

The analyst's interpretations

At a certain point in this process, as part of the "complex and unconscious ways two people play upon each other's idiom" (Bollas, 1995, pp. 23–24) the analyst *decides* to put in a comment, i.e., an interpretation, concerning the patient and sometimes about the patient's relationship with the analyst. "We give the patient," Freud (1910) wrote (and here he appears an *ante litteram* Winnicott[2]), "the conscious anticipatory idea [the idea of what he may expect to find] and he then finds the repressed unconscious idea in himself on the basis of its similarity to the anticipatory one" (p. 142). It would be difficult not to consider this statement of Freud's an exceptional one. It is a postmodernist statement, which could have been put forth today, and is especially remarkable when one remembers it was written almost a hundred years ago.

At the very moment the analyst makes a comment he is interrupting the continuity of a process taking place in the patient's internal world. The analyst introduces his own viewpoint into the *analytic field*, i.e., that area or setting that is the joint contribution of both analyst and analysand. To put this in Winnicottian terms, this is an area where analyst and analysand *live an experience together* (Winnicott, 1945). So interpretation, per se, is always something that separates and is intrinsically a vehicle of otherness.

In my opinion, Winnicott is very clear and convincing about these characteristics of interpretations when he writes:

> It is only in recent years that I have become able to wait and wait for the natural evolution of the transference arising from the patient's growing trust in the psychoanalytic technique and setting and to avoid breaking up this natural process by making interpretations. It will be noticed that I am talking about the making of interpretations and not about interpretations as such.
>
> (1968, p. 219)

This has become one of his most famously paradoxical statements insofar as he subtly distinguishes between the analyst's "making of interpretations" to the patient and "interpretations as such." However empathic the analyst may be while in close contact with the analysand, "identified ... even merged with the patient" (Winnicott, 1960, p. 163), we may say that at the very moment in which the analyst decides to speak, he creates, through separating himself, an object to talk about.

The analyst wishes to leave the analytic field available to the patient. He wants to focus his attention and comments on the patient. The analyst has no intention of speaking about himself and quite often honors this intention. In any case, it is assumed that he is capable of not occupying the patient's own field, while nevertheless guaranteeing his "contribution to the creating and maintaining of the psycho-analytic situation" (Balint, 1950, p. 121).

In this connection, the analyst's *silence* and his *not interpreting* come to the same thing. Here I refer to the technical tradition (which I share) that considers the analyst's tolerance of the patient's regression and the analyst's not interpreting as mutative agents for psychic change that are equally as important as, and in dialectical relation with, the act of interpreting itself as Khan has written:

> The act of interpreting should include also the analyst's reticence – that is, his *not-interpreting* ... To put it paradoxically, un–interpretation is the climax only of interpretation. It is not possible to arrive at un-interpretation without interpreting. It is this that is implied by the statement often made that the basic ego–strength and complexity of psychic functioning has to establish itself in the patient before he can arrive at the point where the non–interpretation of the analyst crystallizes the experience of being in the patient.
>
> (1969, p. 205)

Interpretation is an interference on the part of the other that is potentially mutative for the patient, and since not interpreting, i.e., the analyst's silence, may reduce interference with the patient's privacy,[3] the analyst, in not interpreting, places himself in the service of a process that facilitates the patient's search for a kind of intimacy with himself.[4] In both interpreting and in not interpreting, the analyst's individuality will emerge. In both cases the analyst can manage to get in touch with the patient, can meet his suffering, can *reflect back* to the analysand what he has communicated to him, can *share* with the analysand in finding "a satisfactory definition of his true self" (Winnicott, 1959, p. 50). In other words, the analyst can be for the patient the *other* who will allow him to *rediscover* himself, but only if he, the analyst, is himself; if he claims, as it were, his own boundaries and his own individuality.

The analyst's individuality was radically defined by Winnicott (1962) as follows: "In doing psychoanalysis, [...] I aim at being myself and behaving myself" (p. 166). Like this definition, Bion's (1967a) recommendation for the *suspension of memory and desire* on the part of the analyst is anything but 'technical.' With these comments, neither Winnicott nor Bion is describing a technical strategy, but rather *a position of the analyst in the consulting room*, in the here and now of the session – ways that the analyst may *be-himself* in order to *be-with-the-patient*.

131

So, in spite of his intentions and his discipline in not invading the patient's own field, whenever the analyst decides either to give an interpretation or else to remain silent, he inevitably lets something of himself, something personal, something of his individuality, override these limits. Thus, he reduces the distance and the separation that he has deliberately created in order to communicate, and in doing so, he inevitably reveals something to the patient.

Clinical vignette

Background

I have two goals in presenting the clinical material that follows. Keeping in mind that every clinical narrative reflects the way the analyst experienced the clinical encounter with the patient described, as previously discussed, my first goal is to demonstrate that my clinical narrative *speaks also of me*, even though my attention is focused, more or less successfully, on the patient's material. This may appear to be an obvious statement, but at the same time, it is, in my view, worthy of our consideration, particularly as it relates to the theme of the analyst's subjectivity versus his objectivity.

My second goal in presenting this material relates to what is commonly called *self-disclosure* and its impact on analytic technique, as this theme is part of the larger topic of the person of the analyst. I will discuss the ways in which this clinical material illustrates the effects of self-disclosure on technique after presenting the material itself.

The analysand, whom I will call Giovanni, was a 29-year-old waiter employed in a fine Roman restaurant. He was unhappy with his job because he had completed training for a higher position, that of a *demi-maître,* at a school for hotel and restaurant management. He had sought psychoanalytic treatment following a psychiatrist's referral because of his persistent impotence, characterized by premature ejaculation, which regularly cut off even his rather feeble erections during the preliminaries of sexual intercourse.

During my initial assessment with Giovanni, although I did not overlook his narcissistic-defensive personality organization – characterized by his sense of feeling isolated and not understood, both within his family and outside it, as well as by feelings of contempt and suspicion – I perhaps did not fully appreciate at the time the extent of the impact that this personality organization would have on the psychoanalytic relationship and, in particular, on the very texture of the dialogue between us. For a long time during the first two years of analysis, I found myself focusing internally on the positive aspects, so to speak, of his decision to move to Rome permanently, which required him to confront more than a few adaptive difficulties – a decision that I thought of as signaling the patient's level of investment in his therapy. The move thus seemed to me an index of his willingness to collaborate and of the therapeutic alliance that would later be seen as incorporating a fundamental level of trust that could sustain the analytic work, work that, for a long period of time, felt "tiresome" to him because of his vulnerabilities and his stubborn narcissism.

There is another significant element in the therapeutic alliance that must be emphasized, one that had clandestinely sustained the patient in the analytic work, and that at the beginning guaranteed the work would go forward. This was the idealization that Giovanni reserved for the psychiatrist who had referred him, which I could initially take advantage of as part of the continuity of his treatment, but which was later counterbalanced in the clinical relationship by his devaluation and criticism of me, as I began to feel myself becoming the object of the patient's splitting processes. This idealization, in fact, testified to the existence and persistence in the patient of good aspects of the tie with his internal father (though these were confined to a split and dissociated area), which he was capable of valuing and preserving. As would be evident later in the course of the analysis, these good and trusting areas were tied to the relationship that Giovanni had enjoyed as a child with his maternal grandfather, and more recently with a paternal uncle, a bachelor who lived with the family. His maternal grandfather also appeared as an object who was valued and idealized by Giovanni's mother, and that became significant in the course of the analysis in that it concerned the good and organized aspects of his relationship with his mother, allowing him, furthermore, to internalize a good relationship between a woman and a masculine object.

I think it is important to emphasize here that it was necessary to reach a certain point in the analysis, as mentioned, before I was capable of distinguishing and locating the existence of good masculine objects in the patient's internal world. Retrospectively, I can say that the earlier, limited recognition on my part may have been fundamentally attributable to the above-mentioned 'disturbance' in my usual capacity to understand what I felt initially came from this patient. But, more particularly, I think it was attributable to the fact that in Giovanni's initial narrations, the high esteem reserved for his maternal grandfather and especially his paternal uncle had been in effect camouflaged to my eyes, so subtle and clandestine was the level of positive transference toward me that nevertheless sustained the analysis. In fact, initially, the patient had made nothing more than passing references to these positive masculine characters, while all the rest of what he talked about, abundantly narrated and described, seemed inundated with scorn and criticism.

Excerpts

In a session in the second half of the second year of analysis, on a Monday, Giovanni entered and, after settling himself on the couch, disconsolately pronounced, "What shit, it is all shit," and went on to recount the "usual disaster" with his family, whom he had just visited over the weekend.

When Giovanni said "shit" for the first time, I automatically thought to myself, given the themes of many previous sessions, that "it is he who thinks of himself as shit," he who is rundown and demoralized. I say this to him, exactly in these terms, and too precipitously, but Giovanni is capable of correcting me, the sign of our having reached, at this point in the analysis, a *shared language*. Actually, I was thinking at the time of an umpteenth sexual failure of Giovanni's, and I made an interpretation that it was an example of interpretive *enactment* in my desire to quickly support him.

"It's not what you think," the patient continued in a collaborative way, but he went in another direction, his and not mine, not the one that I wanted to impose on him. In reality, Giovanni was referring to his father, and for a few minutes there was a sort of disconnect between my internal sensation, which was a misleading one, and the patient's discourse. At this point, there were two divergent lines of thought going on in the analytic couple that permitted us to get a sense of how an aspect of *the person of the analyst* could interfere with the patient's discourse: that is, due to my prejudgment of the situation, my thoughts were following a particular line, while Giovanni at that moment was going in another direction. Such an event is not always necessarily a negative interference, but it is evidence, I think, of how imperceptibly the analyst's listening may be 'disturbed' – influenced, that is, and directed by his expectations, his conflicts, and/or his concerns in regard to the patient.

At first it was not easy for me to see that this was the cause of my sense of disconnection, of something coming apart in the analytic couple. In this session with Giovanni, I found that I had to work hard internally in order to put myself back in line with him and once again be capable of listening.

Giovanni said that his father "is really a turd, there's no help for it … he's a turd." He reported having proposed to his father that now was the time they should at last begin remodeling their family home outside the city, at least partially, because the part where his room was located was empty since he moved to Rome. The building was a sort of medieval mansion in which the family had always lived, making use of only a small part of it, which many years ago was transformed into an apartment, while most of the rest of the building was given over to storage.

Giovanni continued, "If he, Papà – no, I mean the turd – would only decide to open up his wallet, I could begin to think about getting the remodeling going so that it would be finished when I return there to live. If I ever *do* return," he added, disconsolate and angry. "Do you know what he said when I proposed this to him? He said that, as usual, I'm being a ball-buster, that I arrive with my big ideas, my delusions of grandeur. Me, a ball-buster? Well, he's a turd, he really is a turd."

I told Giovanni that, "there seems to be an area of opposition with your father, between him being a turd and you being a ball-buster, and it does not appear that there could be any possibility of negotiation, of understanding." "Certainly," I added "you are very disappointed and angry in feeling yourself treated this way by your father, but to consider him 'inevitably a turd' means that you, too, feel like a turd, given that you are his son."

Giovanni's narration continued almost uninterrupted, as though he put aside what I had just said and wanted instead to reaffirm his point of view, to make me understand it, to have my agreement. His father was described yet again as a "colorless, flat, opaque person – dull, continually ready to criticize in a hidden way, but never openly." "He's missing the gift of words," Giovanni continued. "The most he does is grumble, and no one can understand what he says, what he thinks – they can't even establish contact with him."

The patient went on to say that his father was always "closed" and "withdrawn" into his "ugly little workshop," where he made hand-crafted products to order for his clients. According to Giovanni he was always incapable, due to his "passivity" and "fear," of adequately supporting the family.

I told him, "Maybe you feel *me* to be closed and withdrawn also, into my ugly little workshop of analysis – as happened today at the beginning of the session when you didn't feel understood, and indeed even *mis*understood. You felt that I was not in contact."

"Yes, this is true; at the beginning you pissed me off," Giovanni replied. "And I thought … *but he hasn't understood anything, this t …* But at least you don't lack the gift of words, in fact you talk … too much. I mean that I'm not really used to all this dialogue. We are rather closed as a family, few words and many deeds, you might say. My father uses few words, but he also does few deeds."

Giovanni was silent and thoughtful for a time after making these remarks. I told him that maybe he was thinking that to keep himself enclosed, holed up, and silent, uncommunicative, was a characteristic he shared with other members of his family. Maybe he felt that he, too, was like this, and instead would perhaps like to be more communicative, more capable of expressing his feelings. And this was why he felt furious with his father, perhaps because his father reflected a little of him, just as he was reflected in me when I didn't understand him, when I didn't immediately follow what he meant to tell me.

The analytic process

In this period of the analysis, various masculine characters appeared who were analogously criticized and devalued, persons who gradually made their entrance into the narrations, as Giovanni, by now having definitively moved to Rome, continually changed jobs, passing from one restaurant to another. Here the manager was an "exploiter," there "too bossy," there he was "an incompetent guy," or his co-workers "were not professional," "second-rate," or "had the brains of chickens."

My interpretations in this first phase of the analysis were aimed at relating the patient's scorn for his father and other masculine figures with the experience of mortification and shame over his impotence, that is, his sense of lacking an internal penis, and of being continually attacked and ruined by his own scorn. I soon realized, however, that these interpretations were basically ineffective. They were ineffective not so much because direct confrontation with themes of impotence (continually evoked by the patient) made him feel distanced from me, as I had at first believed. In fact, one might say that Giovanni's baseline attitude was already so scornfully distant that only with difficulty could he have felt himself placed at a greater distance. On the contrary, I believe that this type of interpretation, as much as it was devalued and refuted by the patient, may have caused him to sense – as he was later able to tell me – a sort of courage and daring on my part, which for him was not at all something to be rejected.

The sense of shared meaningfulness in our dialogue, which had seemed to be in place since the beginning of the treatment, in an ordinary and apparently satisfying way (as I have tried to show up to this point), progressively led me to feel, during the third year of analysis, that my interpretations, which earlier had seemed to succeed in linking various aspects of the analysand's narrations, had in fact little impact. I became aware that Giovanni had taken in my words as "meaningless," and, in like fashion, they were returned to me as meaningless. I began to realize that my interpretive contribution, however 'formally correct,' had in reality turned out to be quite "colorless" (a characteristic the analysand frequently assigned to his father) and therefore fundamentally impersonal.

For example, I commented several times to Giovanni that he was again finding himself in a job where he was confronted by negative characters whom he could not respect. These comments had the effect of presenting him with an image of himself that he could not respect either, even though he protected himself by remaining on a level of apparent superiority. "Others don't understand anything," he would say. "if I were in the place of that turd of a maître d'hôtel, I would know how to make the restaurant function well." My comments about this came back to me reconfigured, perhaps after two or three sessions, in a mirrorlike way, anticipatory of my response: "As you would say, again this time, I find myself confronted by someone who isn't worth anything," Giovanni would begin. "But the director of the restaurant where I've begun to work temporarily really is a ball-buster – he doesn't understand anything, he really doesn't grasp it, he can't do it ..."

It seemed to me that in this way, Giovanni, acting defensively, actively took the meaning out of my words, stripped them of sense, and made me listen to them repeated back without logic. His 'answers' to what I said, whether they took the form of silence, disorientation, or dismissiveness, were relative to his need to keep me out (as in his eyes, I had already begun to cling to my point of view even before I could express it). They sounded just as impersonal to me and were progressively stripped of meaning.

Only later was I able to realize, to comprehend, that this sense of impersonality, and of an absence of meaning in our communication, hinted at the shadow of the incomprehensibility of emotions that give sense to words. This incomprehensibility was a *deactualization*, a reproduction *in toto* in the transference of a primary relationship with another who "knew nothing" about emotions, who was quite incapable of naming them. For Giovanni, these emotions were oppressive and invasive, but also unnamable and therefore unrecognizable. The maternal world, like the world of femininity, into which he was afraid of being swallowed up, was not ordered and structured by the discourse of the father.

When I realized that this incomprehensibility was a structuring factor in the analysis for both of us, as revealed by continual misunderstandings, that is, when I realized that my interpretations were perceived as meaningless and fed back to me as such, I began to understand that my interpretive contribution was too much for the patient, even though my intentions were, so to speak, good. They were, however, a sort of continuing interpretive acting out on my part, aimed at a*void*ing the *void*, the lack of meaning, the impersonality that infused our relationship. I thereupon began to reduce my verbal interpretive contribution in order to clear the field, as it were, and provide Giovanni with more space.

For example, the patient recounted that he had enthusiastically started to work as a bartender at a stylish cocktail bar because it was a prestigious place frequented by many VIPs of the "*dolce vita romana*." However, the new manager there had revealed himself to be "an incompetent" and "a good-for-nothing." At this I remained silent for some time. I wanted to give him the opportunity to describe the details of this, those most pertinent and specific, the most emotionally explanatory ones, even, in addition, I explicitly asked him for more specifics: "Could you help me better understand what you intend to say, what you are really referring to when you say that the director of the cocktail bar is someone who doesn't know 'how to crucify two words?' What does that mean?"

Giovanni at first seemed to be a little taken aback and disoriented by my listening silences, or perhaps by my requests for more explanation. He began progressively to enter into a state of withdrawal, of apparently pensive silence. Then a new phenomenon presented itself in the communications between us.

The interpretation and meaning of words in analysis

My countertransference during our third year of analysis involved my learning to tolerate the invasion of various quirky 'mental products,' often tortuous and affected, that appeared to stem from the patient's internal disorientation. These phenomena left me with the impression of a certain precariousness of mental boundaries, and there were times when I was tempted to intervene in order to shore him up, but I resisted doing so. Pieces of his unarticulated thinking and fragments of thoughts were shared, and on the one hand they tempted me to ascribe meaning and return them to the analysand, but on the other, they caused me to feel a transient sense of anxiety because I felt responsible for letting him go, without making sense of them. For example, in one session, he said: "I'm thinking about a rooster with colored feathers, I don't know why ... A memory of some writing just occurred to me, from an advertisement in the subway: 'Courses offered in computer skills, typing, and word processing – authorized by the Region of Lazio.'"

Or, yet again, in another session, after a long silence, he launched into the following chain of associations: "Silvia comes to mind, that waitress at the hotel last year. The one whose pants I couldn't get into, as usual. Silvia, Leopardi, Leo, lion, lone, alone, solo, trumpet [Giovanni dabbles as a performer on both the piano and the trumpet], to fuck ... maybe! Sorceress, Circe, one would need a spell, pigs, the *Aeneid*, the Latin teacher in high school."[5]

Giovanni continued his monologue, now launching into a tirade against me: "You don't tell me anything, *nothing comes to your mind to tell me or to explain to me?* In my opinion, you don't understand me, and indeed you *can't* stand me at this point, and *do you even know what I'm telling you?* It is *I* who really cannot stand *you* with your arrogant silence, and with all this crap that you tell me every now and then. I could jerk myself off with what you tell me, and also with what you don't tell me but you think it inside yourself. But mostly *I don't care anything about what you think or say!*"

139

Despite my being strongly tempted to reorder or to explicate the logic of the sequence (Bollas, 1987), which in fact I was able to follow or intuit, or at times invent, or even to interpret his intense apathy toward me, I nevertheless succeeded in remaining silent, deliberately silent, and reducing my comments to a minimal level. For example, I said: "It seems that you delight in chaining together words for their sound, like in a game. Maybe you would like me to participate in this with you, to be like a schoolmate for you to compete with and maybe to beat, as I produce my own sounds in spite of the Latin professor, whom you've said you thought of as inconsistent, which is a little like the analysis that you perceive as menacing, controlling, and intrusive."

I believe that it was my perseverance in maintaining a relatively silent stance that allowed me to see "beyond the mucous" (which sounds strange, but this was the image that came to my mind in relation to Giovanni's loose verbal productions), and then to understand that Giovanni's comments made sense to him, while they also reflected his search to find me.

Of course, in considering my increased interpretive distance from the patient's relatively meaningless verbal productions, I must recognize that there was also something for me to gain by this: an expanded inner space in which to feel and hear from. My intention to remain mostly silent was thus intentional, though one result was that I was unable to stem feelings of boredom, futility, and impotence, as the patient leapt from one silly, pretentious image to another. Eventually, however, I found that as I focused less on the details of his material, his nonsense, which indeed it was, began to acquire a sense of its own. Therefore, from my point of view as well, the expansion of inner space resulted in my ability to make sense of the situation, and also reflected my search to find the patient.

Use of a countertransference dream

My first flash of insight into the configuration I am describing came from a countertransference dream that helped me change my emotional attitude toward the patient. The dream occurred at the end of the third year of analysis, and, significantly, during a long separation from the analysand due to a vacation of mine. I felt that the dream unexpectedly allowed a new, pure image of Giovanni to emerge, a sort of non-analytically biased one that came from inside. In analyzing this dream, I felt first as though I had been 'invaded' by Giovanni's presence, by the patient whom I had supposedly forgotten during the period of separation. The associations that followed had to do with a sense of distance, coldness, and alienation, of not feeling in touch with myself. I then associated the dream image of Giovanni to a part of me relative to the patient, to a coldness and distance in myself; indeed, the image of the patient seemed to represent an attitude of mine, of my person, that I did not want to recognize but that had to be acknowledged in order for the analysis to proceed.

I am touching on something here that is related to what Winnicott is referring to when he states that the patient *has the right to get in touch with the real objective feeling of the analyst toward him*. He wrote: "I wish to suggest that the patient can only appreciate in the analyst what he himself is capable of feeling" (1947, p. 195), and continued, "If the analyst is going to have crude feeling imputed to him, he is best forewarned and so forearmed, for he must tolerate being placed in that position. Above all, he must not deny hate that really exists in himself" (1947, p. 196). Here I would make an addendum: the analyst must not deny hate that really exists in himself *as a person*.

Here the totality and relevance of *the person of the analyst* are put out onto the table, clinically and radically, without infringements and without apology. We see this again when Winnicott wrote: "Recently, for a period of a few days, I found I was doing bad work. I made mistakes toward each one of my patients. *The difficulty was in myself* ... The difficulty cleared up when I had what sometimes is called a 'healing dream'" (1947, p. 197, italics added).

Of course, other psychoanalytic authors have treated analogous themes and made similar clinical observations. However, the way Winnicott puts these things out on the table seems to me particularly subjectively meaningful and clinically useful; rarely are such themes put forward so courageously in the analytic literature.

Now that I have given some associations about my healing dream and contextualized it, let us look at the dream itself. I saw myself clambering up the snow-covered slopes of a mountain. I was breathing hard as the cold became more tiring. I felt lost and despairing in a desolate, boundless landscape. I was standing on the peak of Mount Everest. There, in a kind of niche in the ice, I clearly made out the shape of a man covered by sleet. It was something like a *mirror image* on the ice surface. My first impulse was to draw back in fear. Then I saw the man's head emerging from the snow, and I perceived that it was Giovanni's. Excitedly, I started to blow the snowflakes away from him, but the feeble warmth of my breath was immediately dispersed into the freezing air. Then I began rubbing his body with my hands, taking care not to rub too hard so as not to 'crack' his frozen skin. His eyes slowly opened and his glassy stare became more conscious, more intense. At last I felt confident that Giovanni could be unfrozen.

In my internal perception of the analysis with this patient, the dream became a turning point in the treatment. I felt healed from the illness that I had contracted in the analytic process due to my defense against Giovanni (Bollas, 1987). The dream became for me the source of meaningful images that I could begin to propose to the patient. I started to 'draw off' pieces from the dream (although, obviously, I did not reveal the dream to him) in order to describe to the patient what seemed to me to be happening in our sessions, both with reference to our relationship and his narrations about his external object relations.

In the third session after the dream, Giovanni tentatively described a sense of feeling apart from everything, including the analysis. The gist of my comment to him at this point was that I felt him to be at a very great distance, as though he were "on top of Mount Everest." He replied after a bit, "this makes some sense to me. Maybe not on Mount Everest, but at North Cape, while you are down here, basking in the sunshine of Rome, happy and content." With these words, Giovanni was able to express his feeling of envy toward me for what he felt to be my good relationship with my wife and my capacity to have a satisfying sexual life.

Approximately one month later, feeling depressed about his recurrent lack of sexual success with another girl, for the first time, instead of criticizing both the girl and himself, Giovanni recognized that he had felt frozen while he was with her. I replied that it seemed he felt "closed, trapped into a fridge," referring here to the dream image of the niche in the ice. I added that, "it seems someone should have come to release you from that uncomfortable position." He replied that he was wondering whether the analyst had ever felt, really, what it was like to feel sexually inept and unsuccessful with a girl who was warm and appetizing, as though he were unable to embrace her or even touch her.

In a session approximately two weeks later, I found myself sounding a bit harsh in one of my comments to Giovanni: "As usual," I began, "you have found that your family is insensitive toward you, and that even I do not understand you properly." Both *usual* and *even* were words that hurt the analysand because they were perceived as dismissive and aggressive (which they actually were, as I realized soon after). Two sessions later, when his discourse had suddenly become impoverished and he was rather withdrawn, I was able to interpret that he had perceived my words as "without warmth … like icy breath," and similar to his father's criticisms of him, which were so sharp "they could crack his skin."

It was at this point that the first *phonemes* of a new common language began to surface. I noticed and recorded that the patient, who had evidently felt that my suggested images made sense to him, began to use similar images to describe things that bordered on emotions, or at least sensations. This, of course, occurred sporadically, over quite a long period of time – months, in fact – without the patient explicitly 'letting on.' It was during this period that the 'mucous' in the analysis (an image I mentioned earlier) started to thin out and give way to more coherent communication and narrations about specific events that came up in the analytic relationship, and here Giovanni began to reveal a keen sensitivity.

For instance, a slight adjustment in the cost of his sessions, which I suggested well ahead of time, toward the end of his fourth year of analysis, aroused a deep resentment against me, expressed by his return to a state of withdrawal. He accused me of having left him "dumbfounded" and "boiling with rage," expressions that referred to sensations and feelings that were certainly no longer incomprehensible. At this point Giovanni accepted and agreed with my interpretation of his having perceived me like a boyhood friend of his, Giuseppe, whom he had told me about in the early stages of the analysis; Giovanni had told me he was "betrayed" by Giuseppe, when the other boy suddenly asked him to pay up the money won in games over which they gambled in small amounts. This disruption of trust in the friendship, which significantly was represented *in toto* in the transference, produced in the patient a deep sense of anger, resentment, and disappointment, as well as a sense of expulsion and exclusion, thereby organizing his narcissistic defenses. But even more significantly all these emotions could now be identified and thought about within an ongoing relationship.

143

The analyst's participation, interpreting function, and reconstruction

What kind of participation by the analyst is conveyed by my comments to this patient? From a technical point of view, my clinical presentation aims to show that the analyst does not need to take anything other than a 'standard' approach in order to successfully follow the many tangents – both representational and nonrepresentational – the patient takes in order to make the analyst understand where he is and how he feels.

For some time now, we have been aware that the field of the psychoanalytic encounter, and in particular the analyst's contribution to the creation and maintenance of the analytic situation (Balint, 1950), is wider than first thought. Our 'standard' shared technique may encompass this larger field without significant variations, apart from how we meet the patient's regression and the most primitive level of his communication.

In the case of Giovanni, I think through my dream, which was mine and not the projection onto me of his feelings, I represented something not yet representable for him. In this sense I understand Heimann's (1950) statement that "Countertransference … is the patient's *creation*" (p. 83, italics in original). Through my interpretations to the patient, I think I reflected back to him what he had communicated (not projected) via the means at his disposal (bizarre associations, withdrawal). In reflecting back to him what he had communicated, I inevitably gave him something of mine, i.e., my personal, idiomatic way of representing him. This is what I consider a relational dimension of the analytic encounter, and it is in this sense that the inevitable revelation of the *person of the analyst* is implied.

I am not speaking here specifically of self-disclosure, a topic that many American colleagues have been debating in recent years, sometimes in particularly interesting ways in regard to the variety of clinical situations that are being reexamined against the backdrop of so-called classical technique (Jacobs, 1999). But to my way of thinking there is sometimes too great an emphasis on the *participation of the analyst* in the analytic process and his subjectivity, factors that may seem to us, on the other side of the Atlantic, both self-evident and long-established within the framework of object-relations theory.

Why introduce the concept of the analyst's subjectivity when we already have the deeply entrenched concept of countertransference?

(Manfredi Turillazzi & Ponsi, 1999). I will return to the subject of countertransference later in this paper and discuss it from another point of view.

Because of the enthusiastic neo-accentuation of the analyst's participation in the analytic field, some currents of contemporary American analysis appear to me to be in danger of falling prey to an excessive co-constructivist and intersubjectivity drift. The intersubjective approach – and with it references to the analysand's and the analyst's subjectivities – can thus become a privileged observational vertex that engulfs everything in the analytic situation. In my view, such overemphasis may result in an invasion of the patient's own field in the service of establishing a parity between the two subjects. If too much personal space is taken away from the analysand, then enactment – be it psychic or behavioral – becomes the only chance the subjects have of getting to know what is really happening in the analytic situation (Green, 1997).

According to Green (1997), in the intersubjective approach (in its specific meaning, i.e., as a model for the analytic relationship) the priority granted to enactment is influenced or guided by the neo-Kleinian concept of the ubiquitous nature of projective identification, as well as the concept of the analysand's tendency to force the analyst's mind to do something. Approaching this from a different direction than the one from which Green's criticism stems, I will state that in my view the intersubjective and neo-Kleinian approaches, as well as extremist theories of the analysis as a bi-personal field, may appear to proceed hand in hand, because of their common widespread insistence upon the relational here-and-now as the one and only place in which to consider the events of the session.

Busch (2001) expresses a similar opinion, noting the presence of a

> view that analysts cannot know their own minds, let alone the mind of another. It is evidenced in the lack of interest amongst some analysts in the individual mind of the analysand, except in interaction with the analyst. We see it in the belief that analysis is primarily a co-creation of two minds, both in the clinical moment and as the agent of the change process. (pp. 739–740)

Recent brilliant observations by Friedman (2008), who ironically asked, "Is there life after enactment?" do not conflict with the above-mentioned, tradition-preserving position expressed by Green but represent a way of viewing the same problem from another, more empirical point of view, which takes into account much of the debate that has occurred around this topic. In a way that I find particularly congruent with my arguments, Friedman wrote:

> Having recognized their own libidinal involvement with patients, analysts could not refuse to confess their many subtle collusions.[6] And having gone that far, they were bound to wonder whether enactments aren't, in fact, omnipresent ... whether, in fact, analytic treatment isn't altogether a continuous game of catch-up ... But if enactment is part of the very fabric of analysis and not just an occasional snag, the question logically arises, What would *not* be an enactment? Why use the word at all? What was the error we would have fallen into without the term? (p. 436, italics in original)

In fact, I have posed the same questions in regard to what I feel has sometimes been the too-enthusiastic and uncritical substitution of the word *subjectivity* for the concept of *countertransference,* as though there is a belief that the former sounds more modern and philosophically driven. I agree that countertransference is not a felicitous term in the sense that the prefix *counter* seems to imply opposition between analyst and analysand, but at the same time, I do not think we need be overly literal in choosing to maintain components of our psychoanalytic lexicon that have served us well. Countertransference, after all, contains within it layers of technical and conceptual reflection, so that the bad prefix is blurred by the many other meanings acquired by the term over the years.

Friedman's astute observations proceed as follows: "If recognizing our enactment means realizing that we have been laboring under an illusion, what was the illusion that fooled us? Given the contemporary climate, the handiest answer might be this: 'Not-an-enactment is both parties doing their proper work'" (2008, p. 436).

In a related way, the constant de-emphasis on the reconstructive aspects of analytic work in favor of careful and detailed attention to the phenomenology of what takes place in the session between analyst and patient – on understanding the here-and-now of the session as a projection or actualization of the patient's internal world – not only seems to devalue the importance of the patient's history, but also implies a particular view of the transference that risks giving short shrift to the role of *Nachträglichkeit*. This important concept, also called *après-coup,* denotes Freud's articulated concept of temporality (inadequately translated in English by Strachey as *deferred action*). It implies a movement from past to future that includes the "deposit" of something into the individual, something that takes on meaning only retrospectively (Birksted-Breen, 2003).

Relevant to my discussion here of *Nachträglichkeit* is a comparison of the analytic situation to the patient's repetition of internalized object relations. The *new* scene, or the new object *created* by the analytic relationship, encompasses even the most intense repetitions of historically internalized object relations, but is, at the same time, hierarchically superimposed on them. This new scene becomes the place from which one can observe repetition, and it is the place where the analyst becomes the target of the patient's projective identifications (if we choose to use this terminology), so the analyst is forced to enact the role assigned to him by the patient. It is the place where the analytic work occurs, a place created by the two parties, by their mutual communication, but cannot be considered simply to overlap the repetition of internalized object relations because it is the prerequisite for these to be actualized and then analyzed.

In other words, once the patient 'projects' and the analyst recognizes through his countertransference the role the patient is forcing upon him, in what place does this revelation occur except in the new, constantly changing object relationship to which both parties have contributed? And how does the analyst perform his analytic function *as a person relating to the analysand?* That is, how does he contribute to this relationship by meeting the patient precisely in that place, contributing his personal qualities to the object relationship? Only by articulating the situation with these broader questions am I able to agree with the notion of the transference as a *total situation* (Joseph, 1985).

A new realism, a new reification in postmodern guise, has appeared on the conceptual scene following the demise of the justly denounced reification of the drive and structural model, and of its supposedly solipsistic structure that was attributed *tout court* to ego psychology. The inescapable relationship and the concept of intersubjectivity were summoned to emphasize – and rightly so – the reciprocal contributions, mutual influence, interchange between the two partners in co-determining meaning. The intersubjective relationship was also called upon to highlight the constructivist

147

dimension of reality, including psychic reality, and hence its relevance obviously depends on the relational context. Thus, intersubjectivity itself seems to escape the dimension of the relativity it claimed, at least on those occasions when it is considered out of context, as a thing in itself; in fact, in the hands of its most radical upholders, it risks becoming a sort of basic absolute reality – at once indivisible, a prerequisite, and a prime mover.

I do not intend to discuss self-disclosure, as mentioned earlier, when I state that, whenever the analyst decides to introduce an interpretation or to remain silent, he inevitably admits something of himself into the analysis, and this something is revealed to the patient. But if I am not referring to self-disclosure, what revelation do I mean? What I have in mind is the unpredictable and inevitable *presentation of the unconscious* in the intersubjective communication – the emergence of it from within us, which Freud described in many ways and on many occasions, starting with 'Jokes and their Relation to the Unconscious' (1905). I refer here to the unconscious communication between people that lies at the base of analytic work: a communication *from one unconscious to another unconscious* within the analytic setting. To this communication, the 'listening system' (which analysis essentially is, i.e., the patient's free associations and the analyst's evenly hovering attentiveness) is applied, and this system offers an opportunity for such communication to emerge into consciousness and thus provides the means for its realization.

Here we are faced with the paradox of how an 'intrapsychic' model, i.e., the dream, can function in the service of an essentially intersubjective experience, i.e., the analysis (Phillips, 1989). The analyst's role in this paradoxical arrangement is to provide an environment for creating the dream space. Bollas (1995) described this oscillation from the *intrapsychic* to the *intersubjective* as a sort of *countertransference dreaming*. Ferro (1996) in an original and personal elaboration of Bion's thinking, investigated the concept of dreaming activity during the waking states of both analysand and analyst.

The concept of *the analyst as a person*, or *the person of the analyst*, should be made an integral part of an approach that emphasizes the presentation of the unconscious in intersubjective communication. Such a concept is by no means a new fact to be taken into consideration; it has roots in the very origins of psychoanalysis and is part of its clinical and theoretical status. In short, it is quite simply a fact to be taken for granted, but one that implies establishing a different focus as soon as we begin to discuss it directly. Of course, this change of focus, i.e., explicitly considering the participation of the analyst in the creation, maintenance, and development of the analytic process, marks a pivotal point in the evolution of analytic technique, just as changing conceptions of exactly what its therapeutic factors are become markers of other evolutionary developments in the field.

What I am emphasizing is the continuity in analysis of an awareness of the analyst's influence as a person in the analytic process. In contemporary analytic literature, this nontraditional focus is generally listed under the register of a *paradigm shift*, a somewhat pompous epistemological expression normally employed to announce, and later proclaim, adhesion to a 'new model' of the analytic situation. My interest in this focus is primarily clinical, and it is in fact the clinical experience, and by this I mean the *therapeutic situation, that has provided the basis for modifications in analytic theory and technique*, just as the clinical arena, from the very beginning, gave rise to the model of mental functioning elaborated by psychoanalysis. To put it another way, the central role of psychopathology and its manifestations in the therapeutic situation are the essential source of the data upon which the analytic conceptual model has been built, but unfortunately the significance of this tends not to be recognized, since there has been an effort to downplay it in order to correct what came to be considered an excessively 'pathomorphic' trend in psychoanalysis.

The "dramatic" appearance of the countertransference dimension, i.e., the quality of *the analyst's participation,* has been mobilized by the acceptance into psychoanalysis of a new type of interlocutor who is not like Freud's original patients; these are our so-called borderline, schizoid, narcissistic, and psychotic patients, as well as children. Gradually, as countertransference has begun to reveal 'the other side of the coin' in the analytic scenario, it has also compelled us to rethink and carefully redefine the entire analytic situation, and to rethink and redefine (though in a less radical way), the concepts upon which the model of the mind that it derives from are based.

This eruption of countertransference issues is one of the principal factors of change and development in the psychoanalytic model of the mind and of the relationship.[7] But I would not refer to this as a paradigm shift; rather, I regard it as a slow, progressive and necessary change – a *quiet revolution,* to use Ogden's (1992) expression – that speaks to the vitality of psychoanalysis as a method of cure.

Individuality, intersubjectivity, and intersubjectivism

Both intrapsychic and intersubjective factors participate, dialectically, in the psychoanalytic process. As Green (2000) observed, "Instead of working together, these two dimensions may become the object of a struggle for supremacy in which each point of view, while acknowledging the other's position, strives to secure its primacy, if not its hegemony" (p. 2).

The vision of the dyadic, relational, intersubjective dimension of the psychoanalytic process has become progressively more widespread (and quite fortunately so). I am aware that in stating this I may appear to champion the very perspective that I have been questioning. However, let me explain my belief that, because of cultural differences, the term *relational* may have different connotations to European (and, specifically, Italian) analysts, than it does American analysts. From reading American psychoanalytic literature, I understand that the term refers to a theoretical orientation (and, consequently, a technical one) that might be considered the opposite of a classical or traditional approach. As distinct from this, the European, the Italian – or perhaps simply my personal understanding – is that both *relational* and *intersubjective* imply a particular attention to what is going on between patient and analyst, i.e., on both sides of the analytic couple, but without displacing the primary focus from the patient's thoughts, emotions, defenses, and overall psychic structure.

As Winnicott (1954) put it in his idiomatic way: "In doing psychoanalysis, one is constantly on the lookout for indications as to the main source of the material presented for interpretation."★

And in a footnote he adds: "★Psycho-analysis starts with patient + → develop theme to unconscious co-operation process, growth and use of intimacy, self-revelation, 'surprises'" (p. 88).

As it has become so widespread in the analytic literature, the dyadic, relational vision of the analytic process has tended to transform itself into a sort of metamodel for treatment, which seems aimed at unifying, at 'melting down' varying points of view that may in fact be widely disparate owing to their unique positions in the cultural and geographical matrix of the psychoanalytic panorama. As a metamodel, however, this approach houses an epistemological vice that, in my opinion, resides in the confusion between the 'place' of the analytic process (in which the intersubjective, analyst–analysand dimension is located and realized), on the one hand, and on the other the object (Boesky, 1990), or even the 'aims' of the analytic process, or its 'use,' which, I would say, has to do exclusively with the patient's individuality.

Let us consider some emblematic (but significantly, not so recent) comments about the intersubjective dimension, i.e., the 'place' of the analytic process, through an examination of what is currently unduly considered to be one of the signs of an authoritarian stance on the part of the analyst: the analyst's interpretations. Bion (1977) condensed his views on the vast clinical theme of the *therapeutic alliance* by describing the analysand as the "analyst's best colleague." He wrote that interpretations are "theories the analyst makes on the theories that the analysand makes on the analyst." Nine years earlier, Winnicott (1968a) made what he defined as a "very simple statement" about interpretation, implying a circularity between analyst and analysand:

> The purpose of interpretation must include a feeling that the analyst has that a communication has been made which needs *acknowledgement* ... Giving an interpretation back gives the patient opportunity to correct the misunderstandings ... [In making an interpretation] the analyst *reflects back* what the patient has communicated.
>
> (pp. 208–209, italics added)

Both Bion and Winnicott's remarks quoted above derive from a conception of interpretation whose central aspect is *not* the unveiling of an unconscious fantasy fixed and locked inside the patient, but rather a proposal offered to the patient, or an amplification of emotional and relational meanings, which the analyst in turn transmits back to the analysand in what I would describe as a *semantic circularity*, a dialectical interplay between self and other.

Ferro (1996) advised that the analyst should make an interpretation to the patient only insofar as the analyst believes it will be transformative, a position with which I agree. Whereas Ferro is essentially speaking from a Bionian point of view, I find that Winnicott's expression resonates more with my own; from a clinical standpoint, that is, I have a better understanding of what Winnicott is saying because I find evidence for it in my own experience, though I certainly admire the way that Bion could convey such ideas on an intellectual level.

151

The intersubjective dimension of the analytic encounter is therefore not only inevitable, but necessary and useful, in understanding, describing, and returning to the analysand what is actually happening in the session between two members of the dyad. Bolognini (2008) recently demonstrated this by focusing on the *intrapsychic* and the *interpsychic* as two different ways of considering the same question from different angles, while also indicating from a technical point of view what difficulties may arise if one of these is privileged over the other.

It seems to me that to assign the relational, intersubjective point of view to the highest position in psychoanalytic theorizing is to claim priority for what are basically the qualities of the *analyst as a person,* i.e., his idiomatic way of *being* with the patient and of tolerating his countertransference (Carpy, 1989). In fact, once this point of view has been vaulted to the highest theoretical level (instead of being retained at the clinical level, where it more properly belongs), it seems to me that a dangerous fiction is created: that is, that the analyst's capacity for being sensitive, unobtrusive, and aware of his influence on the patient is *ipso facto* guaranteed.

In effect, instead of a democracy or a parity between analyst and analysand, a sort of *statism* is thereby created, in which everything belongs to the *state* of the intersubjective relationship, and nothing is owned by the individual parties themselves. Such a framework restricts the analyst's freedom to respond to the patient's needs and ultimately hinders his understanding of the patient. Unfortunately, once the analytic prescriptions belonging to a presumed objectivity, such as neutrality, abstinence, etc., are thrown out the door of the consulting room (and not all that politely, either) new prescriptions simply enter in through the window. On a clinical level, Bolognini (1997) did well to highlight a related phenomenon when he stressed the risk of the analyst's empathy turning into *empathism.*

What about Freud's evocation of the 'impassive' analyst, guardian of the rules of the setting, who positions himself in relation to his patient as an 'opaque mirror' who reflects back only what the patient projects? Are we certain that in this famous Freudian metaphor (1912), we can find no more than the sedimentation of obedience to an antiquated, formal orthodoxy? Does this metaphor present us with nothing more than a strictly 'uni-personal' (one-body) perspective (as of course is often seen in more or less classical or traditional clinical accounts)?

Bearing in mind what have been defined as the lost certainties of psychoanalysis (Manfredi Turillazzi, 1994; Kohon, 1999), we might begin to appreciate to what use a Freudian metaphor like the opaque mirror might usefully be applied, and how we might consider such analogies in the light of developments that have transformed psychoanalysis since Freud's time. I believe that this metaphor offers us the chance to see, *a posteriori* (*Nachträglichkeit*), what Kohut defined as *narcissistic mirror transference,* to give one example; or what Winnicott described as the *mirror function of the mother's gaze,* to give another (in which the individual recognizes himself through the other). In the Freudian adjective *opaque,* isn't it possible to find a reference to the clinical concept of the unobtrusive analyst (Balint, 1968), who refrains from invading the patient's own field and does not engage him in obsessive monitoring of the reciprocal, interactive movements of patient and analyst? Moreover, doesn't the word opaque also evoke the *negative capability* that Bion (1970, p. 124) mentions, referring back to Keats (1817), implicit in his recommendation "to suspend memory and desire?"

Then, too, the analyst's privacy, his personal idiom, can come under fire in the analysis. Perhaps with a touch of exaggeration, we might imagine an analyst who is intensely concerned with tracing the relational texture in the analytic material, with pinpointing the reciprocal moves between the analysand and himself in the context of the session, but in the course of this exhaustive task he may lose sight not only of the patient but of himself as well.

What about transference? There can be no doubt that the most important developments in the concept of transference (which remains the central preoccupation of psychoanalytic treatment), that the amplifications of transference that have occurred in many different directions, have all accentuated the dimension of actual, current experience and newness inherent in the concept itself. By definition, transference has been the bearer of these ever since its original discovery by Freud, who saw transference as something newly found. Even in the most classical definition of the transference as a place of repetition, I do not believe that there is an exclusive prerequisite for the blind repetition of fantasy processes. Rather, such distortion, as there is, belongs to the unilateral way with which this concept has been interpreted exclusively in terms of genetic determinants.

Today, even though we do not know much more about what is therapeutic in psychoanalysis (that is, we lack a simple, precise statement about this), we nevertheless question our earlier certainties (Gabbard & Westen, 2003), and we know that the whole issue is much more complex than we used to think or write, as Smith (2000) notes. We know that it is not the transference, nor is it transference interpretation, that is the sole or even main agent of psychic change. The quality of psychoanalytic ecology (space, time, and the presence of the analyst) makes an equally important, if not more important, contribution in working with so-called difficult patients. The entire conception of the psychoanalytic process has changed step-by-step with the amplification and investigation of the transference-countertransference relationship, and this change is by no means limited to recent years.

As I have already stressed, I feel that strict adherence to an excessively relational approach in psychoanalytic technique may tend to obscure the patient's individuality, his search for an intimacy with himself, as I theorized in an earlier paper (Bonaminio, 1996). I also wonder whether, in view of the progressive affirmation of a relational metamodel, we ought not to identify what we might think of as the 'ideological' components of psychoanalytic theory. For example, if we consider postmodern psychoanalysis as having begun with the discovery of the importance of the countertransference, i.e., with the participation of the analyst in the totality of the analytic process, it seems to me that two fundamental movements can be seen. First, there has been a progressive rebalancing in favor of a greater weight and responsibility on the part of the analyst, a factor previously undervalued. A second movement can be discerned in the opposite direction: that is, an overreliance on countertransference, which might be conceptualized as the 'analyst's retreat from the patient's vantage point' (Schwaber, 1999). This is what I have described above as the risk of a subterranean erosion of the patient's space, an erosion caused by the analyst in the service of prioritizing co-participation and context dependency of everything that happens in the clinical situation.

Concluding remarks: Countertransference and the analyst's individuality

I will conclude by briefly discussing the importance of the analyst's 'realness', i.e., his capacity for *spontaneity, freedom,* and *aliveness* in responding to the analysand on the basis of *his own experience*, in such a way that he is not shackled by stereotypical attitudes in observing analytic neutrality (Ogden, 1999).

If the analyst's act of freedom in thinking (Symington, 1983), or his capacity of thinking the unthinkable in psychoanalysis (Coltart, 1985), represents an important factor for therapeutic change, then to what was Winnicott referring? Which clinical situations did he have in mind in making this arresting statement, unless we dismiss it as an offhand declaration? In other words, what interferences and what defenses and resistances may have cropped up in the analysis, and what petrified language did he believe had taken root in the relationship between analyst and patient that stopped the analyst from *being himself* and, generally, from *keeping himself alive*?

The analyst's inner process cannot be taken for granted. It is the result (if indeed there is a result) of a continuous process of elaboration, each moment of which is characterized by what Smith (2000) defined as *conflictual listening*. Smith uses this term to emphasize "an ongoing conflictual process, containing all the components of conflict and shaped in every moment by both the patient's and analyst's conflicts" (p. 95).

Winnicott refers to the work done by the analyst when he writes:

> I would rather be remembered as maintaining that in between the patient and the analyst is the analyst's professional attitude, his technique, *the work he does with his mind.* Now I say this without fear because I am not an intellectual and in fact I personally do my work very much from the body-ego, so to speak. But I think of myself in my analytic work working with an easy but conscious mental effort.
>
> (1960, p. 161)

Here Winnicott is calling attention to the distance and the difference in position between the two partners of the analytic couple in session: one of them enters analysis mainly because he is ill and expects to be cured, while the other one is supposed to be in a position to cure him.

Certainly, the analyst has a subjectivity of his own that leads him to re-elaborate what the other narrates to him, and that makes his listening different from any other listener's. His personal history provides him with a wide range of mental contents that each of his patients organizes in a different way. To put this in the evocative words of Bollas (on whose conceptualization I am largely relying): "Even as an unconscious subject, I am still shaped by another's effect on me. My self is given a new form by the other" (1995, p. 25).

Both analyst and patient unconsciously know that they are contributing, moment by moment, to the transformation of the other's self. Shall we conclude that no other outcome of the analytic couple's work is available to the patient? Although the analytic relationship in itself is of the greatest importance here, and although the analyst's function of *holding* (in Winnicott's term) and *containment* (in Bion's) contributes to the cure, it is through ongoing interpretive work that the analyst opposes and deconstructs the patient's pathological structure. The analyst is required to use his own analysis, training, and professional expertise to distance himself from his subjectivity, and together these guarantee his ability to step outside it.

This is why, in my opinion, we ought to distinguish the countertransference (even, in its broadest sense, including the analyst's theories, interpretations, and unconscious responses) from *the private areas that are the analyst as a person*. In order to develop the image proposed by Winnicott, one might say that, if the countertransference is the analyst's work, "an easy but conscious mental effort" (1960, p. 161), under ordinary or standard analytic conditions, and presumably a much greater effort in circumstances of intense emotional turbulence with difficult patients or in certain phases of all analyses, *then it is the analyst as a person who is conducting this work*.

Adopting a theatrical metaphor here, we might say that the internal relationship between the analyst's countertransference and his *person* is analogous to the relationship between the actor who passionately *impersonates* and *lives* a character on the stage, and the director/playwright who closely but *invisibly* follows the performance from offstage. From this point of view, we might say that the countertransference is largely an unconscious work tool, at the disposal of the analyst's self who is directly involved in the action of the play, onstage, but not utilized by his whole self.

I believe this dialectic between the analyst's countertransference and his whole self was what Winnicott (1960) alluded to in the following:

Ideas and feelings come to mind, but these are well examined and sifted before an interpretation is made. This is not to say the feelings are not involved. On the one hand, I may have stomach

156

ache but this does not usually affect my interpretation; and on the other hand, I may have been somewhat stimulated erotically or aggressively by an idea given by the patient, but again this fact does not usually affect my interpretative work, what I say, how I say or when I say it. (pp. 161–162)

I use this quotation here with an explicitly paradoxical intention. On one hand, Winnicott's assertion that the analyst's interpretive work is not affected "by ideas given by the patient" may be seen, indeed, as naive and outdated in terms of its description of the analytic process and the nature of the analyst's position; today, it is hard for us to imagine that the "analyst's irreducible subjectivity" (Renik, 1993) does not inevitably influence his way of interpreting and responding to the patient, who in turn communicates with him on the basis of his own conflicts, but also in response to what is coming to him from the analyst.

On the other hand, Winnicott's arguably outdated statement is a single, obvious example of the analyst's need to – and, ideally, his ability to – step outside his subjectivity, to keep it separated from the work that he does 'for' the patient, guaranteeing the privacy of both the patient and himself, as well as the patient's right to be fed, so to speak, by the analyst's interpretations. Otherwise, one might imagine that the analyst's stomachache would be put in charge of the patient!

Winnicott's reference to stomachache is useful for another reason: it represents a *personal fact* originating within the analyst, which belongs to the analyst's psyche-soma and is not necessarily a response, however idiosyncratic, to what the patient has made him feel. Here I am thinking of situations that are not ordinary, but neither are they unusual; for example, we are all aware of many descriptions in the literature that describe the influence of illness in the analyst on the course of treatment. Like a litmus paper, such situations may help to make the person of the analyst visible.

In my view, then, the margin between the analyst's countertransference and his privacy (or individuality) is elusive and ambiguous; it represents a border that defines the analyst's activities, his technique and technical attitude, and his presence as a person. Yet these are also two separate concepts. We will function better as analysts if we can work to keep them as separate as possible in our minds.

Acknowledgments: The author is indebted to and wishes to thank several colleagues who carefully read this paper and assisted him in modifying and refining the ideas expressed, especially Dr. Fred Busch, Ms. Anne-Marie Sandler, Dr. Evelyne Schwaber, and Dr. Daniel Jacobs. The author is also grateful to *The Psychoanalytic Quarterly's* three anonymous readers for their helpful suggestions.

Notes

1 An earlier version of this chapter was presented at the Psychoanalytic Institute of New England, East, in Boston, Massachusetts, on February 26, 2005.
2 Of course, it is Winnicott who is 'Freudian' when he states that the object is created where the other lets it be found (1951). Interpretation thus has the characteristic of being *object presenting*.
3 From a technical point of view, the analyst's silence itself, of course, can also be an interference and an impingement on the analysand.
4 See Balint (1968) on the concept of *the unobtrusive analyst*. See also Bonaminio (1993; 2003) for a further discussion of not interpreting. Also relevant are Winnicott's (1958) comments on the capacity to be alone and the role of the analyst in facilitating this capacity. In addition, see Winnicott's (1941) discussion of a *period of hesitation* (presented in relation to the spatula game), a period that allows the child (and, metaphorically, the analysand) to recognize the reality of his desire, to the extent to which a sort of suspension is created: a *not-interference* on the part of the other. In the same Winnicottian tradition of technical thinking, Bollas (1995; 2007), Giannakoulas (2003), and Parsons (2000) have emphasized the analyst's trust of the unconscious process between himself and the patient, as well as the evolution of the analyst's identity.
5 Here the patient was indulging in a very specific series of linguistic and symbolic associations—words strung together by their assonance and double meanings, that highlighted the sexual register and the patient's preoccupation with sexual themes. From the name of the woman he had dated, Silvia, he associated to the poet Giacomo Leopardi (1798–1837), whose famous poem "A Silvia" describes the poet's unrequited love and fascination for an attractive but sexually unattainable woman. From "Leopardi," Giovanni moved to the Italian word for lion, "*leone.*" He then dropped two syllables and easily reached the English word "lone," then to the Italian word for alone, "*solo,*" followed by the Italian word for solo, as in a musical solo: "*assolo.*" "*Tromba,*" meaning trumpet in Italian, also has the vulgar connotation of "to fuck," so that his following this with the Italian word "*magari,*" maybe, conveyed his interest in the possibility that maybe he could fuck. By subtracting two letters from "*magari,*" he arrived at "*maga,*" or sorceress, and "Circe,"

the sorceress of Ancient Magna Grecia in Southern Italy, who forced men to fulfil her sexual desires, hence Giovanni's comment that "one would need a spell" (to succeed in having a sexual relationship). His progressing from there on to pigs referred both to Circe's habit of turning men into pigs, and the animal's Italian connotation as symbolic of a hearty sexual appetite. Thinking of Circe then made Giovanni think of Virgil's *The Aeneid,* typically studied in Italian high schools, and of his former Latin teacher.

6 My clinical presentation of Giovanni aims exactly at this: to show the presence of the person of the analyst as he is involved with the patient.

7 Of course, this eruption began with such notable contributors as Heimann (1950) and Little (1951). Into these relatively early examinations and elaborations of countertransference, Winnicott (1947) too introduced important general considerations, such as "hate in the countertransference." As I have noted elsewhere (Bonaminio, 1991), Winnicott emphasized the necessity for authentic feelings and an authentic presence on the analyst's part, in order for the analytic relationship to be recognized by the patient as a true relationship.

References

Balint, M. (1950). Changing therapeutical aims and techniques in psychoanalysis. *Int. J. Psychoanal.,* 31:117–124.

_____ (1968). *The Basic Fault. Therapeutic Aspects of Regression.* London: Tavistock Publications.

Bettelheim, B. (1983) *Freud and Man's Soul: An Important Re-Interpretation of Freudian Theory.* New York: Vintage Books.

Bion, W. R. (1967a). *Second Thoughts: Selected Papers on Psychoanalysis.* London: Heinemann.

_____ (1967b). Notes on memory and desire. *Psychoanal. Forum.* 2:272–273. Also in: Melanie Klein Today. Development in Theory and Practice. Volume II: Mainly Practice. Edited by E. Bott Spillius. London: Routledge.

_____ (1970). *Attention and Interpretation.* London: Tavistock

_____ (1977). Seven Servants. In: *Four Works by W. R. Bion.* New York: Aronson.

Birksted-Breen, D. (2003). Time and the après-coup. *Int. J. Psychoanal.,* 84:1501–1515.

Boesky, D. (1990). The psychoanalytic process and its components. *Psychoanal. Q.,* 59:550–584.

Bollas, C. (1987). *The Shadow of the Object.* London: Free Association Books.

_____ (1995). Cracking up. In: *The Work of Unconscious Experience*. London: Routledge.

_____ (2007) *The Freudian Moment*. London: Karnac.

Bolognini, S. (1997). Empathy and 'empathism'. *Int. J. Psychoanal.*, 78:279–293.

_____ (2008). *Secret Passages: The Theory and Technique of Interpsychic Relations*. London: Routledge.

Bonaminio, V. (1991). D. W. Winnicott and the position of the analyst and the analysand in the psychoanalytic situation. *Riv. di Psicoanalisi.*, xxxvii:626–666.

_____ (1993). On not interpreting. Two clinical fragments and some considerations for a reappraisal of M. Balint contribution. *Riv. di Psicoanalisi (English edition)*, xxxix:69–92.

_____ (1997). *Squiggles and Spaces: Revisiting the Work of D. W. Winnicott, Volume 1*. Bertolini M., Giannakoulas, A., Hernandez, M., Molino, A. (Eds.). New York: Wiley. 2001.

Breuer, J. & Freud, S. (1892–1895). Studies on hysteria. *S. E.*, 2.

Britton, R. & Steiner, J. (1994). Interpretation: Selected fact or overvalued idea? *Int. J. Psycho-Anal.*, 75:1069–1078.

Busch, F. (2001). Are we losing our mind? *J. Am. Psychoanal. Assoc.*, 49:739–751.

Carpy, D. (1989). Tolerating the countertransference: A mutative process. *Int. J. Psychoanal.*, 70:287–294.

Coltart, N. E. (1986). Slouching toward Bethlehem'…or thinking the unthinkable in psychoanalysis. In: *The British School of Psychoanalysis. The Independent Tradition*. Edited by G. Kohon. London: Free Association Books.

Faimberg, H. (1981). Une des difficultés de l'analyse: la reconnaissance de l'altérité. *Rev. Française de Psychanalyse*, 45:1351–1368.

Ferro, A. (1996). *Nella Stanza d'analisi. Emozioni, Racconti, Trasformazioni*. Milano: Cortina.

_____ (1992). *The Bi-Personal Field: Experiences in Child Analysis*. London: Routledge, 1999.

Freud, S. (1901). Fragment of an analysis of a case of hysteria. S. E., 7.

_____ (1905). Jokes and their relation to the unconscious. S. E., 8.

_____ (1910). The future prospects of psycho-analytic therapy. S. E., 11.

_____ (1912). Recommendations to physicians practicing psychoanalysis. S. E., 12.

_____ (1915). The unconscious. S. E., 14.

_____ (1926). The question of lay analysis. S. E., 20.

_____ (1937). Analysis terminable and interminable. S. E., 23.

Friedman, L. (2008). Is there life after enactment? The idea of a patients proper work. *J.Am. Psychoanal. Assoc.*, 56:431–453.

Glover, E. (1931). The therapeutic effect of inexact interpretation: a contribution to the theory of suggestion. *Int. J. Psycho-Anal.*, 12:397–411.

Green, A. (1997). Smembramento del controtransfert. Paper presented at the "Colloquio italo-francese." *Società Psicoanalitica Italiana e Societé Psychanalytique De Paris*, Palermo, 22–23/11/1997.

_____ (2000). The intrapsychic and the intersubjective in psychoanalysis. *Psychoanal. Q.*, LXIX:1–39.

Heimann, P. (1950). On counter-transference. *Int. J. Psychoanal.*, 31:81–84.

Jacobs, T. J. (1991). *The Use of the Self. Countertransference and Communication in the Analytic Situation*. Madison, CT: International Universities Press.

Joseph, B. (1985). Transference: The total situation. *Int. J. Psychoanal.*, 66:447–454.

Keats, J. (1817). *Letters of John Keats: A Selection*. Edited by Robert Gittings. Oxford: Oxford University press, 1970.

Khan, M. M. R. (1969). Vicissitudes of being, knowing and experiencing in the therapeutic situation. In: *The Privacy of the Self (1974)*. London: The Hogarth Press.

Kohon, G. (ed.) (1999). *The Dead Mother. The Work of André Green*. London and New York: Routledge.

Laplanche J. & Pontalis J. B. (1967). *The Language of Psycho-Analysis*. London: Hogarth Press, 1973.

Little, M. (1951). Countertransference and the patient's response to it. *Int. J. Psychoanal.*, 32:32–40.

_____ (1986). *Transference Neurosis and Transference Psychosis: Toward Basic Unity*. London: Free Association Books.

Manfredi Turillazzi, S. (1994). *Le certezze perdute della psicoanalisi*. Milano: Cortina.

Manfredi Turillazzi, S. & Ponsi, M. (1999). Transfert, controtransfert e intersoggettività. Contrapposizione o convergenza? *Riv. di Psicoanalisi.*, XLV:697–719.

Ogden, T. (1992). The dialectically constituted/decentred subject of psychoanalysis, II: The contributions of Klein and Winnicott. *Int. J. Psychoanal.*, 73:613–626.

_____ (1999). Analysing forms of aliveness and deadness of the transference-countertransference. In: *The Dead Mother. The Work of André Green*. Edited by G. Kohon. London: Routledge, 1999.

Parsons, M. (2000). *The Dove that Returns, the Dove that Vanishes. Paradox and Creativity in Psychoanalysis*. London: Routledge.

Phillips, A. (1989). Returning the dream: In memoriam Masud Khan. In: *On Kissing, Tickling and Being Bored*. Cambridge, MA: Harvard University Press, 1993.

Renik, O. (1993). Analytic interaction: Conceptualising technique in the light of the analyst's irreducible subjectivity. *Psychoanal. Q.*, LXII:553–571.

Schwaber, E. (1999). Travelling affectively alone: A personal derailment in analytic listening. *J. Am. Psychoanal. Assoc.*, 46:1045–1065.

Smith, H.F. (2000). Countertransference, conflictual listening and analytic object relationship. *J. Am. Psychoanal. Assoc.*, 48:95–128.

Symington, N. (1983). The analyst's act of freedom as agent of therapeutic change. *Int. Rev. of Psychoanal.*, 10:283–291.

Winnicott, D. W. (1941). The observation of infants in a set situation. In: *Collected Papers: Through Paediatrics to Psychoanalysis (1958)*. London: The Hogarth Press.

_____ (1945). Primitive emotional development. In: *Collected Papers: Through Paediatrics to Psychoanalysis* (1958). London: Tavistock Publications.

_____ (1947). Hate in the countertransference. In: *Collected Papers: Through Paediatrics to Psychoanalysis (1958)*. London: The Hogarth Press.

_____ (1951). Transitional objects and transitional phenomena. In: *Collected Papers: Through Paediatrics to Psychoanalysis (1958)*. London: Tavistock Publications.

_____ (1956). Clinical varieties of transference. In: *Through Pediatrics to Psycho-Analysis. Collected papers*. London: Hogarth, 1958.

_____ (1958). The capacity to be alone. In: *The Maturational Processes and the Facilitating Environment (1965)*. London: The Hogarth Press.

_____ (1959). Nothing at the centre. In: *Psycho-Analytic Explorations*. Edited by C. Winnicott, R. Shepherd & M. Davis. London: Karnac, 1989.

_____ (1960). Counter-transference. In: *The Maturational Processes and the Facilitating Environment (1965)*. London: The Hogarth Press.

_____ (1962). The aims of psychoanalytical treatment. In: *The Maturational Processes and the Facilitating Environment (1965)*. London: The Hogarth Press.

_____ (1967). The mirror role of the mother. In: *Playing and Reality*. (1971). London: Tavistock Publications.

_____ (1968). Interpretation in psychoanalysis. In: *Psycho-Analytic Explorations*. Edited by C. Winnicott, R. Shepherd & M. Davis. London: Karnac, 1989.

_____ (1969). The use of an object. *Int. J. Psychoanal.*, 50:711–716.

_____ (1986). Holding and interpretation: Fragment of an analysis. *Int. Psycho-Anal. Lib.*, 115:1–194.

6

IMAGINATIVE ELABORATION

"To smell," "to hear," "to see," "to remember" – to portray, represent, and elaborate the bodily experience of the child in analysis.

In this chapter I intend to examine Winnicott's concept of *imaginative elaboration,* which seems to me rather neglected. I will try to reexamine its significance from a subjective point of view through the presentation of the material of a seven-year-old boy's analysis; this child was in psychoanalytic psychotherapy with me three times a week.

In my opinion the concept of imaginative elaboration possesses a certain uniqueness which has not yet been emphasized. The concept has what I could call two symmetrical branches, colored and striped in an identical way yet different from each other.

On the one hand, imaginative elaboration is the internal activity of the child, and more in general of the individual, that which *makes him alive.* It permits him to grasp, perceive, and *interpret* both the internal and the external world in a creative, individual, and subjective way. As such it is a *uniquely Winnicottian version of the concept of the self.*

On the other hand, imaginative elaboration is a specific emotional and psychic activity of the analyst at work. It comes close to, but does not coincide with, the concept of countertransference. And so we have a concept that covers two different areas, that of the individual and the relational. It is a transitional concept with a particular Winnicottian stamp.

What I have defined as the concept's symmetrical or mirroring nature is typical of Winnicott's thinking, and only the creative self-confidence of this author permits it to pass from one 'branch' to another, or from one side of the mirror to the other – without the

DOI: 10.4324/9781003228332-7

need to worry about a more definitive approach, precisely because the interest here is transitional, intermediate.

"A point in technique"

In the essay "A point in technique" – a gem of Winnicottian clinical intuition (and a work to which the editors of the posthumous volume *Psychoanalytic Explorations* [1989] were not able to attribute a precise date) – the author writes:

> I have learned recently to adopt the following procedure in analytic practice.
>
> When the fantasy that is represented in the transference material is revealed I ask myself: what and where is the accompanying orgastic bodily functioning? And, per contra, when in the analytic situation there is orgastic bodily functioning, I ask myself: what fantasy material is the patient telling me about by this functioning? (p. 26)

From a clinical point of view, I have not found in Winnicott a more convincing definition of imaginative elaboration. This definition applies directly to the heart of clinical technique and into the very texture of the psychoanalytic relationship. The interested reader will be able to locate the philology of this term in Jan Abram's useful book *The Language of Winnicott* (1996), as well as the points and meanings with which Winnicott uses it. It is a term, however, that is not widely used in his writings, even though, as I have already emphasized, it is of fundamental importance. Here I can only touch on its relationship to the concept of countertransference, and also the specificity that distinguishes it from that concept; the area of overlap, but also of differentiation, would require a deeper discussion that lies outside the scope of this chapter.

Since Abram's dictionary can provide the reader with the necessary information on the Winnicottian use of this concept, I consider it more useful – and without a doubt, more interesting – to travel through some challenging clinical situations and give them a personal dimension, but one in agreement with Winnicott's formulation. Overall, I would like to show the reader how I understand the concept of imaginative elaboration, so that they might become attuned to a subjective point of view, rather than a systematic, scholastic discussion of the concept.

An initial fragment from a session with Marco

When Marco, aged seven, entered my consulting room at the Istituto di Neuropsichiatria Infantile,[1] accompanied by an assistant, immediately I noted an unusual behavioral style. I see Marco three times a week, on Mondays, Tuesdays, and Thursdays. Usually, he immediately ran to the table where his box of toys was arranged and began to improvise a very simple way of playing, which in my notes I described as "animating the little figures." But this Tuesday he stood immobile, in front of the door, after the assistant had closed it behind him.

With this child at least three or four months of patient waiting and cautious verbal interventions had been necessary in order for him to *very slowly* abandon the pattern of total immobilization that could last for an entire session. He abandoned this stance, one could say, through very small, nearly imperceptible changes: first he approached the toys, then began to touch them, and finally to manipulate them. Sporadic interpretations about his fear of coming into contact with the therapist, and a few rare comments of facilitation and encouragement, plus a very great deal of patience, were the ingredients of what I considered a small therapeutic success, a work in progress.

The capacity for change

When we see signs in analysis of a capacity for change, and in particular the first stirrings of a capacity for play, we know from experience that the prognosis is generally good, and that in psychotherapy the *touch* (*tatto*, in Italian) and the *contact* (*contatto*)[2] (Carloni, 1984) will bear wholesome therapeutic fruit. If the child is not capable of playing there is a need to do something so that he may become capable of playing, after which the psychotherapy can begin (Winnicott, 1971).

Becoming capable of playing

These words have taken on a peculiar power in psychoanalysis, to the extent that they have almost become jargon. The capacity for playing, the capacity for being alone, are central to Winnicottian theory. Perhaps Khan (1962, 1972) is the only author who elaborated on this conceptual dimension – possibly thanks to his closeness with Winnicott – to the point of adding the *capacity for dreaming* as well.

165

Distinct from dreaming itself, the capacity for dreaming considers the dream as a product, as a dream that is dreamed, as text.

Let's think for a moment about the revolution that introduced this term into psychoanalysis: the capacity for playing, dreaming, the capacity for being alone, the capacity for entering into a relationship. I have long maintained – and I have also written along these lines (Bonaminio & Di Renzo, 1996) – that this Winnicottian vision was already outlined in a precursory way in his revolutionary article, 'Primitive Emotional Development' (1945). Here the author says many surprising things, but it is already clear that he is skipping over the A. Freudian/Kleinian discourse about the 'birth date' of the object for the child – whether this is after eight months (as suggested by Anna Freud) or from the beginning of life (as Melanie Klein maintained). Instead, Winnicott deliberately explores the preconditions for which the object can be discovered/found – that is, the capacities for integration, for personalization, and for the acquisition of space/time, as well as maturational capacities or processes. These are all joined with the maternal capacities of *holding, handling,* and *object presenting,* making possible the formation of the self, which in turn sets in motion the capacity for entering into a relationship with the object and thereby discovering/finding it.

Capacities are all to the good. Where, then, is the pathomorphological tendency of psychoanalysis? Certainly not in Winnicott, who is in search of development, of change, not regression or repetition. He writes:

> It is in playing and only in playing that the individual child or adult is able to be creative and to use the whole personality, and it is only in being creative that the individual discovers the self.
>
> (1971, p. 54)

Traumatic reality transformed by the capacity to play

For Winnicott, *playing and reality* exist in a vague dialectical relationship, not in opposition; the capacity to play includes pieces of reality. Reality can be tolerated only if it is *played* by the child, *creatively transformed,* rendered *me/not me* – as a transitional object, in fact, the "first not-me possession."

Modern-day life almost philosophically crushes playing, making it a must or an unnecessary frivolity; 'playfulness' is frowned upon.

In fact, one could say that setting up playing *against* reality, takes space away from playing, suffocates it. This is why it falls to the therapist, Winnicott suggests, to take on the task of putting the child (and the adult) in a position of being able to play, restoring to play and fantasy the space that is its due.

The crash of reality against fantasy (isn't this one of the factors that has led to the striking expansion of the virtual universe as a compensatory escape from the oppressive *reality of reality?*) takes the breath away from creativity, removing a sense of spontaneity and feeling alive. The fact that this crash[3] attempts to stifle fantasy, as well as related themes, is admirably expressed in a beautiful song by REM (the name of this pop group seems to express their way of making music). In 'Überlin' (2011), the group takes up various Winnicottian concepts, almost word for word. This subject had in fact already been dealt with by the Beatles, who were almost contemporaries of Winnicott's later period, in their masterpiece 'A Day in the Life' (1967). Here the frenetic rhythms of a working reality are modulated and juxtaposed with *dreaming* – which, however, because of a sort of hallucinosis, becomes almost a nightmare, and then returns to being a dream in the final, improvised sequence of piano notes.

The Beatles' song famously contrasts the world of dream and fantasy with that of cold, repetitive reality in the episodes sung by John Lennon and Paul McCartney respectively. Lennon's oneiric mode is interrupted by McCartney's robotic petty clerk rushing to work but, having climbed up to the second level of a London bus, the clerk loses himself in fantasizing, which extricates him from the constrictions of his boxed-in life and projects him (back) into an oneiric mode, sung in Lennon's dreamy voice, portraying the self's *other*.

There is an analogous contrast in 'Überlin' by REM.[4] This song portrays the repetitiveness – again, almost robotic – of postmodern man, who has lost himself in a faceless crowd and withdraws into an almost hallucinatory fantasy. Again, the singer's imagination takes flight., this time into the striking nonsense of its oneiric stars and meteor.

Some anamnestic notes on a clinical fragment: A basis for imaginative elaboration

Marco had been sent for therapy within the institute by an organized treatment team which collaborated with our social worker. They requested an accurate diagnosis. The child was very inhibited and barely spoke; even though his vocabulary and linguistic expression were appropriate for his age, he made use of them only rarely.

It seemed as though, as his teachers said, the bare necessities were enough for Marco. The social worker explained to me that they were explicitly referring to 'The Jungle Book,' the animated Disney film that, according to his parents, Marco eagerly watched every day. He hung on the words of Baloo, the easygoing bear who sings about the "bare necessities, the simple bare necessities." Moreover, Marco seemed to identify with Mowgli, who is as thin as a stick in the animated cartoon, just as Marco is. His parents said that they had seen him imitating Mowgli's movements, though only with vague, incomplete gestures, the bare necessities, in fact, of the behavior of *a little boy who was abandoned in the jungle.*

I noted that in this situation the quality of the narration immediately brought about in me a mental image of the child even before I had seen him in person. The memory of evenings spent watching this same cartoon with my own children certainly played a role in this. At that time I was a young father, but my children continued to welcome me with such joy and anticipation when I returned to watch the cartoon with them that I felt I was the center of the world.

"Daddy, can we watch Baloo?" was their very sweet demand, a somewhat imperative one. Naturally, it wasn't only Baloo that first one and then the other of my children wanted to watch, but all the Disney cartoons I bought for them. Baloo, however, and the lively song about the bare necessities, and Mowgli the abandoned boy – all of these experiences were *condensed* within the memory of all these cartoons. (After all, the work of the unconscious is accomplished through shifts and condensations.)

The first meeting that had not yet taken place between me and Marco – the little boy abandoned in the jungle – figuratively represented a key point in my imaginative elaboration about this child, essentially based on *remembering* and *representing.* I felt a sense of tenderness, and the wish to get to know him. I was tempted to pass over another child, Andrea, a psychotic patient who had been entrusted to me for a diagnosis that week.

Who feels he can see a psychotic child lightheartedly? This child was almost the same age as Marco, and one about whom I had little information. The data made me think of Frances Tustin (with whom I had a number of supervisory sessions), who would perhaps have defined him as *confusional:* Andrea licked everything that happened to come into his hands, and the saliva and its acidic odor, which after a while emanated from all the objects he handled, would perhaps be what Tustin called *self-sensual autistic forms*. Tustin believes that only confusional children can make use of these forms, while *shell-type* children, by contrast, *self-sensually* perceive forms as hard objects; for example, feces are held back in the rectum, teeth are clenched in the mouth, or a narrow piece of wood is clasped in the palm of the hand.

For this reason, at the beginning of this paper, I mentioned 'to smell, to hear, to imagine, to represent'; and indeed, where would we start if not from the bodily fantasies of the child who is in psychotherapy or undergoing diagnostic evaluation? The body unavoidably impacts our internal world. We create a mental image of it with our imaginative elaboration, certainly the result of our expectations, of our projections, but also of those little pieces of reality that are transmitted to us when we are told about a child who is going to be diagnosed, but whom we still do not know as a physical person, as a body.

In this case, my imaginative elaboration about Andrea caused me to paint him in my mind as a case to be treated *after* I had experienced some gratification with another young patient, one who was 'supposed to be' easier, simpler, and – let's be frank – nicer. In any event here is the confusional child, whom I am calling Andrea, and whom I still don't know to be truly confusional. The diagnosis will be useful, in fact, to evaluate the nature of the psychopathological disturbance. He has already evoked a fragment of imaginative elaboration in me.

While I am in the ward meeting the cases assigned to various workers, I smell – almost delusional – the stench of acid in the saliva left where Andrea has been. By contrast, what is resounding in my ears is Baloo's lively song: "the bare necessities, the simple bare necessities." I 'see' Mowgli, the abandoned boy of the jungle, who happily imitates the bear's movements and sings softly with him.

I will allow myself here to focus on these sensorial elements: I *smell* the acidic saliva, I *hear* the lively song, and I *see* before my eyes Mowgli, the little stick of a boy, and then there is Marco, whom I still don't know. At least three sensorial channels are activated; we are talking of the body and of a psychic activity in its infancy, still unformulated. It is my psychic activity that is engaged here – my self's activity. One of the meanings that Winnicott assigns to the concept of imaginative elaboration has been pressed into service, so to speak, in this case – that of the apperception of reality, and especially the bodily reality, of my young patients, towards whom there is clearly a disproportionate level of investment. This frame of reference, as I have already emphasized, touches on countertransference, which it overlaps in some areas, but it is not the same; let us say that it is a *precondition*, to use a Winnicottian expression.

I think that here it may be evident to the reader that the concept of imaginative elaboration has a dual core: it is actually the activity of the analyst's self that is directed toward the patient and invests him, but it is not yet countertransference; and, simultaneously, in a mirrorlike way, one could say that, through primary identification, it is the self of the patient that is presented to the analyst. It is in this sense that the concept of imaginative elaboration is an *individual/ dual* one, with two branches – a concept that connects, but at the same time maintains uniqueness. It is not a co-construction; it is a meeting – if it happens between two individualities. Paraphrasing Winnicott (1945), one could say that there are two phenomena: the imaginative elaboration of the analyst and that of the patient. These two do not enter into a relationship with each other until there is a common experience, until there is a certain psychic intensity (Bonaminio & Di Renzo, 1996), and until they meet and are drawn toward each other – or, conversely, until they move away from or are removed from each other (attraction/repulsion).

The concept of imaginative elaboration

For Winnicott, the concept of imaginative elaboration takes a step beyond representational, Freudian metapsychology. In my opinion these words, *imaginative* and *elaboration,* have a developmental potential yet to be fully considered. The adjective pairs with *Deutung,* the activity of *guessing,* and especially the psychic figurability that Freud speaks of in *The Interpretation of Dreams,* which was taken up and admirably re-examined by the Botellas (2004).

It is not true that psychism, as Freud portrays it, hinges on representation. (The foregoing remark is directed toward detractors of psychoanalysis, to the enthusiastic supporters of implicit memory – absent from Freudian theorization – and to critics of the representational as the center of everything in Freud.) One could say that in Freud there is a long ontogenetic history before representation (and certainly before imaginative elaboration), as I have partially outlined up to this point, which is part of it and yet a new development at the same time. In other words, the *pre-representational* and the *representational* actually exist along a continuum, and as such they must be seen jointly, as a unit.

Let's return to the clinical material, to Marco and Andrea. In fact, it is in daily clinical practice that I have begun to truly understand the meaning of this expression and the concept of imaginative elaboration; for as much as it is deeply, intrinsically Winnicottian, it is not often used in his own vocabulary, nor is it as frequently utilized as his other clinical concepts, and it is not uncommonly twisted or jargonized.

But the destiny of other psychoanalytic idioms is no different; we might recall, for example, some of Bion's equally authoritative and creative contributions, observing that a quantum of alpha functioning is necessary in order to transform beta elements: a little bit of containment here, and small transformations grow ...

These expressions often crop up in clinical discussions, with a greater or lesser degree of relevance – like jets of water in an Italian fountain, ingeniously conceived but by now somewhat worn out. In the same way, parts of presumed transitional experiences spring up, as well as pieces of 'good enough mothers,' fragments of 'subjective objects,' evocations of 'fear of breakdown' – as though one were dealing with adhesive labels to affix here or there, and not, on the contrary, with concepts. After all, these concepts grew out of the blood and sweat of the relationship with the patient, and ultimately came into being through the patient's associations, his inhibitions and anxieties – *imaginatively elaborated* by the analyst at work.

The practice of inappropriate labeling, or using 'psycho-analyses,' takes us to the cinematographer Moretti, who ridicules the psychoanalyst for his incurable narcissism in the film *Habemus papam* (2011). But does Moretti accurately represent the analyst's character? Is it possible that psychoanalysts do not have within themselves the antibodies with which to defend against this jargon?

Here is a point to strongly emphasize, to throw into relief: imaginative elaboration is always born out of a clinical basis; one could say that it is born of the *pulsating body* of the analytic framework, of the concrete relationship between analysand and analyst, of the anxious or spitting or inhibited child and the analyst who tries to understand. But in order to understand, and possibly go on to interpret, one must first *take in, participate,* and *support.*

171

Not by chance do I use the expression *pulsating body,* for two reasons: the first is because I have insisted on the subject of the body in regard to the particular meaning that Winnicott gives to the term *imaginative elaboration.* The second is to emphasize through the adjective *pulsating* that it is not imaginative elaboration that gives life to something that is devitalized (or at any rate stuck); on the contrary, imaginative elaboration takes life and develops it, engulfs it in order to multiply it from the existing level of vitality, which is often hidden, encapsulated, even in the closest of analytic relationships.

With the illustrative cases of Marco and Andrea (which have wandered a bit, perhaps, and the latter case was only hinted at), I have wanted to refer precisely to this: the child is the carrier – even before being physically seen – of fragments of his own psychic life, of idioms, as Bollas (1992) would say. These fragments must become the target of the analyst's listening, of his attention; he must prove himself capable of fitting in with the patient and gathering signals, like those from a radio beacon. He must orient himself to the patient, like an airplane in search of a vector point that defines its route, in order to come closer and understand a little more. In the meantime, the *psychic intensities* (again, to use Bollas' [1995] term) emanating from the patient will have activated the analyst's own psychic intensities within, and these can be joined or not with those of the patient. But the enormous, incessant process of *cracking up,* the dissemination of the unconscious, which originates in the patient, will be intercepted by the analyst. "Baloo," the "bare necessities," and "Mowgli, the abandoned boy of the jungle," for example, give form to an image and permit the analyst to take in something and connect it with his own experience.

Marco, a little stick of a boy like Mowgli, brings to mind my own children, and I understand his experience a little better through the sweet, nostalgic memory of when I was a young father. Perhaps, in looking at myself again, I see myself for the first time as the easygoing Baloo – carefree in a way that I no longer am – and as someone whom my children clung to, practically climbing on top of me, forcing me to watch the cartoon with them (then perhaps our play would begin). Marco may have been the abandoned, neglected child, like Mowgli lost in the jungle, but I, too, am Mowgli, and Marco may be "abandoned" by my children, because they are now grown up. How else can I explain the powerful identification that I immediately felt for him?

All these elements – especially the sensorial ones, but also the ideational, figurative ones – contribute to the imaginative elaboration we are talking about, which in some way brings me in tune, *ante litteram,* with my young patient even before I have even met him. In the first clinical fragment I reported, taken from the seventh month of analysis, I demonstrated how this element persisted and was transformed.

Imaginative elaboration, then, is that psychic activity that develops out of the analytic relationship, from the meeting between two subjects. I am making statements here that I consider to have a certain polemical tone because they have to do with the necessity of rethinking what we could define as the *tendency of countertransference,* that is, the analyst's mental activity, the analyst's mental framework – sometimes pompously evoked – that in the words of its supporters could give meaning to something that does not have it, and that if it doesn't, could lead us to paralysis. Imaginative elaboration, like other levels of countertransference, actually draws its strength from the relationship with the patient, from participation in the encounter with him.

An important point in the way I see things: imaginative elaboration is that psychic activity that *adds meaning,* but does not *give meaning,* because meaning is already there, though unexpressed. It is a much more of a craftsman-like activity, and more humble than we might want to believe. It is a little like the work of a carpenter who must use a rasp and planer to make a decorative spiral on the front of a drawer, and in order to do so, exploits the grain of the wood, the natural curvature, adding to what is pre-existing. In encountering the wood, he looks at it, scrutinizes it, touches it with his artisan's hands, and understands both its roughness and its smooth parts. From these, the basis is formed for beginning to imagine how the spiral might come out, then perhaps he will have to change its form in the course of the work. He will be satisfied if the spiral he has imagined, starting from what the wood itself is like, corresponds sufficiently to what he had glimpsed, what he had guessed at from that curvature.

Isn't this a form of 'found-created'? Doesn't the creative analyst deceive himself? Imaginative elaboration is not a creation of his, *ex novo,* from the patient's inert body or from the analytic relationship, but it is an addition, certainly a significant one, that enriches the meaning of the experience undergone by the patient and the analyst together. Winnicott chooses his verb with great care when he speaks of *experiencing* as the "possibility of *living* the experience" itself – both with the child and the patient in analysis. It is an enlivening process, a revival of something.

Melanie Klein described the importance of taking in the transference first: that is, first of all accepting it before understanding or interpreting it. Winnicott speaks of the necessity for the analyst to preserve his psychosomatic integrity in order that he may take in the patient's "need to be known in all his parts" (1945).

For me, imaginative elaboration is furthermore all the psychic activity that is set in motion in order to fill this gap, and which never fills it. I am referring to the gap between the patient's need for his transference to be taken in first, and the analyst's attempt to take it in – between the "patient's need to be known in all his parts," and the obstacles that intervene for the analyst so this can happen. It is this space into which imaginative elaboration penetrates – between body and mind, we could say, between the clinical and the theoretical. It is this restricted space that it slips into in order to open it up. I think that we are here in the area of a sketchy form of *countertransference before transference* – a topic about which I have recently written.

Returning to Marco, I think that a kind of imaginative elaboration was mobilized in me that gave a soul to this little body, to this small sad heap of bones, as I represented Marco to myself – even before I saw him. What set in motion this type of "primary paternal preoccupation?" I think it may have been the description of his body, of his slow and inhibited movements, which made me feel the presence of a child without a soul, one who functioned at a minimal level, with only the bare necessities.

Clinically, I think that here, as far as Marco is concerned, we are in the area of that phenomenon, of that area of experience that Winnicott calls – with a terminology all his own, and very complex in its content compared to how it might appear at first sight – *imaginative elaboration*. As I have said, this concept forms part of the phenomena of countertransference, but in my opinion, it needs further exploration. Imaginative elaboration was positioned by Winnicott both as a function of the analyst who thinks, imagines, and *dreams* his patient, we could say, and, more specifically, as an equivalent of psychism, the self – which always begins from the body and from endophytic perceptions.

Marco's parents have a daughter, Giorgia, who is younger by three years, to whom they seem to devote a great deal of attention, neglecting Marco a little. They consider him more able to manage on his own, while on the contrary it is evident that the boy's behavior is impoverished, as though he has been numbed. I am struck by this neglect. My negligence in not explaining the origin of the noise in the hall to Marco – for him a traumatic experience – represents precisely that environmental failure that I recognized in the here and now through imaginative elaboration, bodily animating that elaboration before the lifeless image of a neglected child.

Notes

1 The Institute of Child Neuropsychiatry is now known as the Department of Pediatrics and Child Neuropsychiatry at the University of Rome ("Sapienza").
2 In Italian, there is a pun (untranslatable in English) between *tatto* and *contatto* even though the meanings are different but the sounds similar.
3 A well-made film by Paul Haggis, entitled 'Crash' (2004), portrays this dimension of contemporary postmodern society from another perspective, in part complementary to what I am describing. Human relationships are no longer possible, and if they are, it is only through physical crashes between people, sometimes in the form of traffic jams or collisions, at other times in casual knocks against others in a crowded city, and still at other times, in deliberate intrusions. Emotional contact is missing; only a crash is possible. In these crashes, however, the need for human contact persists as an expression of hope.
4 "Rapid eye movements," the very quick ocular shifting that indicates dream activity, is in itself a revealing name for the group, as already mentioned.

References

Bollas, C. (1992). *Being a Character.* New York: Routledge.

––––––––– (1995). *Cracking Up.* New York: Routledge.

Bonaminio, V. & Di Renzo, M. B. (1996). Giocare e sognare come potenziali esperienze complete del sé. *Richard e Piggle,* 4:9–22.

Botella, C. & Botella, S. (2004). *The Work of Psychic Figurability: Mental States Without Representation.* London: Brunner Routledge.

Carloni, G. (1984). Tatto, contatto e tattica. *Rivista Psicoanalitica,* 30:191–205.

Haggis, Paul, Director. (2004). *Crash.* Lions Gate Films. 1:52.

Khan, M. M. R. (1962). Dream psychology and the evolution of the psychoanalytic situation. In: *The Privacy of the Self.* London: Hogarth, 1974.

_____ (1972). The use and abuse of dream in psychic experience. In: *The Privacy of the Self*. London: Hogarth, 1974.

_____ (1976). Beyond the dreaming experience. In: *Hidden Selves* London: Hogarth, 1983.

Klein, M. (1992). *A Contribution to the Psychogenesis of Manic Depressive States in Melanie Klein Love, Guilt and Reparation and Other Works 1921–1945*. London: Karnak Books and The Institute of Psycho-analysis.

Lennon, J. & McCartney, P. (1967). *The Beatles. A Day in the Life*. London: EMI Records.

Moretti, N. (2011). *Habemus Papam*. 01 Distribuzione.

Reitherman, Wolfgang, Director (1967). *The Jungle Book*. Walt Disney Productions. 1:18.

Winnicott, D. W. (1945). Primitive emotional development. In: *The Maturational Processes and the Facilitating Environment: Studies in the Theory of Emotional Development*. London: Hogarth, 1965.

_____ (1955). Clinical varieties of transference. In: *The Maturational Processes and the Facilitating Environment: Studies in the Theory of Emotional Development*. London: Hogarth, 1965.

_____ (1971). Playing: creative activity and the search for the self. In: *Playing and Reality*. London: Tavistock, pp. 53–64.

_____ (1989) *Psychoanalytic Explorations*. Cambridge, MA: Harvard University Press.

7

THE ADOLESCENT'S DISCOURSE

New Forms of Civilization's Discontents

I have been treating Fabrizio, a young man of 18, for a few months. So far what strikes me most about him is that he is a very *lukewarm* patient: he is lukewarmly depressed, he is lukewarm in his social involvement with peers, lukewarm in his occasional (though ongoing) consumption of street drugs, and lukewarm in his sexual encounters with girls. Equally lukewarm is his interest in music, though he plays guitar fairly regularly.

One day Fabrizio breaks out of his lukewarm mold and is suddenly eager to make me see a connection between the lyrics of two songs written 25 years apart. Actually, the connection is obvious – and one I had been aware of – but my *lukewarm* analysand tells me he has made a "discovery all his own," which prompts him to suggest an alternative "conclusion" to the songs, different from what either songwriter had in mind. According to Fabrizio, his conclusion is far more consistent with the earlier lyrics of both songs than their actual endings.

In the first song, 'God – Part II,' Bono, U2's singer and songwriter, pays homage to John Lennon with a variation on one of his lesser-known songs, 'God,' written at the time of the Beatles' traumatic break-up. (I would add that this break-up was traumatic not only for Lennon, McCartney, and the other members of the band, but for an entire generation.)

In Lennon's song, a torrent of words pours forth in a furious, repetitious crescendo, listing all of the values Lennon believed in, but no longer does. He goes so far as to renounce the Beatles themselves. At a certain point, the music suddenly stops. There is a pause,

177   DOI: 10.4324/9781003228332-8

and then, from out of a disquieting but necessary gap, it resumes in a more relaxed vein. Lennon speaks the last line, saying that all he believes in is himself, and Yoko.

> "Now here," Fabrizio jumps in with his opinion, "Lennon should have gone on yelling, 'I *don't* believe *in me*, I *don't* believe in Yoko and me.' To be consistent, he should have created a desert around himself and out of himself; but he didn't have the courage! He should have destroyed everything, including himself, even though 'the only thing left standing' – himself – was later tragically and violently destroyed from outside."

Quite frankly, my patient hurts me with these acerbic words because I really like the music of Bono and U2, and am also a fan of John Lennon.

It is interesting that in describing these two singers – who for Fabrizio are *cultural objects* – he focuses more on the latter, assuming that I can share more of what he is saying about Lennon than Bono. "But I can understand Lennon," he continues. "Of course, he recorded this song in the 1980s, before I was born; for me it's *pre-history*. But still I can understand him."

I can't help thinking that for me, in contrast, John Lennon is *history*. But it seems that what Fabrizio has to say is expressed in a language I can understand: sometimes destruction is necessary in order to preserve a part of the self, after which the self can be reborn. *Separation is necessary in order to exist.*

> "But Bono, now," my patient goes on, "his homage to Lennon ends with a whole list of 'don't believes': 'I don't believe in the devil, don't believe in cocaine, don't believe that rock'n'roll can really change the world.' And he ends with 'I …'" (Here the patient pauses.) "'… I believe in love.' So where does he go to get that love? Where the hell would you find it around here? He, Bono, 'leans on' Lennon – he uses him, misuses his words, and falsifies him."

Here the heart of what my patient is saying becomes clear. He is making a sort of social commentary.

> "Bono wanted to impose a continuity from Lennon onto himself," Fabrizio continues, "a continuity that doesn't exist; because

now everything has cracked and shattered, fallen to pieces, the world is in a complete mess. He, Bono, changes one thing into another. Lennon may be scared, but he's real. Bono believes he can convert the masses; it's an instance of a *show that becomes a person,* or rather *a person who becomes a show* – along with the Pope, Bush, Mandela, Obama, the whole darn bunch of them – *olé!* Bono sees the rottenness but he alters it, he throws something 'good' over the top of it, but really it isn't there at all!"

And I'm bound to admit that my patient's description of society as a sort of "global show" soundly hits the mark, in my perception.

In reporting this brief extract from an adolescent's communication, I am well aware of how much it follows the normal course of things for the listening analyst. There is nothing particularly illuminating in the words of my intelligent teenage patient, who shows a remarkable capacity for reflective thoughts on culture – that is, on a piece of culture to which he can attach an 'historical interpretation,' a piece we are both immersed in and of which both of us form a part.

And yet I feel his communication bears traces and imprints of the superficial nature of generational objects[1] (Bollas, 1992) today – their changeability, their fleeting nature, which renders them nearly ungraspable. But this is no longer the *form* of generational objects; instead these attributes have become their *content.* As psychoanalysts we are not so much better as "judges of things" because of our supposed closeness and familiarity with the unconscious, but our work as psychoanalytic practitioners positions us at a unique point from which to observe what Freud (1930) called 'civilization's discontents.'

But as analysts, we are not only able to observe rapid and continual social and cultural transformations taking place, forged according to a social and cultural reality quite distinct from the present; we must remember that we are also part of these transformations ourselves. We must not fool ourselves into thinking we stand on a riverbank in a flood – i.e., entirely out of the water. The so-called 'crisis of psychoanalysis' – about which psychoanalysts are sometimes heard to lament, even masochistically consulting one another in this regard – comes from the crisis of thinking of ourselves as not being part of global society; this in itself is an aspect of civilization's discontent.

179

In this context, as psychoanalysts, we should regard adolescence as our one privileged area of observation because of its function as a cultural link between generations. Adolescence gives us the chance to see, almost in real time, how rapid, overwhelming, transient, and difficult to grasp are today's changes in ways of thinking, of representing inner and outer reality. This period of life highlights aspects of civilization's discontents and along with them the discontents of the analyst who has to face them. In working with adolescents, we can appreciate Kaës' (1994) belief that what he calls *new forms of civilization's discontents* are upsetting the structure of psychic life and especially its transformative functions.

Listening to the adolescent's discourse and reporting it allows me to focus on an issue I believe is central, which is that *trauma* can be considered on two different, though intertwined, registers: (1) the impact on the ego of what is not yet representable, i.e., those elements that fall outside the ego's realm and with which it is unprepared to cope, even though these elements affect and alter the ego's structure; and (2) the consequent undeveloped differentiation between fantasy and reality, sometimes extending to a virtual absence of the transitional area between the two, and even at times an equation of fantasy with reality.

An example of this situation can be seen in the case of another teenager, aged 15, a boy named Antonio. In our first interview, he asks me not to schedule appointments for him on Mondays because he is always "bushed" after weekend parties, which leave him "done in," "spaced out," and "squashed" like a bunch of grapes – a condition he has every intention of remedying by attending more of these events the following weekend. He finds a stupefying pleasure in these parties, "zoning out" to their deafening music and mind-altering drugs. Even though they cause him to feel that "something is drilling into my stomach," and "as though I am floating in a milky liquid." Antonio doesn't even consider the possibility of giving up the parties, since they constitute the sole reason for living through the rest of the week.

Another young patient, Franco, in his final year of high school, tells me he is amazed to find that he sometimes cannot understand the slang of some boys at his school a few years younger than him. "I had to ask what some of their words meant because I simply didn't know," he tells me, obviously shocked by the experience. "There were whole sentences I couldn't understand – already they're speaking a different language to ours!" (By "ours" he means the language of 18-year-olds.)

Franco continues, "Even kids of twelve or thirteen, still in middle school – they've got it all figured out. They've already caught up with us. Sharing a joint or looking around for our first fuck was a big deal for us in the first or second year of high school, but these guys ..." His voice trails off as he attempts to control his anxiety brought on by these accelerating changes.

In learning to cope with cultural instability, Franco is creating the environment he lives in (Winnicott, 1971), populating it with objects he has encountered. In doing so he is distinguishing and further developing his own identity – the fundamental task of adolescence.

The rate of cultural change has become so fast and furious (partly as a result of rapid technological change) that adolescents may have great difficulty finding their way. As a result, the adult may experience a sort of internal crumbling, a "laceration" of the transitional "tissue" that lies between inner and outer, between fantasy and reality. This inner sense of crumbling is often what leads a patient to enter analysis.

Indeed, the discontents of which Freud spoke have themselves become a real illness; the very idea of a civilization in which we live our lives has been called into question. When psychoanalysis first came into being, there was great optimism about the possibilities of its influencing culture in a positive way, but today, by and large, we no longer have faith in this idea.

In passing from one type of acculturation largely linked to the family circle and written culture, to an acculturation based on audio-visual media (Ahumada, 1997) – which creates the *illusion* of seeing reality, but actually does no more than *allude* to it – the adolescent must succeed in the arduous task of stabilizing connections and sorting out what appears to oscillate between inner and outer. The transitional space, needed as both a container and a divider, has become a tenuous membrane.

The sensation of feeling "bushed" after a wild party becomes the same as the feeling one has while setting out to look for that sensation before and during the party. We might say, in Antonio's case, that "a piece of the psyche" – quite a large piece, at that – is involved in his being bushed at the party. Another "piece" turns up in the session. And another one is "always feeling done in," but without evidence of much actual fatigue. I wonder if this is the fragmentation Freud had in mind when towards the end of his life he penned the enigmatic sentence, "Psyche is extended; knows nothing about it" (1938, p. 300).

The last century has been called the short century (Hobsbawm, 1994) because of the incessant multiplicity of historical, social, cultural, and technological events and transformations. If we look at the past through this lens, surely the final decades of the 20th century and the first one of the 21st were even shorter; actually they flashing by like lightning. Time has sped up so much that we – like my 18-year-old patient, Antonio – have felt this period was largely unintelligible. Our modes of thinking for establishing order in reality are working tirelessly, yet they are "breathless" in their attempts to handle the task, to keep up with the speed of change. "Postmodern" culture, of which we are all a part, reflects this situation in a double sense: it describes and documents the twilight of one set of ideologies – the crisis of certainties – and the competition between different though perhaps compatible truths; but intrinsically it is itself affected by the very transient fragmentation it attempts to describe.

For the psychoanalyst in the consulting room – which is our inescapable location, and the data obtained there should be the sole source on which we are entitled to speak in our function of reducing psychic suffering – his discontents with his culture join with his discontent at the inadequacy of his tools. In the consulting room the analyst finds himself face to face with what Kristeva called *les nouvelles maladies de l'âme* (1993). And yet it is possible for us to be of great help to our young patients in coping with such a profound change – provided that we see this as the goal of analysis. An opportunity to accomplish this goal is presented by our clinical work and our method, and we must take seriously the responsibility it entails as we embark on this unique venture with our patients.

Note

1 By generational objects, I am referring here to a concept used by Bollas (1992) that I consider to be of highly heuristic value, especially for the understanding of some aspects of adolescent processes and how adults (the ruling generation) elaborate them in terms of comparative memories of their own adolescence. Each generation, Bollas maintains, selects its own objects, persons, events, and things that have a particular meaning for their identity. These objects contribute

to what Bollas calls a generational identity, which is formed in the space of approximately 10 years, from the turbulence of adolescence through to the age of 30.

References

Ahumada, J.L. (1997). Disclosures and refutations: Clinical psychoanalysis as a logic of inquiry. *Int. J. Psychoanal.*, 78:1105–1118.

Bollas, C. (1992). *Being a Character.* London: Routledge, 1993.

Freud, S. (1930). Civilization and its discontents. *S. E.*, 21.

_____ (1938). Findings, ideas, problems. *S. E.*, 23.

Hobsbawm, E. J. (1994). *Age of Extremes: The Short Twentieth Century, 1914–1991.* London: Michael Joseph/Penguin Group.

Kaës, R. (1994). Psychic work and unconscious alliances in therapeutic institutions. *Brit. J. Psychother.*, 10:361–371.

Kristeva, J. (1993). *Les Nouvelles Maladies de l'âme.* Paris: Fayard.

Winnicott, D. W. (1971). *Playing and Reality.* London: Tavistock.

8

PARENTAL PREFABRICATION OF THE SELF

An Account of the Analysis of a 30-Year-Old Man

From analysis to dream, from dream to analysis

Analytic space and individual dream space through a clinical fragment

I was in my Land Rover on the freeway heading for X. I was driving with my foot steadily on the gas down this long straight road with flat countryside all around. Everything was going smoothly and easily, as though nothing were wrong. I glanced in the rear mirror, as I do from time to time, and to my surprise saw this huge truck behind me. Right out of nowhere, because a moment before it hadn't been there. It looked like one of those enormous "on the road" American trucks, the kind you never see here. But I kept cool and drove straight on down my lane. Again, I glanced in the rear mirror and there was the truck still on my tail, but much closer this time, its headlights winking incessantly. I could almost hear them clicking on and off. It was just about to crash into me, almost touching me; but I was able to shake it, because now I found myself heading straight for the turn-off for Y (the town close to his holiday home). I accelerated, shot into the exit lane, and that was that, because I could see the truck streaking away to the left. Did you ever see that Spielberg film, 'Duel?' Well, it was just like that... By the way, yesterday I happened to see 'Close Encounters,' another masterpiece of his.

DOI: 10.4324/9781003228332-9

When he had finished telling me his dream my patient, in the third year of his analysis, resumed a rigorously detailed account of his day.

Federico, a 32-year-old scrupulous medical professional specializing in otolaryngology, arrives on the dot for his sessions carrying his "real leather" briefcase, which he places carefully on the chair. The same ritual is observed almost every time: two quick pats, first with the right hand then with the left, on the back pockets of his trousers, as he pulls out his driver's license and wallet. These he places beside the briefcase, before turning to the couch where he stretches out and invariably starts with: "Well, nothing important to talk about today," but not before informing me, as he usually does, where he has parked "the tank," meaning of course the Land Rover he is so proud of. The emotion that overcame me when he was telling me his dream took me by surprise. My attention suddenly sparked up, out of a rather flat and predictable calm, which Federico tends to establish session after session, in spite of my efforts to arouse some feeling in him.

But now it was Federico who jolted me. For the first time I felt real emotion with this patient. It wasn't that I had never experienced some unsettling reactions over the two years of analysis with Federico: a sense of impotence, boredom, alongside the feeling of solidarity for him, as he was obliged to live beneath a "democratic façade." But the point is, these feelings were mine alone. I mean they were all within me, without any awareness on my part, or hardly any, of the possibility of the patient's relating to them in any way. He appeared to be entirely extraneous to the way I felt.

One might say, *a posteriori*, that Federico's *extraneousness* in his relationship with me represented the dissociation of the self which Winnicott was the first to speak of in connection with schizoid phenomena (1935, 1954, 1960). But what I wish to bring out here is that we find this dissociation reproduced *in toto* in the transference, through the patient's manic defense during the session, as a *clinical fact* of the psychoanalytical relationship. This phase may be more or less long, or else can even occupy the entire analysis, which then risks being usurped as an experience for the patient. So, this phase can be very much a phase, i.e., transitory, only if the impasse is overcome and the patient is allowed to have the experience of dreaming, then it is an important contribution towards overcoming the impasse.

I am here introducing one of the arguments of this paper, namely, that the dreaming experience coincides with the patient's experience in analysis, and that the transformation of the clinical configuration of the patient's dissociation and manic defense is a model for describing the dreaming experience, and vice versa. In the phase of analysis I have just referred to (the phase before the dream described), the analytic scenario becomes a sort of *orthogonal projection* of the patient's dissociation: on the one hand we have the patient with his manic defense who is dissociated from a part of himself; on the other hand we have the analyst who might be said to harbor in his own countertransference some aspects of that dissociated self which the patient is unable to reintegrate.

In this phase, even narrating his dreams may amount to nothing more than a variant of the patient's attempt, on his own account, to maintain omnipotent control over his inner reality, by obsessional control of language and material, "not letting language and metaphor elaborate or change his experience" (Khan, 1978). To paraphrase a well-known expression of Lacan's (1966), here we find ourselves in an area where the analysand "speaks to the analyst *without* speaking of himself." Clinically, I visualize that *without*, just like that absence in the patient's communication (his manic defense) as the *negative* Green speaks of (1995) which, one might say, is still awaiting *connection*.

This is why, in a previous paragraph, I have deliberately written the contraposed form, "on the one hand the patient... on the other hand the analyst," to draw attention to the fact that it is the *leap* in the level of communication (the *feeling* that so surprised the analyst on hearing the patient describe his dream) that creates this connection; in other words, it is used in order to emphasize the role and meaning of the dream, or rather the *dreaming,* as an aspect of the work of the negative (Winnicott's *not-me,* Bion's *no-thing*) i.e., the transformational potentials of the dis–continuity (in clinical terms, the surprise) of the psychoanalytic process.

It seems to me neither adequate nor satisfactory (not to say supersaturated) to define this configuration in the more general terms of "transference/countertransference vicissitudes" because, as a description, this would refer back to a complementarity, a two-way reflection, a "flow or transition of projective identifications" between patient and analyst; in a word, an interaction which would mechanically flatten, from a descriptive point of view, the experience of himself which the analysand is potentially able to have (or not have) in the analysis. This is also why I have described, above, the extraneousness of the self to himself on the part of the patient

186

(his manic defense), as something which is re-proposed *in toto* in the transference, leaving the analyst's countertransference to do the 'work' that involves the personal feelings and thoughts arising from his preconscious, which become progressively accessible to his awareness, work that also includes something about the patient, something alluding to that dissociated self which the patient (still) knows nothing about (Winnicott, 1935] "denial of inner reality," the "flight to external reality," and "suspended animation," as clinical characteristics of the manic defense).

It is in this frame of reference that I believe we should read Paula Heimann's (1950) original statement, according to which the analyst's countertransference is not only an integral part of the analytic relationship, but also a *creation* of the patient, and part of the patient's personality.

This expression, "creation of the patient" – often understood as a linguistic variant of what, in the years immediately after, began to be described as a sort of effect of the patient's projective identification onto the analyst – is in fact precisely what is pertinent to dreaming and its transformative potential for creating images. Therefore, in my opinion, this creation of the patient has to do with what Bollas (1987) has developed much more recently, in the wake of Paula Heimann and Masud Khan, in terms of "evocative or expressive use of the counter-transference"; especially as "the transfer of 'the unthought known,'" a form of knowledge that has not yet been dreamed or imagined, because it is not yet mentally realized" (1987, p. 246).

In Federico's case, my sense of boredom and impotence were that something. They alluded to the dissociated part of the patient, which was extraneous to him and of course to his analyst as well. In these terms, seen from 'the external' (to use one of Winnicott's enigmatic expressions) the situation is impersonal for the patient (Federico's sense of impersonality, of which I was only too well aware when listening to his relentless narrations). The patient's subjectification is still to come from there. It is his potential point of arrival through the course of his experience of the analysis and of dreaming, not the point of departure, which is taken for granted.

To put it in other terms more congenial to me, it is the potential personalization of the experience of the self, the individual process through which the patient, in whom the phenomena of the dissociation of self prevails, can make the interpersonal experience of the analysis as a two-fold set-up with an absent third. The paradox

187

of psychoanalysis is that the person can know, or recognize, himself only by means of the other. But the other is not, in actual fact, the analyst. He is the absent third who continually turns up at the borderline of the self and the relationship with the analyst. The focus I am proposing in this paper, on the *transformation of the clinical configuration of the dissociation and the manic defense as a model to describe the dreaming experience* and vice versa, seems to me a useful extension to a clinical definition which, in general but highly evocative terms, Bollas (1990) crystallized as follows:

> It is no accident that Freud took the dream as the cornerstone of psychoanalysis, where the person splits into two basic structures: the simple self who is the experiential subject inside the dream; and the organizing intelligence that creates the dream environment and gives it meaning. This mirrors the split of fetal and infant life, of a simple self-immersed inside a complex intelligence, a structure which becomes part of the nature of intrapsychic life [...] In the dream a simple self is repeatedly inside a highly complex theatre of eventful thoughts and allegorical personages with constitute an intrapsychic warrant for the treatment alliance.

Dream as a transformative way of thinking

Listening to Federico telling me his dream, I actually felt excited because I realized it was the first time he was talking about us. This still didn't add up to any kind of intimate experience, and yet it marked the beginning of a potential development. While he was telling me his dream, I was aware that something (a *duel*) – I shall shortly come back to this event – had not simply come of the blue, as though everything was going smoothly and easily in the analysis, as though there were "nothing important" to talk about. In fact, it was taken by the patient from analysis and transferred inside himself, into the individual dream space, (re)created on the basis of the space made available by the analytic relationship. And from this internal space, the patient was now able to 'send me back' something in return, something represented in the dream: so, now a path had opened up, *from the analysis to the dream and from the dream to the analysis.* Perhaps, it was this newly acquired permeability discovered in the course of this previously impenetrable path, which created my unexpected emotion in response to the dream rather than its latent transference content barely dissimulated by the manifest content.

In this dream there is an equally significant sense in which the dream is an opportune response to the configuration which had been created in the analysis at that specific moment. As usual, the week before the dream, Federico had delivered his relentless report on his daily life: his work, practically anything that had happened to him, and mentioning one or two difficulties that cropped up in his social relations. And as usual in this period of the analysis, I had been trying to piece together what struck me as common elements scattered through the material, in an attempt to make it possible for the patient to see himself, something I considered an essential contribution of my analytic function. In particular I had got him to see that intentionally calling in at the studio of Caterina, the young architect he was in love with, but whose offer of love made him feel threatened – and telling her he just happened to be passing by – was perhaps one of the ways through which he created the distance between them which he felt so powerless to breach, but which was obviously necessary for him to protect himself from a contact he felt was threatening. I had also hinted, but only incidentally, at a transference connection with me. Clearly, this interpretation was aimed, at least in my conscious mind, at providing the patient with a viewpoint on the state of his self, rather than on the conflict (in this case, the implicit defensive scorn directed at Caterina and thus at me): an interpretation, and more generally an attitude, that was only seemingly oriented in this direction. But what Federico picked up, or else interpreted, from it was a prompt – an impingement on my part – that he should "do something" to get closer to Caterina, do something to get closer to me. What I had not mentioned because I had overlooked the circumstance was that our separation the following week, i.e., the week of the dream, would be longer owing to a public holiday.

A posteriori, through the answer supplied by Federico's dream, I realized that his "happened to be passing by" ploy was not, as I had interpreted, an attempt to steer clear of contact with Caterina and myself, but quite the reverse. This was the only degree of nearness to the object which he could bear, once he had saved himself by the prospect of separation in a safe place, inaccessible both to me and Caterina where he could protect himself from the burden of a contact that he felt was nagging at him.

Because of Federico's dream, I am able to see myself, thanks to him. I am able to see *where* I am placed in respect to the patient. Again, through the medium of the dream – which crystallizes the

189

configuration of the psychoanalytical relationship – I saw that I had occupied the place of his internal object (the mother) who intrusively solicits him for contact. My over-attentive and controlled interpretations *behind him* are perceived as that insistent blinking of headlights on the huge truck which tried to crash into him and from which he was able to protect himself thanks to the "exit lane" of separation.

The fact I didn't include this question of separation was a *blind spot* in my countertransference, and it coincided with the "blind area" beyond the "beam of light" which belongs to the object trying to run him down or, in other words, his being run down by one or both parents. This blind spot could be understood as something of him which is not-seen and which allows him to live and offers the chance to look after himself in a separate place. "Y," the place where his summer holiday home is located, is the very place where Federico can cultivate something that really is his own – perhaps his true self – and survey the work in progress, finding more satisfactory solutions, and above all tending his fine Mediterranean garden (a significant metaphor for an intermediate, transitional area).

The creation by means of analysis, and the means for experiencing the dream of this not-seen place which was presented by his absence during the brief vacation, coincided with the creation of the dream space where the experience of dreaming, the experience of himself and the other was realized. As a not-seen place this dream space is, so the speak, mute: it really is not-seen (fortunately) in the transference by the analyst as an observing and interpreting figure; at the same time it is not-seen, i.e., not visible, insofar as it exists away from the eyes of the analyst. In this sense the private space lies outside the analysis, but at the same time it is fully in the analysis, in the same way as this dream space is outside the *text* of the dream, and at the same time is fully *in* the dream, or rather *of* the dream. This of course is not represented in the dream, but only alluded to by means of the exit lane, the way out, which as we saw, led to this other space, this *other scene of the self.*

The dream space outside the text of the dream, but which belongs to the dream because it *allows dreaming,* is obviously beyond interpretation by the analyst who, paradoxically, remains excluded.

Equally obviously, it is *unknowable.* In the words of Marion Milner's comment on a work of Khan's, "It could be also necessary to look for the dreamer's wish to relate himself to *what feels like non-being as part of the process of coming to be.* By the way, Bion has used the symbol 'O' (or zero) for this ultimate reality both of analyst and patient" (1975, p. 277, my italics).

A turning point

A leap of quality in the psychoanalytical process and relationship. The formation of a dream space.

Of course, it was hardly possible for me to take all this in while I was listening to the dream, but I am not simply reporting it for its value as a description of a precise phase in Federico's analysis. As already mentioned, it provides a much wider point of view, for two different reasons. First of all, in the story of this analytic experience, because of the repositioning it involved, it formed an important *turning point* in the work, a leap in its quality, a *dis-continuity* which extended the confines of the emotional field, gradually making itself accessible to the patient in the analysis.

Secondly, it offers a favorable angle for describing the clinical configuration and its transformations in the psychoanalytical process, which I consider central for the patient's internal experience: I refer to the *vicissitudes of being, knowing, and experiencing* in the psychoanalytical situation, where early, repeated intrusions into the self, of substantial expectations and fragments of the internal world of his parents, have led to a distortion of the ego in terms of a rigid and almost de-animated false self, and a dissociation within the personality defensively reorganized around obsessive control.

In this context, for the purposes of exposition, I shall leave the latter dimension more in the background.

In my opinion, this dream represents and indicates the formation of an individual dream space which can be recreated on the basis of the space made available by the psychoanalytical relationship. Khan's contributions (1962, 1972, 1976) suggest that "it is the incapacity in a patient to use dream-space to actualize the experience of the dream process that leads to acting out of dreams into social space (...) I am also suggesting that we should consider a patient's compulsive dreaming and reporting them in analysis as a special type of acting out, which screens the patient's lack of dream-space in his inner reality." By contrast, "the psychic capacity in a person to actualize such experiences in the dream space enables them to curtail acting out of unconscious internal conflicts" (Khan, 1972, pp. 314–315.).

191

This psychic capacity is related to his concept of "the good dream," taken up in terms of "unconscious psychic work" by Bollas (1987; 1992; 1995), but also developed in adjacent directions by Pontalis (1974) with his distinction between "dream-object" and "text-dream." In the development of the capacity for a good dream as personalization of the dreaming experience, the creation and use of the dream space can be compared to the creation and use of the transitional space and the potential space. Khan wrote:

> I began to discover in my work with adults that they can use the dream-space in exactly the same way as the child uses the transitional space of the paper to doodle on [*the squiggles*]. Furthermore, it was important for me to distinguish between the *process of dreaming* which articulated unconscious impulses and conflicts from the *dream-space* in which the dream actualizes this experience. I have also gradually begun to realise that in many patients for a long time the process of dreaming can be available to them but not the dream-space, hence they derive very little satisfaction from their dreams and have a very poor sense of the experiential reality of the dream dreamt.
>
> (1972, p. 314, my italics)

Further on, differentiating it "from Bertram Lewin's (1946) instructive concept of 'dream screen' ... as something *on to* which the dream imagery is projected," Khan states that "the dream space is a psychic area *in* which the dream process is actualized into experiential reality" (*ibid.*). In this sense, for Khan the dream space is "the internal psychic equivalent of what Winnicott has conceptualized as the transitional space which a child establishes to discover his self and external reality" (*ibid.*).

Here, I am interested in emphasizing the coincidence of different levels of experience that can be visualized in terms of *overlapping circles* (Milner, 1977): dream space, transitional space, potential space, and analytical space. Recently Hernandez and Giannakoulas (1997), writing "on the construction of potential space," have observed that the term "area" in Winnicott was initially linked to transitional objects and phenomena. With the substitution of "space" for "area" and then "potential" for "transitional," Winnicott defines a conceptual plane both in terms of the transitions which can take place in it, and the confines of these transitions. In a paper on the analysis of children and adolescents (Bonaminio & Di Renzo, 2000), we have begun to deal with this topic of playing-and-dreaming as "potential experiences of the self" discussing Winnicott's distinction between play and playing, which is analogous to that of dream and dreaming:

> [The] area of playing is not inner psychic reality. It is outside the individual, but it is not the external world (...) Into this play area the child gathers objects or phenomena from external reality and uses these in the service of some sample derived from inner or personal reality. *Without hallucinating* the child puts out a sample of *dream potential* and lives with this sample in a chosen setting of fragments from external reality (...) In playing the child manipulates external phenomena *in the service of the dream* and invests chosen external phenomena with *dream meaning and feeling.*
>
> (1971, p. 60, my italics)

The analyst's contribution is not only to give meaning to the dream content (and/or play), by co-determining it with the patient, but to point out the *potential personal experience of the self*, which the individual can have in subjective terms through dreaming. According to Khan "[Freud's] statement (1925) 'those dreams best fulfil their function about which one knows nothing after waking' seems to imply more than merely the function of preservation of sleep" (1976, p. 45): i.e., it is crucial to differentiate, even conceptually, the dreaming experience, that is beyond interpretation, and the meaning of the dream text, that is remembered and thus made available for interpretation.

Beside this statement of Freud, mentioned by Khan, I would set another, taken from a note added to Chapter 6 of *The Interpretation of Dreams*:

> I used at one time to find it extraordinarily difficult to accustom readers to the distinction between the manifest content of dreams and the dream-thoughts. Again and again, arguments and objections would be brought up based upon some uninterpreted dream in the form in which it had been retained in the memory, and the need to interpret it would be ignored. But now that analysts have at least become reconciled to replacing the manifest dream by the meaning revealed by its interpretation, many of them have become guilty of falling into another confusion [...] They seek to

find the essence of dreams in their latent content and in so doing they overlook the distinction between latent dream-thoughts and *dream-work*. At bottom dreams are nothing other than a particular *form* of thinking, made possible by the conditions of the state of sleep. It is the dream-work which creates the form, and it alone is the essence of dreaming – the explanation of its peculiar nature.

(1925)

It was therefore from this viewpoint in the previously mentioned paper on playing-and-dreaming, we used the dream of *Alice in Wonderland* as a metaphor to explain the multiplicity of the function of the dream. Alice's journey-dream as she falls down the rabbit hole describes a 'geography of the mind' which implies, as Meltzer (1983) would say, the possibility of living in different worlds, visiting different regions of the self and objects. This dream-journey also alludes to the dimension of the dream as "theatre where various scenes unfold, where different characters appear and express themselves in story plots, as has in fact been emphasized on quite a number of occasions" (Bezoari & Ferro, 1994). But Alice's dream also brings another dimension of the metaphor. Her dream is represented as a journey where the accent is placed not only on the places and inhabitants whom she meets and gets to know, but above all on the process of travelling. The journey itself, i.e., the dreaming, is a path of knowledge but above all it is a piece of experience whose "full course ... is allowed" (Winnicott, 1941), and as such it is a search for, and an experience of, the self. Inherent in the narrative structure of Alice's journey in Wonderland is the element of being 'surprised by herself' which in Winnicott's paradoxical way of describing the subjective experience, comes to the unexpected and unforeseen autoperception of the self.

Dream-space requires the conquest of the developmental process of personalization facilitated by the experience of maternal holding and caring: the psychoanalytical scenario can facilitate this process by constructing a space for the *dreaming experience*. Here we face the paradox of how an *intrapsychic* model, which is the dream, can function for an essentially *intersubjective* experience, which is the analysis (cf. Phillips, 1989). The analyst's position in this paradox is that he procures and creates the environment for making the dream-space. Now if we look once again at Federico's dream, the incipient experience of the self (as well as of the object) leaps into the foreground

194

and represents the turning point in the analytic process. With the building up of this internal space for dreaming, the patient can take a look at the state of his self at that moment and begin to personalize his own experience. This experience can now be reintegrated and narrated in a more coherent way: the *flat countryside,* representing the de-animation of the self, and later his *keeping cool and driving straight on down his traffic lane so that everything was going smoothly and easily* even through the mechanisms of denial (*as though nothing were wrong,* which is very similar to that "nothing important" at the beginning of the session). The rigidly defensive organization of the self (again, the "keeping cool in my traffic lane") serves to guarantee his massive control (the *rear mirror*) over what he feels as an intrusion, like the words of the analyst, as well as the parental objects, that he "almost feels," in spite of, but also thanks to, his defensive armor (his *Land Rover*/tank).

The storyline of this narration of the self, which is now possible, is 'Duel': a crushing conflict but at the same time the representation of the analysis as a couple relationship. *"And that was that"* recalls the retreat into dissociation (schizoid phenomena), in a place where he is not seen (dream-space), where the potential self can be cultivated.

Finally, I wouldn't like to pass over the peripheral placement at the end of Federico's dream of the film 'Close Encounters,' which appears to have been fished up at the last moment. Placed as it is at a borderline point, his reference to the film seems to constitute a second-level glance at the dream. Now the danger of intrusion on the part of the analyst with his interpretations can also be seen in another perspective, as those *close encounters* (not only between himself and the analyst, but also between parts of the self) which he can acknowledge. With this close encounter begins a new phase of the analysis as a twofold collaboration.

Some elements of Federico's story

How his parents consciously and unconsciously affected, or 'prefabricated' his personality.

From this intermediate stage, let us take a look at events which led to the development of this phase of the analytic relationship.

Federico is the only child of an averagely wealthy middle-class couple. The father is a doctor who has just retired, although he still practices privately with some of his clients. The mother, who is younger, is a former principal of a secondary school. She too has retired and left behind a working life that was intense and varied. Before she became a teacher, she worked as a tourist guide.

The analysis was set up as the "mother's business." It is the mother with whom Federico says he has a very close and trusting relationship, who made the effort to ask around among her acquaintances, in search of "someone reliable" for her son to consult about the difficulties he had told her he was having, but which she "had always known about." And in fact, Federico's first contact with me was preceded by a phone call from one of his colleagues, a doctor at the university whose most important credential was as the "daughter of a friend of a friend of his mother" – as the patient stressed from time to time in the early days of the analysis.

In this session he talked about the therapy being needed urgently so he could "put things back in line," but he also alluded to the fact that it was "an idea that came to mind between him and his mother." They had talked about the need for him to consult a psychoanalyst because of the "unexplained anxiety reaction that I had, many months before, at the prospect of a more serious emotional relationship with Caterina." He was in the habit of distancing himself and had experienced a number of physical symptoms, the sensation of wanting to vomit, of his "stomach being tight," and a sense of alienation and unreality. These symptoms had persisted for a long time and "unbalanced" him. Regular contact with Caterina seemed unsustainable.

Already, in the first interview, I realized that his "inexplicable and unreasonable anxiety" was the least of his symptoms related to anxiety about contact with his mother. He had separation anxiety upon entering the first grade, characterized by gastro-intestinal problems, which occurred on the occasion of his going away from home for a week on a trip to the Dolomites; and this led to a sense of the "closure of my stomach." He also mentioned "some difficulties" during adolescence when he travelled which he did not elaborate on, but which seemed to have something to do with "two families being together," his own and a friend's of the same age.

These symptoms relating to separation anxiety immediately appeared significant to me and seemed to suggest an early claustro-agoraphobic organization of the personality. Psychoanalytic treatment was therefore required to help him gain some insight into how this organization limited his object relations. Federico maintained that he was "difficult to love," an attitude in which he stubbornly persisted during the early part of the analysis. In reality, that "instability," that loss of equilibrium which "anxiety" – i.e., emotions, not otherwise nameable and knowable – represented in comparison to the rigidity of his personal disposition, which should have mastered it, had immediately appeared to me as the "way in" being offered by the patient to himself and to me, so as to question his conventional way of being in the world and the "false narrative" he was making about it.

The complaisance of the "regular family guy," the "prefabricated image" with which Federico presented himself, had made itself known from the start of the analysis ever since he had "readily" accepted the suggested rhythm of four sessions a week, willingly reorganizing his work schedule, which had in fact been messed up by the timings of the sessions, and not asking to renegotiate them.

This general eagerness to please had almost reached the level of a "lie" – one evidently produced to protect a most private nucleus of the self – when, during the first months of the analysis, I received from Federico's own accounts the "acknowledgement" of that sense of inauthenticity and falsity that I had perceived in the conventional façade he was presenting: cultural interests, sporting activities, or hobbies that might have given him "qualities" were practically non-existent, or barely featured. That top layer of conventionality – which, being a top layer, is quickly dissolved in analysis – "talked" in the transference about his compliance with the demands of his environment. *I'm the way you want me to be*: this is how Federico had set up a self-image on the basis of what he believed I expected from him – a repetition in the transference of the image that was "acceptable" in his parents' eyes, and especially his father's – but here the adjective "acceptable" is provisional; an image into which he had "molded" himself in response to their expectations.

While what I have mentioned is only a fragment, and a superficial one – the tip of the iceberg in the initial analytic interaction – of a false-self structure, the unfolding of the narrative of Federico's history during the first years of analysis offers a steadily more detailed picture of how he had organized this compliant response to his parents' expectations and intrusions in order to protect his hidden "true self" in a dissociated place.

While, as I expected, the early part of the analysis featured Federico's persistence in developing the rock-solid policy of representing himself to me and to himself in a highly compressed fashion, keeping the two of us at a due distance, we can say, looking back, and putting it slightly differently, that the "discovery" of the lie constitutes a first narrow *gap*, a slight ungluing of what seems a perfect fit between the conventional self-image and the other's expectations: a hiatus that is directly achieved in the consulting room and has to be included in that "unbalancing," which, as I said, constituted a way into psychoanalytic work. This hiatus is a fore-runner, a first tiny building block for creating a more intimate space in the analytic scenario. On the other hand, and on another level, as I indicated in relation to my thoughts about the initial dream, my "exploitation" of this hiatus also had a place in the unfolding of the analytic process during the middle phase as the "repetition in the transference" of contact, relating, closeness as impingement.

But I don't want to return to this second aspect so much as to stress how the achievement of this first 'ungluing' – a new and unexpected feature for the patient, though he did not recognize it on this level – began to make more disjointed narrative material start to flow; or perhaps it would be better to say that it allowed me to listen to the patient's narratives with a different ear as a result of an adjustment in my attitude towards him.

The intense, endlessly repetitive flow of Federico's speech in sessions, always along the same lines – a speech that leaves no room for me and rebuffs every attempt I make to relate to him verbally, and makes me feel that what I say to him "doesn't take" – slips away and is lost in the void: this iron curtain I feel I've been shut behind, condemned to boredom at its repetitiveness, gets me wondering where I have been located for Federico in the transference.

The boredom I feel – and which, curiously, I also start to observe in Federico in the "chance" yawning that happens every time one of my interpretations goes on for longer than a single sentence – makes me gradually understand that in the transference I am the child faced with the unstoppable flow of the mother's words, which you can only escape by being physically absent. In that unbroken talk Federico is his mother, that mother who is brought concretely into the session, and not only via the leather case that he enthrones on the chair.

"I wonder if you're using these yawns," I say after noticing how they recur, "to communicate how bored you feel by the effort of taking in what I'm saying to you." "Careful, it's not like that," he says, raising his hand in an obvious 'halt' which, I realize, fulfils the distancing function even more concretely than the yawn, a 'halt' that is evidently necessary because my intervention is premature, and also surprising. "It's not like that," he continues in a slightly affected manner, "Maybe I didn't get enough sleep last night … I shouldn't say it because it's not nice, but my mother snores loudly at night, and sometimes it wakes me up and I can't get back to sleep.

In the manic defense as Winnicott described it (1935), in order to deny his internal reality – or to withdraw it from the relational field, as we could say in a more modern Winnicottian language (Bollas, 1992) – the patient feels the need to freeze any possibility that something might "happen." The activity of compulsive thought, writes Winnicott (1971), is a negation of psychic reality, "absorbing energy but not contributing-in either to dreaming or to living," an attempt, as Masud Khan says in his introduction to *Holding and Interpretation*, "to maintain 'suspended animation'" (1978, p. 1).

Extending this original concept of Winnicott's and applying it to the psychoanalytic situation, Masud Khan (1978) observes that the analysand "who compels boring narrative on us is not letting language and metaphor elaborate or change his experience. He creates a space of discourse where both he and the analyst are paralyzed by the technique of the narrative as well as its monotonous and repetitive contents." Tiring and boring, Khan goes on to say, are interconnected "techniques of coping with inner stress. The boring patient is trying to maintain omnipotent control over his inner reality by obsessional over-control of language and material. His narrative is a petrified space where nothing can happen" (p. 3).

Earlier, in the concept of "false reparation" – which "appears through the patient's identification with the mother" – Winnicott (1948) had indicated that the "dominating factor is not the patient's own guilt but the mother's organized defense:" the baby who is busy "managing" the internal world of the mother (and the parental couple) with whom he is identified, is denied the possibility of finding his own personal idiom and the authenticity of his own experience (distortion of the ego in terms of the false self). Whatever is boring or tiring in the psychoanalytic situation, as Khan makes clear, is implicitly inauthentic for both patient and analyst. The analyst's task is to "tolerate" this falsified discourse, this intense mental activity from which the patient would like to be relieved. This laborious mental busy-ness, which results in a significant inauthenticity, brings with it the traces of a specific failure in the area of the primary relationship, a "memorization" which constitutes "the essence of the technique of the patient who is boring. Such patients twist and abuse the analytic process we offer them to impose upon it an arid technique of relating ... Behind it, as Winnicott (1952) points out, there is an ungraspable fear of madness in them" (Khan, 1978, pp., 5–6).

The mother's madness, I would add: that is, a bizarre and uncontrollable element – with which they are identified – that must be "kept at bay," as I begin to understand from this reference to snoring that I have just quoted. The "different ear" for listening to Federico's 'falsified discourse' is therefore prompted to listen by these "concretions-of-sensations-and-relational-emotions," as I would define them, which are left there, almost in passing, in the dense and laborious fabric of his narratives.

The picture gradually becomes clearer, other pieces are added to the mosaic – or rather, it is possible for me to "fish up" other "concretions" in the discourse. His mother "talks loudly" because "she's a bit deaf" and "doesn't realize it;" people "turn around" in the street and he has to "give her tug on the arm." Sometimes when he comes home he finds "the volume of the television turned up to maximum" and has to "run and turn it down" because otherwise "it will upset the neighbors." And "mother hen," as he calls her affectionately, isn't very bright because "she doesn't really understand" certain words "we use here in Rome" and so "she comes out with some rude words ... blunders," which means he is "forced to correct her" and "explain what they mean."

There is a "scene" recounted at a later point in the analysis which significantly coalesces and sums up the identification with the mother and, at the same time, the need to hold back its overwhelming tendency and to distance himself from her.

We are in the fourth year of analysis.

Thursday.

He arrives on time but a bit out of breath. He tells me he was nearly late today getting to the private out-patient's clinic where he works as an otolaryngologist. As he was leaving the house, his mother was coming home for lunch, "all sweaty" because of the heat

(Federico has a "problem with embarrassment and shame" about his own "greasy, clammy skin" which – as a dermatologist colleague has told him – is "constitutional" and "there's no cream you can apply to make it go away"). He follows her into her bedroom as she goes on talking, "going on and on" in detail about everything that had happened during the morning, giving him "every possible detail." He adds in passing that, when she wanted to take something out of her handbag, his mother upturned it onto the bed so that its entire contents went "all over the place." A few objects even slipped onto the floor and under the divan, and he made himself late "gathering it all up and putting it back together again ... that's how she is, there's something a bit funny about her, her very own way of being," he added at the end.

Spurred by that "risk of being late" to analysis, the communication of this "factual account" hit me like an illuminating "big scene,"[1] which suddenly turns the spotlight on the play's two main characters, bringing complete clarity to what has been going on. So I feel an intense excitement and a feeling of solidarity and closeness to Federico who has admitted me to this internal scene. Caught between the interpretative caution that I have had to learn with this analysand so as not to risk pedantic intellectualization, and the sensation that I mustn't let slip this opportunity to reflect back to the patient the emotion he has stirred up in me, I decide to go for an intermediate solution.

I tell him that I have heard that "fact" which was in danger of stopping us meeting as if he had been telling me a dream where he felt unable to resist the job of putting back together the scattered bits of his mother: that is, her states of mind, her impulsiveness, her strangeness, so as to try and give them sense and coherence.

By bringing up the idea of dream, I think I was trying to invite the patient not only into an intermediate area between him and me in the analytic communication at that moment, but also into an intermediate area that might support him in acknowledging his internal world: intermediate, in other words, between the concreteness of emotions and their nameability.

Federico's response to this comment is a rather disoriented silence: but a silence nonetheless, one of the few he ever allows, a space in the incessant flow of this thoughts. Then he lets the matter drop.

The interpretative work around his constant effort to "put back together" the pieces of a perilously scattered internal mother, a mother "who comes out with things," who must be kept at bay and controlled because of her "strangeness," would be long and slow, and would above all require progressive adjustments of tone on my part. Indeed, the analysis of this very intense and powerful identification could only be felt as an attack on his privileged relationship with his mother, and thus as a "demand," a demand for separation. (Who separates? The father.) The immediate effects of my comment are in fact felt when analysis resumes the following week.

Monday.

Settling himself on the couch after searching for the most comfortable possible position, Federico mentions his house by the sea: before going out that morning he spoke to the gardener who, as Federico feared, had told him it was already too hot to plant the shrubs along the wall. Then he adds that, after a weekend of "blessed peace," his "symptoms" had returned: tight stomach, nausea, a certain "feeling of unreality"; he wonders what these disturbances are to do with.

I tell him he felt "disturbed" by me and by the comments I had made on Thursday, which in his opinion had nothing to do with his story. I am to some extent rebuking myself because he felt what I had said as urging him to break free of his mother, rather as if I wanted to tear him away from her. I add that the feeling of sickness and a tight stomach came over him when he separated from his mother.

P: "That's got nothing to do with it. No, it's not true, but it isn't nice to be seen as such a mummy's boy, I've told you this before."
A: "And then the gardener told you it was too late ..."
P: "It's true, when I talked to the gardener before 8 this morning I'd already got up feeling sick and upset ... so you can't bring the gardener into this."

Then off he goes again, telling me about his plan to buy a portable computer to take with him when he goes to his house by the sea: "I'll sit under the portico, so the view of the sea will relax me as I write."

I think to myself about the "mobility" of the portable computer and his need to equip himself with an internal tool for dealing with separateness. But I make no comment.

P: "Dr. Bonaminio will be thinking, 'Why the computer and not a girlfriend, a young woman?'"

That is certainly not what I was thinking just then. Instead I was thinking how convenient it would be to have a computer that you can carry around without having to depend on all that paraphernalia, screen, keyboard … However, since he has suggested this thought to me, why a computer and not a girlfriend?

A: "No, no … and yet the girlfriend might come onto the terrace with a nice cup of iced tea and say, 'Do you want some, Federico?'"

I have cited this fragment of analytic interaction because, in spite of the fleeting contact that Federico allows himself, and me, there is nevertheless an obviously greater intimacy in the analytic communication which even permits him to come up with a daydream. The micro-fracture provoked by my comment on Thursday is healed not only through the connection with the symptoms that I cause him and for which I admit to being 'co-responsible,' but also by Federico himself who, via the image of himself as a "mummy's boy" can use the viewpoint provided by analysis to observe himself, as is also evident in the (humorous) assertion about what he thinks I am thinking about him (the *complex* or *reflective Self* that Bollas (1990) and Fonagy et al. (1991) talk about in connection with the concept of the therapeutic alliance).

But beyond the immediate effects of my comment on the 'big scene' (*scena-madre*), the activating of a great capacity for containing and tolerating his own internal existence is evident in the reflection that he brings to sessions in the next few days, and which also constitute a recovery (emotional rather than cognitive) of a memory to which I shall return several times.

Tuesday.

After the usual account of the events that have occurred since the previous day, he says that on Monday it occurred to him to probe his mother on the problem of separations. His mother had reminded him about something that he actually already knew and wasn't sure if he'd told me: this is the fact that he had been separated from her as a baby, aged around eight months. His parents had had one of their spats about the usual problem (which I already know about and will now refer to) and his mother had taken him with her to northern Italy, determined to return to the work she had given up when he was born. She had had to leave him in a kind of orphanage or institution for about ten days until she could sort out better accommodation, but when she went to collect him he had lost weight because he wasn't eating, and he didn't recognize her.

The image of his father which, from the start of the analysis, Federico transmits to me in his stories is one that I would now call a majority shareholder, whose brief, apart from any other contribution, is to release liquidity exclusively to a rigid, superegoic character structure which must "tighten its belt" in order to produce interest. This image is not a fantasy and neither has it come by chance since financial investment is one of the few ways that Federico's father is prepared to relate to him, though not without criticism, leaving Federico to "trail after" him in search of the approval that never comes.

And never has come, even back in his university days when "he could have done better" in every exam; even at school; and even further back to the time of his first emotional difficulties when as a child he would be sick at every separation; his primary school, his first skiing trip. He always felt criticized for these difficulties, to say nothing of his present ones at the start of the analysis – a maternal matter, as I said earlier, which he deliberately kept hidden from his father for a long time. Federico paid for his therapy from his current account – jointly held with his mother, naturally – at a different bank from the one where his father and he tended their substantial "nest egg."

Approval and goodwill were always withheld so that Federico would "function to the best of his ability": this was the explicit philosophy of the father whom Federico nicknamed the "owl" – in opposition to the broody and receptive "mother hen" endlessly "dispensing" eggs. The image of the "owl" – a true controlling superego like a bird perched high up – is one that Federico will only be able to bring to analysis, along with the other building blocks I mentioned earlier, in a later phase of the treatment; that is, when the feeling of intimacy and collaboration with me begins to appear, permitting us to begin a long task of analyzing his identification with that superegoic internal object.

Of course, even in the beginning I hadn't missed the wooden rigidity of Federico's relationship with his father, in contrast to his mother's ubiquitous "presence." From his initial account I had noted that Federico specialized in the same variety of self-presentation as his father, by no means an unusual fact but significant, nonetheless.

Instead, I get a first "surprise" about what I will later discover to be the extent of this young doctor's "prefabrication" when, having paid for the first month's analysis, Federico – who is naturally an expert accountant, both for professional reasons and by obsessive inclination – asks me if on future invoices I would kindly not indicate his date of birth under his name. Standing by the couch before lying down, and so with the casual manner of an expert talking about something that has nothing to do with analysis, he explains that since he may one day tell his father that he's in analysis, he could then pass the invoices on to him so that his father could "deduct" them from his taxes, given that Federico and he have the same Christian name. The same applies to his professional visits, he adds, once he is on the couch, where I have meanwhile invited him to lie down: he invoices for them as fees paid to his father, "because my father and I make no difference between ourselves as far as tax is concerned: same name, same specialism, consulting rooms in the same place."

Quite apart from the content of the analytic communication I just mentioned – the complexity and force of which I only appreciate later on (Federico is also healing his father by means of his analysis) – this surprising piece of news quite quickly makes me realize, on the basis of further accounts of his personal history and that of his parents, that Federico has been thought of, "prefabricated indeed," as a clone of his father.

There is no need for me to go into detail about these aspects of the personal and family history because Federico brings me a piece here and a piece there in a de-animated and factual manner, like an unavoidable introduction whose conventionality and "normality" must nevertheless be defended while, on another level, he shows me the coldness of its composition. The facts, especially those narrated during the first year, will receive a retrospective emotional significance and a further psychic amplification in analysis, but only later on, as if his objective, bloodless way of recounting them at the start were the only possible narrative for the self: a self in plaster, barely able to move, as his almost robotic ritual gestures and rigid muscular posture made clear.

More than anything else, I would say it was a silent, subterranean process, the effects of which slowly but surely appeared in a later phase of the analysis: i.e., when his intimacy with the mother he had to take care of, when that "same–idea–as–her," previously taken for granted, began to be called into question.

In terms of Federico's social life, this corresponded to a greater "mobility" in the outside world: some journeys, not without anxiety but nevertheless spontaneously "planned"; more time spent with friends; and attempts to "replace" the "Caterina problem" with less demanding flirtations with other young women. There starts to be some actual sexuality, recounted with shy pleasure: sexuality which had until then been confined to masturbation – activated by "recalling" his one previous erotic relationship with a foreign girl, or fired by some alluring character in the theatre – and yet withheld from the analytic field so that, in the beginning, it had not been even remotely possible to explore its corresponding "fantasies."

But in terms of the psychoanalytic process, more than all these slow, uncertain changes, the most significant confirmation of his gradual differentiation from his mother was a slow achievement of intimacy in his relationship with me. The quality of the transference – in which I felt I could sometimes achieve the mirroring condition of a 'friend and confidant' – also contained an evolution towards what I would call 'the formation of the father.'

In a dream from the fourth year of analysis he is "in a printer's workshop, correcting the error-strewn proofs of an article for publication." In his associations he makes clear that the article does exist: it is a chapter on the prevention of ear diseases in childhood, part of a self-help manual for parents that he is writing with colleagues, commissioned by an important medical publisher "in contact with his Professor." The printer, however, does not exist: "Maybe," he says, "it could be a 'daytime residue,' an image taken from who knows where." (Some time ago, the patient had read, without much interest, some of the psychology books that his mother had purchased at the beginning of the analysis in order to master it.) Then he goes on, "Don't tell me you are the printer ..."

"But that's what I do tell you," I reply, although in my next comment I emphasize the features connected to the more immediate material in the *hic-et-nunc* of this phase in the analysis: i.e., his indication of errors that the printer–analyst may be making in transcribing and receiving his text, and restoring it to him; in other words, I add, his personal experience, his idiom.

I intentionally keep to myself the theme of the analyst as corrector of negative experiences, the indicator of a productive, idealizing, positive transference onto me (the Professor). I keep to myself the theme of 'collaboration' which he can now recognize as an aspect of analytic work, and the connected theme of analysis and his own internal elaborative process represented as "prevention of childhood diseases" and as a process of differentiation from the parental imagos. Naturally, the "manual for parents" still carries the fingerprints, so to speak, of the manic defense, of having to work for his parents (his deaf mother; his being an otologist) but it is equally obvious that it is now occurring in the context of self-help, "everyone for himself": we also glimpse here an aspect of reparative fantasy in which the analysis, by healing him, also heals his parents.

But leaving aside this last observation, what I mean to emphasize is that the decision to keep certain "secondary" considerations about this dream "to myself" was the result of a conscious reorientation based on previous "errors" (maybe the errors revealed in the dream). In fact, various micro-impasses in the analytic work had made me realize that, for this analysand, an excess of interpretation on my part acted as a sort of wedding invitation, a banquet he already knew about, a table already laid and providing food that had been collusively requested: in other words, the excess of thinking, which might be a complete repetition of the mother's offloading, brought with it the risk of "intellectualization" and a "false" analysis that would set itself up in place of the authentic emotional experience which the close encounters of the first dream had signaled as being possible.

This keeping certain thoughts about him "to myself" also answered my need to guard and preserve a private, intimate, personal space: a space for my fantasies and emotions, a "dreaming" space that is so hard to maintain in the presence of such a "busy" and ritualistic analysand; a space for *reverie*, if you like. However, as I have pointed out on other occasions, in terms of conceptualizing what happens clinically in the consulting room, I do not find this admittedly beautiful image of Bion's very satisfactory. It has been too abused and saturated with meaning because of the claim, certainly not made by Bion, that it can be applied like a master key, along with "containment," to the analytic stance as a whole.

In any case, for the reasons I have already given, in the clinical work with this specific analysand, maintaining such a private space for the analyst, using it as a boundary to the work of interpretation, certainly acted as a boundary for differentiation from maternal intrusiveness. But it was also identified on the horizon by the analysand as that "paternal function" which the analysis could *use* (adopting this term in Winnicott's specific sense of "use of an object," 1969): a father's regulatory function in relation to the primal (intrusive) pre-Oedipal rapport with the mother, a function that was as absent from his internal world as it had been in his personal history.

This is also clear from the oneiric scenes of that period. For example, in a dream from the fourth year of analysis, I am represented as his university professor inviting him onto a boat. He is embarrassed at not knowing how to handle these strange ropes, and feels subtly criticized and mocked by the professor and his colleagues. Federico knew about my role at the university, although he later called my "position as a non-medic in a medical clinic strange, or at least unusual."

Later on, this academic role of mine, as an outcome of the transformative processes in the analysis, was 'rediscovered' as a positive attribute by means of which he passed through a certain idealization and appreciation of me as an "enviable university researcher": that is, as the object of an idealizing transference he could identify with in order to support his aspiration to "get into the university," a path that, as a young doctor, his father could not follow. It is also evident here how analytic work offered the chance to dig up, behind the criticisms and devaluing judgements, some "good aspects" of the "paternal mandate" with which he could identify in terms of an ideal ego, and pass – as a fundamental contribution to his sense of identity – through a process of dis-identification. The university career could still be cultivated very much as his father's aspiration, but one he had never achieved. This is another aspect of the dialectic between "being like" and "not being like" identified in my "strange position" as a "non-medic" in a "medical" clinic.

Clearly this "dialectic," this "calling into question" of the father, is an elaborative aspect, a tendency which – together with other threads of his previously rigidly petrified internal world – comes to the fore in the analytic work when it enters its concluding phase (sixth year): feelings, emotions, thoughts, and plans were circulating with a certain fluidity; but also anxieties about the prospect of "having to manage on one's own," "moving sooner or later into a flat of his own" (which he does in fact start trying to do, with help from his mother). And he was also trying to face the emotional commitment and responsibility of married life "one day," a less remote possibility after he consolidated his relationship with Valentina, a journalist from a "good family," living in Venice, with whom he had established a romantic relationship "with no ties" and who had made him feel "the same as any other young man of his age."

Note

1 In Italian, "mother-scene" – *scena-madre*.

References

Bezoari, M. & Ferro, A. (1994). Il posto del sogno all'interno di una teoria del campo analitico. *Rivista di Psicoanalisi*, XL, 2:251–272.

Bollas, C. (1987). At the other's play: To dream. In: *The Shadow of the Object*. London: Free Association Books.

_____ (1990). Origins of the therapeutic alliance. *Paper Read at* Week-End Conference for English-Speaking Members of European Societies. London, 12–14, October, 1990. Also in *The Mystery Of Things*. London: Routledge, 1999.

_____ (1992). *Being a Character*. London: Routledge.

_____ (1995). *Cracking Up. The Work of Unconscious Experience*. London: Routledge.

Bolognini, S. (1997). Empathy and 'empathism'. *Int. J. Psychoanal.*, 78:279–293.

Bonaminio, V. D. & Renzo, M. (2000). *Creativity, Playing, Dreaming. Overlapping Circles in the Work of M. Milner and D. W. Winnicott. in: Art, Creativity, Living*. Edited by L. Caldwell. London: Karnac.

Fonagy, P., Steele, M., Steele, H., Moran, G. S., and Higgitt, A. C. (1991). The capacity for understanding mental states: the reflective self in parent and child and its significance for security of attachment. Infant Ment. Health J. 12, 201.

Freud, S. (1925). Some additional notes on dream interpretation as a whole. *S. E.*, 19.

Green, A. (1995). *Seminari Romani*. Rome: Borla.

Heimann, P. (1950). On countertransference. *Int. J. Psychoanal.*, 31:81–84.

Hernandez, M. & Giannakoulas, A. (1997). On the construction of potential space. Paper presented at the international congress "Lo psiche-Soma. Dalla pediatria alla psicoanalisi," Milan, April 1997. In: *Squiggles and Spaces. Revisiting The Work Of D.W. Winnicott*. Volume 1. Edited By M. Bertolini, A. Giannakoulas & M. Hernandez. London and Philadelphia: Whurr Publishers, 2001.

Khan, M. M. R. (1962). Dream psychology and the evolution of the psychoanalytic situation. In: *The Privacy of the Self*. London: Hogarth, 1974.

_____ (1972). The use and abuse of dream in psychic experience. In: *The Privacy of the Self.* London: Hogarth, 1974.

_____ (1976). Beyond the dreaming experience. In: *Hidden Selves.* London: Hogarth, 1983.

_____ (1978). *Introduction to D. W. Winnicott, Holding and Interpretation. Fragment of an Analysis.* London: Karnac, 1989.

Lacan, J. (1966). *Ecrits.* Paris: Editions du Seuil.

Lewin, B. (1946). Sleep, the mouth and the dream screen. *Psychoanal. Q.,* 15:419–434.

Meltzer, D. (1983). *Dream-Life. A Re-Examination of the Psycho-Analytical Theory and Technique.* Reading: Clunie Press.

Milner, M. (1975). A discussion of 'Masud Khan's paper in search of the dreaming experience'. In: *The Suppressed Madness of Sane Men.* London: Tavistock Publications, 1987.

_____ (1977). Winnicott and overlapping circles. In: *The Suppressed Madness of Sane Men.* London: Tavistock Publications, 1987.

Phillips, A. (1989). Returning the dream: In memoriam Masud Khan. In: *On Kissing, Tickling and Being Bored.* Cambridge, MA: Harvard University Press, 1993.

Pontalis, J. -B. (1974). Dream as an object. *Int. R. Psychoanal.,* 1:125–133.

Sharpe, E. (1937). *Dream Analysis.* London: Hogarth.

Winnicott, D. W. (1935). The manic defence. In: *Collected Papers: Through Paediatrics to Psychoanalysis (1958).* London: Tavistock Publications.

_____ (1941). The observation of infants in a set situation. In: *Collected Papers: Through Paediatrics to Psychoanalysis (1958).* London: Tavistock Publications.

_____ (1948). Reparation in respect of mother's organized defence against depression. In: *Collected Papers: Through Paediatrics to Psychoanalysis (1958).* London: Tavistock Publications.

_____ (1954). Withdrawal and regression. In: *Collected Papers: Through Paediatrics to Psychoanalysis (1958).* London: Tavistock Publications.

_____ (1960). Ego distortion in terms of true and false self. In: *The Maturational Processes and the Facilitating Environment.* London: Hogarth, 1965.

_____ (1971). *Playing and Reality.* London: Tavistock.

9

"THESE ANXIETIES ARE NOT MINE"

Adolescence, the Oedipal Configuration, and Transgenerational Factors

Vincenzo Bonaminio and Mariassunta Di Renzo

Part 1

Back to the future!

The scene opens with a running shot over clocks that cram the room: they all tell the same time. The problem of time is thus immediately placed centerstage, like the axis around which the story unfolds. The protagonist's ambiguous voyage in time, which is progressively transformed into a sort of double helix – in which the present and the future retrospectively influence the past, as much as the past influences the present and the future – is a kind of synthesis expressed by the film's plot.

Of course, I am speaking of Robert Zemeckis' film 'Back to the Future' (1985). I'll take for granted a prior knowledge of the multiple and surprising narrative temporal mechanisms that configure the film (and its two sequels), like a complicated but fascinating timing device.

In short, as we can deduce from the film's presentation of the past, Martin, the protagonist, is a typical American middle–adolescent boy of the mid-1980s, who unenthusiastically attends a small–town high school. He forms a close friendship with Doc, an archetypal bizarre scientist and genius, partly because of his unsatisfactory and disappointing relationship with his barely consequential parents; they are opaque and unidealized so as to contrast them with Doc.

211   DOI: 10.4324/9781003228332-10

Briefly, the director introduces us to Martin's family and school and the social milieu of which he is a part.

Summoned by Doc, who wants to show him his most astonishing and important invention, the *time machine* – a modified DeLorean – Martin witnesses Doc being killed (at least, it seems so to Martin and the viewer) by Libyan terrorists, from whom the scientist has stolen plutonium, the essential fuel for his machine. To escape the risk of being killed himself, Martin leaps to the wheel of the DeLorean. Pursued by the terrorists, Martin pushes the machine to its limit, forgetting in the heat of the moment that Doc had pre-set a special instrument with a certain date. The machine thus reaches a critical velocity of 88 miles per hour, and Martin finds himself catapulted to 30 years earlier, in the same place. Here it is interesting to note that the film's fundamental mechanism is a variation in external time, while the place and the internal narrative remain the same.

Martin thus finds himself in the past, before his birth, at the roots of his origins, and in his attempt to return to the future, he comes into contact with the adolescents who will become his parents and with the "prehistory" of his nuclear family.

The plot of the film brings us directly inside the epistemological theme relative to Martin's own origins. Visiting his own past makes it inevitable, as well as risky, that there will be interference with history as it has already happened, but this inevitable interference is resolved in a transformation of Martin's own past. *He actively contributes to the construction of a new history,* of a new narration.

That Oedipal situation is the model for transformation. The dangerous but sincere falling in love, revisited, for the adolescent girl who will become his mother, and the attempt at valorizing the timid and uncertain adolescent boy who will become his father, leads Martin to the active creation of an Oedipal couple, to the configuration of a primal scene from which he can be *regenerated.*

In this Oedipal scene, in which cognitive relationships are interwoven with libidinal and aggressive object relationships, a new interplay of identifications and dis-identifications with primary objects is made possible, i.e., in the movie it is a metaphor of this process, and Martin is capable of generating new, richer, and more articulated representations of internal objects, of the self, and of their relationships.

Through this interpretive and imaginative inscription of Martin's history, his sense of self and identity, we find him at the end of the film modified, broadened, enriched, and articulated. In that moment of fleeting surprise and discovery in which we catch him returning to the future (that is, to the present), when he again comes into contact with his family – that is, his population of internal objects and their relationships, no longer the same population that he left – it is possible to see the development of more authentic potentialities of the self that were earlier inactive. After the suspension, after the fracture of the present, subjective time has taken a new and different course.

The visiting ego and the visitors of the ego

The film is an effective metaphor on many levels. Visualized as a passage in the course of life, it is evocative of those adolescent transformations that can be achieved when basic conditions exist for psychic development, given an environment that is in Winnicottian terms *good enough*. Given the tradition of our clinical work, it is impossible for us to look at an individual *per se* without simultaneously looking at his environment, understood as a quality of *the contribution of the other* that the subject can enjoy and benefit from and in which the individual becomes exactly that. It is only in this perspective that it is possible to think about adolescence as a phase of individuation leading to autonomy, the second *separation-individuation,* in Blos' (1967) terms. This vision, which can be defined as *binocular* in focusing on *the-individual-and-the-environment*, finds in the psychoanalytic situation, in its quality of a relationship between two persons, the central axis of therapeutic change.

If we explore the theme of the film more deeply, we will discover too a further evocation on the same level. Martin's re-visitation of his past, his history, and his elaboration and transformation are rendered possible by the fact that his objects *let him visit*. Personifying the psychic scenario, one could say that there is an observing ego *visiting* and internal objects that welcome this visitation. In terms of deep emotional relationships inside the family, the adolescent also *calls on* his parents to reenter into contact with their own adolescence, to relive it, sometimes to live it for the first time – the transformative meaning. The result of that process of continuity and change in the construction of a real sense of identity, specific to the adolescent stage, is thus also dependent on parental availability. We can imagine in the *other scene* – in the complementary one, that is – the parents whom Martin finds as adolescents are also the parents who re-find their own adolescence through Martin.

In analysis, this unavoidable "summons to adolescence" required by the parents of the adolescent analysand, i.e., the revisiting of the parents' own adolescence, if they are open-minded enough and not rigid, can be seen as one of the nodal points for the clinical process, or as one of its impediments or obstacles when missing. Certainly, one of the principal therapeutic factors of analysis with adolescents resides in working through the countertransference of this specific challenge. With Baranes (1991), we can see that adolescents are experts at not leaving the analyst the same – in forcing him to reopen the psychic 'areas of construction' that have remained closed up to that point. As a *new object* for the patient, the analyst finds himself in the impossible position of being an intersection between the past, present, and future. In offering himself as a dialectical pole through which the adolescent can historicize his own subjectivity, the analyst must tolerate the paradox of being the demonstrator of a historical period for the adolescent, who claims instead the absolute currency of his experience. At the end of the 1960s, Mick Jagger of the Rolling Stones sang, with unashamed adolescent omnipotence, that *time was on his side.*

A further metaphorical level of this film, in our opinion, relates to a register along which the psychoanalytic process unfolds in situations where the analysand who hosts relatively unspoiled internal objects (through the therapeutic alliance, in the function represented by the character of Doc – that is, the analyst) is given the possibility of an experience of re-metabolization, representation, and historicizing of what has come to him from the contribution of primary parental objects.

We would agree, of course, with the observation that we are describing the circularity of this process as occurring fluently, which in a way is too simplified an account of what happens in the analytic process. Nonetheless, the metaphor offered by the film lends itself to an emphasis on the contribution of *transgenerational factors,* virtually always present, to the transformative construction of individuality and identity, as elements that can be, and are, worked through, elements not recorded as such but silently present as elements of continuity of being in the patient's discourse. In clinical analytic work, on the contrary, the transgenerational appears as a break, as the result of a failure of this working-through, a tangle of unelaborated elements that shatter the continuity of individual discourse. The transgenerational then appears as an intruder, an alien, an uninvited guest or a 'cyst' that settles somewhere and whose effects can be discerned in the defensive system organized to delimit and circumscribe it.

If in the metaphor we can imagine an ego that visits its internal objects, as in 'normal' and mildly disturbed patients, on the contrary with very disturbed patients it is the objects which become visitors of the ego. We are referring here to the concept elaborated by DeMijolla (1981), who uses this very suggestive figurative image to describe the intrusion into the subject of the parental objects, another way of describing what other authors (Faimberg, 1985; Bollas, 1989; Green, 1992) define as "alienating identification." These intrusive visitors of the ego claim collusive space or silence. They demand that a secret be guarded, and they expect some working-through that has been missed will now take place. Paradoxically enough, they demand that it *not* take place. The powerfully alienating identification of these patients with these visitors to the ego – what we might call their personal and determinative contribution to their formation and their maintenance – constitutes the clinical and technical knot (not to mention the psychopathological one), the intricate tangle that we as analysts have to face in terms of transgenerational factors.

Severe pathology in adolescence, significantly linked to problems of identity – though we also refer to the retrospective view of adolescence in adult patients in analysis – is the locus in which these transgenerational factors take on greater visibility in the analytic process, but it is probably also the point at which they appear or are structured in a more organized fashion because of the undeniable, specific function of linkage between generations that adolescence performs.

The Oedipal scene

We have considered that the Oedipal scene may be a model of evolution and transformation, or, alternatively, of arrest and distortion. Revisiting the myth of Oedipus (which for us, of course, is no longer a kind of psychic oracular truth), assigning *metapsychological value* as much to the *Oedipal subject* as to the *Oedipal objects,* and keeping in mind the narcissistic dimension as well – as is suggested by the Oedipal *concept of configuration,* proposed by Faimberg (1993) – allows us to redefine the psychic topic of a dual intrapsychic and intersubjective orientation. Taking this perspective in revisiting the myth as

215

a metaphor for the central psychic experience in the development of our emotional and mental life reflects the evolution of, or at least a change in, vertices from which we think about the experience that is generated and developed in the analytic encounter with the adolescent.

Among our patients, isn't it perhaps the adolescent who most challenges us to tolerate the subjective/intersubjective dialectic, the narcissistic dimension/object dimension, pre-Oedipal experiences/Oedipal experiences – a crucial and decisive dialectic for psychic change, for the evolution and construction of a sense of identity?

Isn't it perhaps an adolescent Oedipus who turns to the oracle of Delphi (on the front of which is written "know thyself"), and when he asks it about his future, enters into the paradox of having to discover and recover his past, in order for him to be able to proceed developmentally and undergo a process of becoming? An adolescent Oedipus, who, moved by a cognitive impulse and posing an interrogative about the future, puts forward an unexpressed question about his own identity, his own origins, his own destiny. In the question that Oedipus poses, there is an implicit dilemma about whether the future keeps the past for him – whether his future *is* his past, or whether, on the contrary, his future can be generated by his past as a process of integration and transformation. The riddle Oedipus will confront and resolve is one that the Sphinx poses precisely to adolescents at the doors of Thebes in order to have access to the scenario of adult life, on pain of death if there is no resolution. If we consider that the riddle represents a condensation of some fundamental dimensions that characterize psychic development – identity with its dialectical aspects of continuity and change, the problem of birth and death, the vital cycle of the passage from dependence to autonomy and once again to dependence and generational time that involves its own placement in the interior of subsequent generations – then adolescence becomes a crucial phase in the process of growth, as well as in the constitution of the sense of self and in the assumption of subjectivity. Adolescence as the period of reactivation of the Oedipal configuration, as it is of generational time, is the characteristic place and time of transmission between generations.

The encounter of Oedipus and Laius in the mountain pass epitomizes both the encounter and clash between generations. As clearly explained by Baranes, this encounter has an inherent transformative potential, which positions the young Oedipus in his personal tragic history. However, at another level, we may also say that it carries anti-evolutionary values and risks of stasis and repetition. In other words, on one side there is the subject's embodiment into the story (its historicizing function), and on the other side the risk of the timeless repetition of Oedipal links. In this encounter or clash in the adolescent moment there is a *repetition* of Oedipus' long-ago wound, propagated by Laius (the wheel of Laius' chariot runs over Oedipus' foot,[1] already pierced at birth by the father who abandoned him on Mount Cithaeron), making it impossible to re-signify and transform what has occurred through a historicizing process of *après-coup* (*Nachträglichkeit*).

A myth is generated by other myths, and in turn it generates further myths, so the myth of Oedipus, precisely because it concerns the issue of filicide and parricide, becomes more comprehensible to us if we appreciate its descent from the myth of Laius. Laius, considered by Faimberg as the paradigm of the *narcissistic father,* is perhaps not really such in view of the narcissistic injury and object loss that he himself experienced and transmitted to Oedipus – elements deposited like imprints of traumatic events registered in the self, but not psychically elaborated, not symbolized.

We can also conclude that the oracle who pronounces the prophecy (that Jocasta's son will kill his own father) – as a sort of delusional theory in Laius' internal world – induces him to attempt filicide, mutilating himself in the areas of generativity and creativity, as a continuation of his own childhood experience in which the premature death of Laius' father comes to correspond, in reality, to his unconscious fantasy of having killed him and of deserving the death of his own son in turn. One could say that the body of Oedipus *knows* what his mind *doesn't know* and cannot think.

Oedipus *actualizes* the oracle's prophecies, causing his desires and anxieties to materialize in the present – the desires and anxieties of Laius (parricide and incest). He puts into action his own unconscious experiences, interwoven in an undifferentiated way with his father's unconscious experiences that have been transferred to him, those of a parent who has, with his son, retroposed his own boyhood events, which he could not elaborate and transform.

In this *repetition of relational patterns between generations,* a transmission takes place, not only of fears, fantasies, expectations, and desires, but also of defensive modalities implemented in the face of anxiety, the violence of emotions and psychic suffering – operations like splits, expulsion, denial. How is it that a pronounced split exists between Oedipus' body and mind, a split also maintained by the experience of the extraneousness of the adolescent body, while a split between the family in Thebes and the family in Corinth does not exist? Laius' experience in regard to parenthood and Oedipus' existence and subjectivity determines a destructive realization.

It happens that parents actually abandon their children, and we enter into contact with this abandonment in our psychotherapies with adopted children. What we would like to propose is a fuller explication of what can happen in the parents' internal world and in the quality of their relationship with the child.

The Oedipus who is adopted by Polybus and Merope is not only the rejected, wounded, expelled child, but he also concretizes Laius and Jocasta's rejection and expulsion of their individual aspects of a terror and hate, which are not integrable and cannot be metabolized. At the same time, the fostering of Oedipus implies fostering trust in those ideal aspects of the parents' selves, who know nothing of the destructive aspects and raise their son in an idealized and idealizing way, which – if it is maintained in an exclusive manner and prolonged beyond that necessitated by the developmental process – does not permit anything other than a false reparation of the basic injury.

If we think of Winnicott's statement – in 'Hate in the Countertransference' (1947) – that the mother hates the child before loving him, even before the child hates her and before the child can know that his mother hates him, we realize that it is necessary that a mother can tolerate hating her child without doing anything about it, without negating it or acting on this affect that can be expressed and represented in the transitional space of lullabies, play, and fairy tales.

It is in the period of adolescence, in which a movement of de-idealization and disidentification in regard to the parents is activated (the inner voice which instigates Oedipus' doubt about not looking like his parents) that Oedipus finds himself embroiled in the dual orientation of the developmental and transformative push of individuation, and of the maintenance of non-integration and alienated identifications with split and negated aspects of the parents.

It is that period of adolescence, as mentioned, in which the son invites his parents to make contact with their own adolescence. We think of the image of Laius behaving so provocatively and aggressively toward Oedipus at the crossroads, so that he cannot give recognition or space to the emergence of the adolescent son whom he perceives as unknown and extraneous, an image that stands in contrast to the one Kohut (1977) proposes, of the parent in the Oedipal situation who can hear and demonstrate 'a sparkle of joy and pride' in the face of the son's steps toward conquest of a new and richer capacity for affect and assertiveness.

The assertiveness that we see in Oedipus is transformed into destructive aggression. Parricide, the murder of the symbolic function of the father, has incest as a consequence, which mixes all the generational relationships and therefore all the logical relationships between predecessor and successor, between cause and consequence (Green, 1992). If in regard to incest we are led to consider Oedipus' psychic blindness, we cannot fail to think at the same time of Jocasta's blindness: she is a woman cast as a mother who does not see, does not recognize Oedipus' scar as a sign of his identity, maintaining him as an incestuous son, a son originally generated by her narcissistic need (Jocasta had conceived Oedipus through deceit, by making Laius drunk, as narrated in some but not all versions of the myth). The myth concentrates the essential power of its representation – as Green asserts – precisely on the transgression of the rule of rules, incest with parricide. We think that, paradoxically, through its power of representation, the myth reveals to us the effects of non-representation, of non-symbolization.

The intergenerational modalities of splitting and denial contribute to determining those characteristics of ambiguity, of falsity, that are present in the characters of the myth. It is these modalities that impede the processes of integration of self and objects, which therefore cannot be experienced as internal and true, as authentic, and that obstruct the constitution of a potential space for the dream.

The Oedipus myth, in fact, brings us inside the paradox that as it describes what tragically and concretely happens, indicates what can be accomplished as a complex, organizing experience of the self only in the oneiric space of fantasy and representation. Analogously, adolescence, as a privileged time and place of the reemergence of the Oedipal and transgenerational configuration, brings us into contact with the critical equilibrium between reality and fantasy, action and thought, acting out as a dream not dreamed and the dream as a transformed acting out.

At this point we should recall that Winnicott, in his book *Human Nature* (1988), maintains that in the Oedipus Complex, each component of the triangle must be an entire person, especially the child. In addition, in the chapter, 'Reality and Fantasy,' he describes the Oedipal situation not only from the child's side, but also from the parents'. And, in regard to the children, while he considers that the healthy child becomes capable of having true dreams of genital sexuality, and describes this complex articulation, he states in regard to the parents that

> Parents who are otherwise satisfactory may easily fail in child care by being unable to distinguish clearly between the child's dream and fact. They may present an idea as a fact, or thoughtlessly react to an idea as if it had been an action. They may indeed be more frightened of ideas than of actions. Maturity means, among other things, a capacity for tolerating ideas. (p. 59)

In a fragment of the notes for his autobiography, Winnicott considers how difficult it may be for a man to die without a son who kills him on the imaginary level and survives him.[2]

And in now reconsidering the theme of our film, it is possible to see in the scene of Doc's death, from its oneiric quality, the Oedipal representation of the killing of the father (projectively attributed to Libyan terrorists, who represent Martin's aggressive aspects), which permits, through the fracturing of time, the beginning of a journey, a *subjectifying* trajectory of the adolescent protagonist.

Temporality and trauma

In proposing the metaphor of the film 'Back to the Future,' we introduced the image of a room full of clocks that tell the same time (which are also behind the actual hour) in order to emphasize the centrality of the dimension of adolescent time. In fact, adolescence, as Baranes (1991) maintains, opens up a *new temporality* through bodily transformation, access to adult sexuality and the discovery of genital love, and also through a series of mournings: the loss of the illusions of childhood, the renouncement of the omnipotent fantasy of the internal parents, the abandonment of imaginary narcissistic bisexuality (which includes having to face incompleteness), and the difference and complementarity of the sexes.

Adolescent time encounters adult time, the parents' time, in a reciprocal process thrown into crisis – that short-circuits the times and differences between generations (adolescents make their parents older), which includes – as we have just indicated – the potential for change,

220

but also the risks of stasis and repetition. Points of alteration and arrest, on the parents' part – in the psychic inscription and symbolization of events and experiences relative to the complexity of the Oedipal configuration – remain active and traumatic, so that unprocessed and thus unelaborated *traces come back,* through the phenomenon of repetition. In our opinion, a configuration of this type can be evidenced in certain forms of pathology that arise precisely in this phase of life.

In adolescent clinical disturbances (taking into account different degrees of seriousness), the problem of temporality is truly in the foreground. Adolescent pathology can indicate a delay in time, its arrest and even its absence. In borderline states and especially in psychoses, the time of differentiation is absent – that of individuation and personalization, of becoming and projecting with the future in mind.

In this regard, we think that the psychoanalytic experience can re-establish and again set in motion adolescent time through a *process of posteriority,* in which new meanings generated in the encounter between the adolescent and the analyst give meaning and representation, retrospectively, to the past, which can therefore be transformed (Baranger, Baranger & Mom, 1987). We believe that the recognition and comprehension shared with the adolescent of some traumas can contribute to the activation of a process of *subjective reintegration* of one's own story. We are referring to those events and experiences that were not metabolized and integrated into the *parental environment.* More recently, Baranes (1993) noted in the previous decade, "the transgenerational has acquired the right of citizenship" in the psychoanalytic field, whilst making reference to the risks of seeing arise again

> under the 'transgenerational' subject, a double theme that is profoundly unanalytic: that of an *etiological linear causality* that assigns to a precise external origin certain impasse of symbolization in the treatment, as well as that complementary to the preceding, of a reparative and projective aim that infiltrates that which becomes an untried process … to the preceding generations, rather, that assumption of the intimate stranger in everyone.

From the risk of a simplified linearity in which attention to the transgenerational can aid comprehension of clinical phenomena, we would need to emphasize the complexity of the fact that the single individual, although subjected to the chain of generations like a ring

221

of transmission, must in reality *actively acquire* (*erwerben*) what comes to be transmitted to him through psychic heredity. As Kaës et al. (1993) notes there may be significance in Freud's passing reference to a line in Goethe's *Faust:* "What thou hast inherited from thy fathers, acquire it to make it thine" (1940, p. 80).

Advised of this risk of a simplified linear causality, one can, however, emphasize that interest in this area undoubtedly involves an opening of new perspectives, both in regard to the dimension of psychoanalytic epistemology and the theory of technique. It promotes a further profitable vertex of observation in the psychoanalytic process, to which both the analysand and the analyst contribute with their relationship, a relationship in which subjectivity and intersubjectivity are articulated. It can stimulate the identification of differences, the comparison, and eventual possible integration of different conceptual models.

There are some nodal points at which consideration of the transgenerational seems applicable, albeit problematically, to the extension of theory and clinical practice which are part of the current frontiers of development in psychoanalysis, although in different clinical and theoretical paradigms. One of these may be a more or less radical reconsideration of the genesis of individual pathology, seen not only in terms of intrapsychic conflict, but mainly in terms of the organization, development, and distortion of object relationships.[3] Another frontier of current development in psychoanalysis is the progressive reconsideration of the centrality of projective processes in establishing the connotation and quality of internal objects, with the foreground given over to mutual cross–projective identification processes within the relationship.

Independently of the specific paradigm of self–psychology, which has contributed much on this topic, greater attention to narcissism and to the processes of forming an individual identity can be seen as a common trend in psychoanalytic research, and this too is linked to the transgenerational theme.

Finally, there is another cluster of development, which seems, by the way, the most specific to research on the transgenerational. It concerns articulation of the process by which the *object* transmits unconscious phantasmatic reality, as distinct from the process by which the subject receives this, and the consequent identification of the mechanisms and effects of those processes.

In looking at the panorama of international literature on this subject, one can see many differing conceptual and clinical accents.[4]

222

They range from the purest and most extreme positions, which view the transgenerational as an embedded repetition in the individual of an unelaborated psychic scenario of earlier generations (though it is somewhat refined by its ironic connotation, in the image proposed by Diatkine (1984) of a child inhabited like a castle of ghosts), to positions that emphasize what we define as *unelaborated elements* (see Bonaminio, 1987; Bonaminio, Carratelli & Giannotti, 1989; Bonaminio, Di Renzo & Giannotti, 1993) that are transferred – and absorbed via identification processes – into the broader sphere of the contribution that the parents' inner world makes to the formation of the individual self. It is interesting to underline the fact that, independently of these different accents or meanings, what nonetheless appears to be emphasized in regard to transgenerational factors is the element of trauma inherent in the unconscious transmission, and the characteristic of extraneousness, of alienation.

In my previous works, I [Vincenzo Bonaminio] have in particular emphasized the traumatic effects of the transmission of the object's phantasmatic reality in the organization of psychopathology in terms of ego-alien identifications, especially in reference to Winnicott's (1969) conception.

It is common in psychoanalysis, when specific subjects are addressed in depth – as with the transgenerational – to experience the revelation that Freud *has already talked about it*. In fact, one can observe that the major portion of classical concepts in psychoanalysis revolve around the theme that today we call transgenerational, which by rights, then, forms a part of psychoanalytic doctrine and its development. Among the many relevant citations in Freud's writings, we choose in this context to mention the following reference to his theory of the process of identification – specifically, the "origin of the ego ideal … for, behind it lies hidden an individual's first and most important identification, his identification with the father [or rather with the parents, as Freud adds in a footnote] in his own personal prehistory" (1923, p. 31).

Part 2

Clinical report by Vincenzo Bonaminio

I will refer to the ideas of this specific conceptualization in the clinical material that follows: the case of Osvaldo. This case exemplifies the intrusion of the parents' unelaborated fantasy on the individual, in the very texture of the here-and-now clinical relationship. My experience with Osvaldo caused me to reflect on the nature of anxieties and persecutory defenses, and on their function of integrating the self, when threats of disintegration and annihilation do not find a more sophisticated way of being contained. In other words, the acute sense of persecution – supported by environmental action as well – plays a role in becoming the 'armament' of the self, indispensable for its psychic survival.

This consideration is tightly interwoven with two other clinical aims that underlie my presentation. First, I will try to show the *active expression of these persecutory anxieties in the transference and countertransference* through the use of projective identification and the effects that it engendered in the analyst. Personally, I am not a supporter of "projective identification" as an early and ubiquitous primitive mechanism, underlying all psychic functioning in the consulting room. In fact, I believe that a similar expansion of the concept which has found a place in certain areas of contemporary psychoanalysis may in effect dilute and water down its meaning. Rather, I am in favor of a more restricted and limited use of the concept, helpful in situations in which there is a predominance of powerful psychotic anxieties of disintegration and loss of identity.

My second aim, which I hope is also clinically evident, relates to psychoanalytic technique, and especially to the change in technique necessitated at a certain point as a result of the transformations that the powerful bombardment of the boy's identification brought about in the analyst's attitude, activating in him a different *comprehension* (both emotional and cognitive) of the patient's communication.

Background of the case

Osvaldo began a three-times-weekly analysis at 16 years of age. He was referred to me by a colleague who had an initial consultation with his parents. My colleague also met with Osvaldo on one occasion. He had always been a studious boy with good results in school, much to his parents' satisfaction, but his performance had gradually begun to slip. At the beginning of treatment he was in his penultimate year of a private high school.

The parents were civil servants in their early 50s, his mother a math teacher and his father a senior administrative employee. The

224

family, which included a daughter two years older than Osvaldo, had "always been very close-knit." But father's "important job" "forced" him to move to a different city every six or seven years. In fact, the father's move to the north of Italy, and Osvaldo moving with him to attend university there, caused the premature conclusion of his treatment after approximately four and a half years of analysis.

There is a prologue to this story. The first time I spoke on the phone with the father, I noticed that he never directly mentioned the nature of Osvaldo's problem, although the reasons he had been recommended for analysis had been clearly stated by my psychoanalyst colleague. The parents had consulted my colleague in the first place because the boy had broken down in tears a few months earlier and "confessed" to his anxiety about being homosexual, causing the parents to feel "desperate and confused."

The analysis was to reveal that Osvaldo's anxiety about being gay was actually "an unthinkable thought" long shared in the family. And the episode of his weeping was a kind of collusive falsification that generated the temporary revelation of a secret, one designated as Osvaldo's problem. I will say more about this later and I will try to show that the boy was able to make use of the secret by staking out a private space for the self. In regard to the secret as a constructive process of the adolescent mind, it is worth considering the etymology of the word: it comes from the Latin *secernere*, "to sift or secrete," yielding something taken out and set aside, something distinct from a pre-existing matrix.

Osvaldo felt threatened by anxieties regarding his sexual identity and by his unrelenting persecutory fantasies. These fantasies focused on schoolmates making fun of him, scornfully calling him "sissy" or "queer." He was anxious because he didn't know whether his friends were looking "through" him and seeing that he was a homosexual or if he were only homosexual because they made him feel that way.

He had a limited group of friends, consisting of a few former classmates from grammar school and two girls of his age who lived in different cities and were his "pen" and "telephone" friends. With these two girls he felt at ease, believing he understood them and they understood him. He felt strongly attracted to but at the same time rejected and despised by his schoolmates. He wanted to but could not share anything with them: afternoons at the disco, rides on a motorbike, clothing, sports.

After a few months of analysis, I began to picture some prevailing features in Osvaldo's social life. They were not recounted to me in terms of a consistent self-experience, in the way I am relating them now; rather, they were *discharged* into sessions as bits and pieces of interactions, mixed and confused chunks of the patient's fantasy life, his thoughts and anxieties.

I mention the way Osvaldo presented in the early stage of analysis in order to show how this mode made it gradually possible to single out some areas of the patient's functioning – and of the transference and countertransference – that were marked by what I consider alienating identification with aspects of the primary objects that intruded on his self, which was organized chiefly around paranoid-schizoid anxieties and defenses.

Our first meeting

My first meeting with Osvaldo occurred in the courtyard of my office complex. We had arranged the appointment by phone for a Wednesday afternoon at 1:30 p.m., but I was detained at the university clinic where I work in the mornings. Breathless, I arrived at the building with five minutes to spare. I was concerned that I would encounter my potential new patient outside. In fact, more precisely, I had the fleeting sensation of being watched, outside my awareness, from a hidden point near the building. By now on the home stretch, I noticed from a short distance away a man in his 50s next to a younger figure of the same height. It seemed that both were examining the row of buttons below the intercom at the main door.

As I reached them, the man asked me if I knew Professor Bonaminio, with the rhetorical and falsely questioning tone of one who already knows who is before him. When I introduced myself, what I got instead of a greeting was the man's swift movement to his left, as if to free the field, while his right arm, from around his son's shoulder, almost shoved the boy in my direction: "This is Osvaldo."

I saw a tall boy with a proportionate build but hair styled in a manner that was different from the current fashions. The wavy hairdo framed a face almost as pale as wax – an ageless face, neither young nor old, neither male nor female, with an ineffable expression. He greeted me with a kind of impenetrable grimace.

Once in the consulting room, Osvaldo was immobile, almost paralyzed, in the armchair in front of me, his face ashen and his eyes fixed on me. I was about to formulate a facilitating comment but before I could put it into words, there was a sudden change in the atmosphere. Osvaldo dropped his silence and said: "I know *what* you are: a psychologist, a psychiatrist ... *something* like that ... but you can't help me." I told him I understand he knows *what* I am, but maybe he is scared about not knowing *who* I am. "I didn't want to come here," he continued, "but it was my parents, my mother, who brought me first to another doctor, and he sent me here ... My mother couldn't come; she works at this hour ... My father had to come get me at school ... But do we always have to meet at this time? The other days I finish at 2:30 ... I can't be here at 1:30."

I told him that he was also asking what I wanted from him, whether I would restrict him to coming at a time that was inconvenient for both him and his mother. Is this why he thinks that I can't help him?

"You can't help me because my things are not psychological, and besides I can't come at this time – I will be at school or at lunch," he retorted.

"You are telling me," I said, "that you can't come at this time, which is indeed inconvenient for a student like you. But you are simultaneously making me understand that maybe you expected to be able to come at other times, more adaptable to your schedule." His friends, he replied, would *suspect* if he always left school early, and he has no intention of letting them know that he goes to a psychologist; they would say he's really crazy ... not even his sister knows that he came here today, and he doesn't want her to know that he goes to a psychologist either.

To myself, I thought that this potential patient, who had suddenly awakened from his cadaver-like immobility, was almost forcing inside me the sensation of a contrast between external requests and his own needs, which he did not know how to distinguish from those of his parents, with whom he felt confused. I limited myself to recognizing that this time was indeed a little unusual, and in reality I had thought of being able to see him later in the afternoon – assuming, of course, that he was available to come and begin to talk to me about himself and the reason he accepted his parents' proposal to consult a psychoanalyst.

He told me the other psychoanalyst was older and had a moustache, looked at him with a fixed gaze, and asked a heap of questions. Osvaldo told him everything, he "discharged" himself, and that was enough. Of course, he will tell me everything, he said, and of course we will talk to each other. I am younger and maybe I

227

would be able to understand more, or maybe not; on the contrary, who knows if I have ever seen cases like his?

I said that he seemed to have an idea of who I was, and maybe was less certain that I could not help him. Perhaps – I said to him – he could take personal responsibility for seeing whether this arrangement was possible, and I proposed that we meet another one or two times, then he could decide. (To myself, I added that I considered him my interlocutor, not his parents, and that if they wanted to, they could consult another psychoanalyst.) I said that I had learned he was very worried and anxious about something that pertained to his sexuality, and it was for this reason he was recommended for analysis.

Osvaldo flushed when I pronounce the word *sexuality*: he sat forward on the chair, as though he wanted to get up and leave but at the same time get closer to me. He also seemed reassured by what I had said about his parents and what I knew about the other analyst. His redness and his movement on the chair – strangely contradictory – expressed a contrast between his being able to trust the object and run away from it.

The patient told me that the other psychoanalyst's office was full of books, like mine, but the building was nicer: from the main door one entered immediately into his office, and there was no need to go through a building as there was here. Everyone could have seen him from inside this building, from the windows, as he waited to come up. But if I opened the main door to him immediately, maybe they would think he was going to see a friend or an acquaintance.

At the end of the session I told Osvaldo he was taking into consideration the possibility of assuming responsibility to see me, but under certain conditions that I had better keep firmly in mind.

I felt that during our first meeting "something had happened," yet I was not sure if he would come back. At the following meeting, scheduled at a later time, he arrived on time and out of breath, which also happened the following week. He said he would accept therapy, "taking for granted" that this was his only course of action. Nevertheless, he often said he "cannot be helped by words" or by "a psychological treatment" because his "problems are not psychological."

The first phase of the analysis

In retrospect, I can say that with these words Osvaldo was "pre-announcing" to me his terror about *physical* and *bodily* sensations, particularly in the perineal area. These sensations were related to

228

a fantasy of his having a vagina near his anus, "another hole" from which, when he was excited, "a fluid" came out. All of this made him feel ashamed. He felt dirty and loathsome, different from others, and he did not know whether he was "male or female or homosexual." There was only "this palpitating hole" and "excitation getting at his throat," followed by shame and loathing for himself, and the conviction that others "know" and "see" all that is occurring within him.

Osvaldo would need time to be able to put into words and thereby communicate his unnamable and unrepresentable physical sensations. I needed some time to create a facilitating environment in the sessions so that he could start giving form to these persecutory physical sensations. Such a forum made it possible to name and recognize the sensations and relate them to a fantasy. At the beginning, these persecutory and foreign physical sensations could only be *discharged* by evacuation onto me.

In the first phase, in fact – approximately the first ten months of treatment – clinical communication was characterized by what I would call a persistent emotional turbulence in the countertransference. For example, during some sessions, I felt invaded by his "machine-gun-fire" way of talking. Often, in the constant stream of talk, he chewed his words. At times, the slight but automatic reaction on my face – a spontaneous expression of my emotions – clearly signaled my struggle to catch his missing words. My facial expression then became the focus of his near-delusional attention: "What's wrong? What happened? Why do you look at me like that?" he would say. At that point, his very bright and darting eyes would look carefully at my whole body, at times looking around it, until his gaze rested near my right hip. In this way, Osvaldo seemed to be trying to block the *origin* of my emotional expression, which he felt as very persecutory.

The first time this happened, I looked at the table on my right-hand side, as though I had left something embarrassing on it. Later, the inhibition of this micro–acting-out, triggered by my observation of Osvaldo's eye movements, shifted the action to another level: the discharge now moved inside me, making me experience transient and fleeting sensations of alteration in my body structure. As though in a manifestation of depersonalization, I felt some kind of a growth – or, alternatively, a hole, a pit – in my right hip.

Quite often, aside from these episodes where the intrusion of the patient's words actually altered my inner state, my countertransference

229

was one of feeling examined, scrutinized, and controlled. I realized that Osvaldo was making me feel exactly what he feared he would get from me: control, examination, and bodily inspection; and that, in the complex situation of transference-countertransference, there was a reversal of his relationship with his primary object, felt as an intrusive, penetrating disorganization with a traumatic quality. But in the beginning this consideration was only a thought, a necessary clinging on my part to a clinical model – which did not, however, generate the calming, emotional resonance in me that knowledge sometimes brings, being constricted as I was by the concreteness Osvaldo induced.

My interpretations of this configuration in the here and now of the session did not seem to help with his desire to "loosen the grip of the vice." Rather, it was more important for me to find a space in which to position my speech, given his torrential, uninterrupted output. Nor were there any nonverbal signs indicating his availability to listen. When I did succeed in inserting myself into the dialogue, by advancing an observation on what in that moment seemed to be happening between us, Osvaldo instantly walled himself off in silence, gazing in my direction in an empty and "watery" way – as though he were temporarily without a mind but an inert body was present.

The recurring image in my countertransference was of an inanimate mechanism set up in order to keep me at bay. I realized my attention to the quality of his communications, crucial to me surviving his narrative flow, made my presence too "hot" for him, and made it necessary for him to turn our relationship into something mechanical.

A vignette from a session in the seventh month of treatment illustrates this, as well as my beginning awareness of the need to change the orientation of my comments. Osvaldo arrived on time, rushing in like a runaway. He talked about a schoolmate who "whispered something" about him while he was walking through his classroom the preceding day. He added that his grandmother criticized his spending too much time watching television and thought he should study more. She "doesn't mind her own fucking business." The previous night he was up after everyone else had gone to sleep watching TV. He talked on the phone with Linda, who was already planning her 18th birthday party, although he hadn't thought about doing that for himself at all.

The patient piled story upon story faster and faster, so I could hardly follow him. When I was able to get in a word, I told him he seemed to be saying he was worried about the thoughts induced by watching late TV shows. Maybe he was afraid I would criticize him, like his schoolmate or his grandmother. Perhaps he was also afraid I wouldn't think his thoughts suitable for a 17-year-old. Osvaldo retorted that he was not worried at all and that my comment was irrelevant. Then he went on as before.

He added further tales and impressions: at school, everyone wears Levi jeans and bomber jackets, and he wondered what he would look like in them; maybe they wouldn't look good on him. He should resume tennis training. On TV, he saw tennis players training with a machine that "spits out" balls. (I thought to myself that maybe he is scared by the lively way in which I put together bits of his speech, giving them a potentially "dangerous" meaning.) I told Osvaldo that he has let me know he doesn't agree with my way of combining the things he has told me. He seemed not to take heed of my comment, but then said his mother "thinks she knows everything" about him: she watches how he eats, knows how many phone calls he makes; she is just as worried when he goes out as when he does not.

Which of the two of us, at this point, had dangerously reduced the distance between us? Me, with my comments and recognition of connections? Or the patient, equating me *tout court* with his mother?

I understood at this point that if I were to make a transference interpretation, I would immediately become that "omniscient mother" from whom the patient was trying to escape. I asked him what he meant when he said his mother thinks she knows everything about him; he replied that he feels pursued by her – she is always "on him." I suggested this might be a reason why he watches TV late at night, in order to be on his own for a while. For a moment, he seemed to feel relieved by this different view of the situation. "My mother," he said, "is eaten up by anxiety! This is why she is so skinny – my father says that, too. He is calmer, but he pretends ..."

This passage from a session represents, albeit schematically, an initial turning point in the analysis. That is, directing my attention to the content of the patient's accounts, to noticing his daily disagreements with his parents, the fights he has just had with his sister, his schoolmates' persecution of him – *without relating these to the situation of the relationship between us* – gradually determined a transformation, in the sense of a reduction of the pressure of projective identification, which modified the atmosphere of the sessions. Osvaldo began to show interest in expressing himself in a way that – without losing

231

the characteristics of a river pouring forth, as described above – nevertheless assumed a more tolerable cadence, not only for me but also for Osvaldo himself.

The penetrating alien as an unspeakable secret

With this new climate established, Osvaldo started to bring in feelings like shame, the sensation of being loathsome, feeble, without boundaries – a "horrible secret" about himself. Externalization through enactment of this horrible secret swiftly alternated with tales about it. Uncertainly presented at the beginning, these tales became increasingly elaborate.

Two major themes emerged and were distinguishable only in retrospect: his masturbatory fantasy and the "unspeakable secret." I will start by outlining Osvaldo's primitive sexual fantasies, often accompanied by masturbation, which took two forms: one was explicitly anal and the other was the rhythmical movement of his legs until ejaculation occurred, experienced as a flow of a disgusting and dirty fluid. It was possible to reconstruct a central fantasy from the bits and pieces Osvaldo offered, which included slight varieties in content: the exciting sight of an erect penis followed by submission to it through anal penetration. This was represented as a "pounding jackhammer," penetration with a mechanical and unceasing rhythm.

A long period of analytic work was necessary to reconstruct the narrative of this central fantasy and give it meaning. At first, Osvaldo brought a feeling of shame only in the physical sensations he experienced as external and overpowering: the impact of seeing the form of the penis, the thumping rhythm, the emergence of the penis tip (the "notch") to "fill" his anus, and so on. Only after the disconnected pieces were put together into a sequence – showing, for example, the relationship between the sight of the penis and subsequent anal penetration– was it gradually possible to propose a more articulated interpretation to Osvaldo.

I think for him, the erotization of bodily openings (anus, mouth, and even eyes) was a way to capture and control the object. For instance, the erect penis was threatening and exciting at the same time. Because of its intrusive quality, anal incorporation became the only way to control it from inside and to keep it at bay. The diffuse sensuousness of various areas in his body and the erotization of partial objects were felt as the only way to cope with a sense of loss,

232

waste, emptiness, and non–existence. The "palpitating hole" was the patient himself, his lonely and abandoned self.

The other theme in this phase of the analysis was the unspeakable secret. Physical sensations related to the masturbatory fantasy over-powered Osvaldo and were felt to be an unspeakable secret, which everybody knows, or anybody can come to know. A "transparent inside" was felt as available to anyone wishing to enter it with their penetrating gaze (as I was to interpret to him on more than one occasion). This secret could not be protected by any barrier, despite the high constraining psychic fences he erected to hide it. Moreover, Osvaldo did not just talk about it as a personal problem. He wore his problem, as it were, in the transference relationship with his analyst – a problem which insinuated itself constantly in persecutory fashion.

I realized after some time that the patient's gasping "machine-gun" speech was not just a way of controlling me, after having avoided and hesitated about the confession of his "sodomization" (the patient's own word) fantasies. It seemed increasingly clear that his way of speaking was that of a person in flight, someone fleeing from something, or someone who wanted to hide, a person who revealed his secret without, however, ever being able to say it all before it was too late. His way of speaking hurriedly and insistently, and therefore at times incomprehensibly, seemed to be that of a person speaking excitedly whilst running to catch a train. Some of these images were gradually represented to the patient and contributed in some way to soothing the atmosphere that had been unceasingly breathless, making Osvaldo feel understood.

The configuration of the unspeakable secret theme seems here to have a special quality of its own. The paradox in which Osvaldo was entangled was that coming to therapy meant, to himself and his Oedipal objects, the revelation of a secret that should have remained hidden, which linked up – as a personal contribution to the paradox of his own identity – with the injunction to represent an aspect of parental identity that had to be kept secret, but was instead being revealed by him. In other words, a split-off aspect of the object's psychic reality was transmitted and delivered with the request that it be kept secret. But this split-off and rejected aspect, this inadmissible, cast-off element demanded the existence it had been denied, in a kind of return of the repressed; it demanded its rights of citizenship like someone under house arrest. Osvaldo was the location of this house arrest, and he was contaminated by it.

In a session during the second year of treatment, the patient came in breathless and gasped, almost unable to speak, "I got her, I didn't let her get me, sorry, but I don't want to –". At first I didn't understand the meaning of his words, though I sensed he was telling me he avoided someone or something. I said: "You seem happy about something that just happened, something you managed to avoid, but I don't know what. You talk as if I knew, as if I were always with you. But you have to explain to me what happened, otherwise I can't understand. Or perhaps you want me not to understand?"

The patient retorted angrily: "Always this psychological *jerking off!*[5] Too much is too much!" I said he could not tolerate the smallest distance between himself and me; it's always too much. "Only if you feel I am inside you or you inside me, do you feel sure to keep me at bay," I remarked. Osvaldo stopped short for a moment, apparently under the effects of a "burst of heat" – some strong affect that I was not immediately able to identify. He looked at me, almost smiled, and said: "No, nothing – the usual mental *jerking off.* Something came to my mind ... no ... nothing." There was tension in the air. Silently I made some associations: mine is "psychological jerking off," while his is "mental jerking off." I think his burst of affect expressed a sodomization fantasy induced by my words "inside you." I felt "crisscrossed" by perverse fantasies.

Osvaldo told me that, while he was about to press the doorbell of my office, he had turned around and seen that "she" was coming, motioning toward the door with his head. He meant my colleague – whom he had immediately recognized as female, since the beginning of analysis, because of her soft steps in the corridor, although he had never met her. "I was sure she would come in here, too, and in fact she inserted a key. But I didn't want her to see I was coming here, to a psychoanalyst. I didn't want her to know I am your patient, because she might understand that I come here because I am a queer, because of my thoughts ... So I moved to one side and pretended I was combing my hair, using the glass door as though it were a mirror ..." When he showed me how he touched his hair, I noticed him moving in an effeminate way, like someone who was ridiculing gays, a behavior he did not usually show.

I told him: "It must be a terrible sensation to be always on the verge of being discovered, because you cannot be safe anywhere, safe from gazes that 'read inside you.' But in order to mask what you don't want seen, you are forced to display it through a caricature of yourself." I was hinting at the fact that this caricature, which he wore like an outfit, at least provided him with boundaries, limits and a certain identity.

When I said "read inside," he added that he felt "like an open book." He said this with a feeling of surrender. But then, with triumph and revenge, he said that he also "figures it all out" himself.

"So," I said, "you understood who that woman was following you. And you are just as sure she understood you were going to a psychoanalyst because you are a homosexual." Angry, Osvaldo said only women and queers go to psychoanalysts. The persecutory and intrusive quality of the emotions surrounding this episode, enacted on the doorstep, revealed his feeling of being a runaway who had to keep a secret – or rather, that he himself was the secret that must be masked, but in fact could not be hidden.

An early psychological meaning of the patient's strange sensations

The end of high school was fantasized by Osvaldo as freedom from his schoolmates' persecutions. At college, he said, he would be a *new person*. He would be able to start over again. Unfortunately, that was not the way it turned out; those friends who had so cruelly teased him at least gave him boundaries and identity, while the lack of them felt to him like a loss and left him confused. His new colleagues at the university were "faceless" persons: they brushed past him without seeing him, and for Osvaldo, feelings of desperate loneliness and sadness emerged.

The next session I will describe, occurring at the end of the patient's second year of analysis, revealed how the process of a gradual realization of strange physical sensations related to his orifices – and the sense of desperate abandonment and loneliness that could not otherwise be represented – which now made an appearance in Osvaldo's transference relationship to me.

It was the first session after a weekend separation. Osvaldo said that during the weekend he was "at home alone." He did not go out at all. He did not lunch in a restaurant with his parents. He did not even go for an outing with the Catholic youth group he sometimes joined, because Carlotta would be there, and he thought she liked him. Last time, she was "too loving" with him, and he did not want to feel terror and disgust with himself as he did on that occasion. Carlotta started to hug him when they were alone. She took his hand and made him touch her breast. He understood that he "should do something," so he fondled her breasts a little, then moved his hand down and Carlotta let him do it. He reached her pubis and felt a deep terror. Carlotta put her hand inside his trousers. He could not say if his penis was erect. He only knew he was sweating "around there." He did not feel anything.

But this was not what he wanted to tell me. He wanted to tell me he had "a terrible thought during the weekend, which, if it were true, would be the end." The thought was that I could be included among the persons whom he fantasized about sodomizing him. It could not be so, he said. It would mean that he had no restraint, and it would be confirmation that he is "definitely a queer." In addition, he was disgusted with himself because he was contaminating me. He felt like shit. If this was the way things were, then it would be better to give up everything and let himself go.

This was the first time Osvaldo reported a fantasy and did not feel it arriving with the usual foreign and persecutory quality. I said that I didn't really think this thought meant he was "definitely a queer." I added that he had made me understand how lonely he felt during the weekend – alone with his feelings, thoughts and fear of Carlotta, and also abandoned by me. To think of my body, my penis, including me among his sodomizers, was a way of feeling less alone and abandoned, to feel he had some meaning and was not a "nothing."

"What do you mean, 'nothing?'" the patient asked, half-scared and half-curious. I said that at times, he felt he did not exist; he is *no-thing* and has no meaning. By incorporating my penis within himself, in his anus, he felt himself to be included in me. With his anus, like a mouth, he took hold of me and does not let me go.

At first Osvaldo was perplexed by my words, and then said I had already said something similar. But it was not possible, he went on, for him to have these thoughts about me. "And what if I get excited? The session would be … No! No! It is not possible." He was ashamed of coming here with such thoughts. Then he said: "I wish it were as you say – loneliness, abandonment, sadness … it would be better for me. But the only truth is that I am a queer!"

I told Osvaldo he was afraid of feelings like loneliness, abandonment, and sadness because these feelings could not be controlled, while bodily sensations could.

It was clear that passive erotization and *the need to be intruded upon in order to be included* were the modes used to recover a sense of existence in the relationship, following the sense of exclusion and evacuation, which was disorganizing for the self. To get in contact with these experiences of abandonment, of non-existence, coincided in this phase of analysis with a change in Osvaldo's relationship with me. During the sessions, his persecutory fantasies were less strong and the pressure eased. It seemed that things gradually opened up after this crucial point, inaugurating a stage in which thoughts, memories, and fragments of current interactions were brought to the analysis – a period in which the image of passivity and homosexuality that was ascribed to the patient and made him anxious did not correspond with the experience the boy had of himself. And the quality of the transference also began to change in this direction, in the sense that he seemed more cohesive and less anxious, as if he were finally creating a sort of order in himself. In a similar fashion, the quality of my countertransference improved: my emotional turbulence declined and my listening became calmer. There was more space for the privacy of thoughts and emotions, and I had the sensation of having before me a very sad person who was certainly suffering – not simply a patchwork heap of highly erotized fantasies as the only modality through which the self and the object could exist.

In this new climate, a distinction emerged for Osvaldo between his feelings and those of others, between the "me" and "not me." This was exemplified by a session in the third year of analysis. The patient brought in a memory that came to his mind after a fight with his father. For his seventh or eighth birthday, he was given a much-desired tape-player. His father, commenting scornfully on his joy and excitement, cut off his intense pleasure by saying that he was "acting like a girl" and that "he looked like a queer." Osvaldo remembers that he hid in the bathroom, felt humiliated, and reverted to an autistic-like ritual that he had used as a small child to calm himself: he rolled up a towel and twirled it rapidly in front of him.

More recently, during tennis practice, which his mother usually attended, Osvaldo had demonstrated a particular backhand shot to impress her. He had told her it was "like Gabriella Sabatini's backhand." His mother's reaction, however, was to scold him: she said Osvaldo would do better to compare himself to a male player like Lendl, because the other boys or the tennis coach might hear him and, by inference, would think badly of him for saying he was like a woman player. From that moment on, the boy said, he pretended to be a fan of several male tennis champions to please his mother and calm her anxieties. But inside he felt that his preference for female players grew stronger, as a kind of silent but individualizing opposition to his mother. Osvaldo later related this relational dynamic to much earlier episodes, events, and sensations – for example, the humiliation he felt when he was in nursery school and was made to go to dance class with his sister at an all-girls' school.

Speaking of the patient's fight with his father, I told Osvaldo that he was trying to understand which were his own feelings and which were his father's feelings – just as, in his memory, his overwhelming joy was different from the scorn he felt coming from his father. Of course, what was important in these accounts was not the factual reality (which I was inclined to believe), but the quality of subtle discrimination between the patient's own and his parents' feelings and experiences, as well as the subsequent process of giving new meaning to their mental contents in the act of discrimination between *me* and *not me*. This sort of revision of the self and its objects evolved with the process of individualization appropriate to adolescence.

Then I said to Osvaldo that perhaps he wondered what *my* feelings for him were. He replied that he had always "taken for granted" that I felt the same disgust and scorn for his fantasies he himself felt. But now he thought that, when I listened to him, maybe I was not doing it only for the money.

At this point, a certain objection did not escape me – which I posed for myself at first, in hearing the account of these episodes and memories: that is, that I could be witnessing the boy's delusional interpretation, projected onto his parents, with the aim of arousing in the transference a sort of "collusive belief." An inclination of this type could not be excluded, but it must be seen on the inside as a circularity of projections, in which the boy attributed disgraceful qualities and characteristics to the object in a mirroring reflection of the humiliating attributions of which he was the recipient.

On the other hand, it also seemed evident that in being able to bring to the analysis memories and experiences such as those described, where Osvaldo appeared capable of exploring in a more articulated way the image of himself assigned to him, he allowed himself to put forward his own experience during this phase of the analysis, his own vision of the parents' internal world, in particular his father's, with some of the passive connotations attributed to him.

The entry into analysis of another memory image – which had the features of a screen memory – offered a picture rich in articulated relational experience, no longer flat and one-directional. I considered it in terms of the transference one of the scenarios of "multi-entrances" that Laplanche and Pontalis (1964) speak of. Osvaldo remembers playing with his sister on the grass near the apartment building where he lived as a child in a rather poor neighborhood. The two children were constantly bothered by a teenage bully who stole their ball. The children called their father for help, but when he came out, the youth taunted him with name-calling and threats of a sexual nature. So, the father "turned tail" with the children and went upstairs, after vainly seeking help from the janitor. The offensive young man rang their doorbell, continued to shout insults, and dared the father to come down.

The patient remembered the sense of undefended humiliation in that episode which became the prototype of other events in which his father's "passivity" was something he was tainted by. In a subsequent session, revisiting this episode and seeing it in relation to his current anxieties about his fantasies of being sodomized, Osvaldo commented, "these anxieties are not my own," they are like ghosts, and perhaps they are "the same ghosts that my father had, when he was my age, and who knows – maybe my grandfather Osvaldo as well."

I think the expression "these anxieties are not my own" was the culminating moment, so to speak, in which – in the interior of the analytic relationship – the beginnings of a discrimination between the patient's own emotions and those of the other were at last achieved. His own internal world could be distinguished from that of the other – a discrimination that could be realized only in the analytic relationship because it could be said to the analyst and felt in some way as something outside the self. In addition, this distinction was meaningfully tied to the destruction of the secret, whose "end," so to speak, had been announced when Osvaldo catastrophically revealed that, if the thought were expressed that his analyst could become one of the objects of his fantasies of being sodomized, then that would be "the end."

Concluding remarks

In selecting this clinical material for presentation, I realize that I have not done full justice to the richness of the psychoanalytic process and its multiple facets. My aim has been to show some aspects of the patient's fight – as well as the analyst's struggle in the countertransference – to begin to integrate foreign sensations and alien affects, and to reach the first realization of the distinction between "me" and "not me."

Osvaldo's analysis continued for one more year, but it was the work in the first three years that was crucial in allowing him to make these early integrations. I am aware that the premature termination of treatment was not only due to the external factor of the family's move to another city.

Reflecting on the course and outcome of this analysis, a statement by Winnicott (1962) on the aim of psychoanalytic treatment gives me some comfort. He observes that in psychoanalysis with some patients, one has to ask not only *how much* one can be allowed to do, but also *how little* needs be done.

I began this paper by describing my countertransference experience and the dynamic of the clinical relationship with Osvaldo in order to convey the traumatic quality of the experience of an object that intrudes, penetrates, disorganizes, evacuates, and deposits split-off parts the subject is then forced, as it were, to deal with through pathological identification (alienating or ego-alien identification). I think my quasi-persecutory countertransference feelings with this patient and the concrete, albeit transitory changes in my bodily sensations give a sufficient idea of how unelaborated parental objects may be reproduced in the analytic scenario – as veritable foreign bodies that must somehow be circumscribed and/or absorbed.

I shall conclude by describing a subsequent episode that shows the concrete way in which parental objects intruded on the clinical setting by way of acting out, an unexpected and unforeseeable enactment that raised quite a few technical problems. I should like to make it clear that I do not ascribe a wholly factual meaning to the episode, rather I tend to see it as the performance and intrusion of an emotional construct of which Osvaldo was a part, as both recipient and contributor. Moreover, in complex and serious situations such as the one I will describe, acting out contains emotions and relational configurations which cannot be thought about or represented, and can only be communicated through acting out, until the time is ripe for them to be represented and transformed. The therapist's function should be to take in these emotions and relational configurations, to think about them and transform them, even if the technical challenge – which is the analyst's, not the patient's – is not to retreat defensively from them, and at the same time not collude and reproduce the acting out by intruding on and usurping a private space.

This was the episode, the single additional brief encounter I had with the patient's parents – or rather the encounter that was forced on me. Significantly, it took the form of an intrusion on the setting established for Osvaldo, during a session when Osvaldo did not come. For a moment, they took his place and invaded his space. Osvaldo was to attend his last two sessions before leaving for a study trip to the UK. When I heard knocking at the door, expecting to find Osvaldo, I was surprised to see both of his parents, asking timidly to enter and explain something. My worry, beyond my surprise, was to preserve Osvaldo's setting and, at the same time, not mortify his parents. So, in a clumsy and uneasy way, I said, "please enter, but only for a few moments, because you know this is Osvaldo's space. I will tell him that I met you." They replied that the study trip had been modified suddenly, so Osvaldo had to leave immediately. Instead of calling me on the phone, they thought it would be better to come and say so directly, also because they wanted to meet their son's therapist. I understood that it was clearly a quasi-conscious enactment, however, for the reasons described above, and I decided to let them enter without any further comment.

After I had made some suggestions about the meaning their intrusion might have for their son and their relationship with him, the father made room for himself, as it were, by shoving a message toward me, an intrusion of his unconscious, just as he had done at our first meeting. I took the occasion on parting to recommend that he consider the possibility of therapy for himself.

"This has nothing to do with the situation," the father blurted out, "but I was wondering ... you're an expert ... I read in the papers that a 50-year-old man with a wife and two children discovered he was ... homosexual – he left his family and started a new life. Is something like that really possible? How is it possible not to realize sooner? How could he have a wife and two children?"

Portions of this chapter were translated by Gina Atkinson.

Notes

1 The version of the Oedipus myth we are referring to can be found in Tripp, Edward (1970). "Pelops at Olympia." *Crowell's Handbook of Classical Mythology.* New York: Thomas Crowell Company, 93–103.

2 This fragment is included in "D. W. Winnicott as a Person," written after his death by his widow, Clare Winnicott (1977).

3 Of course, this has been the so-called "relational turn" in North American psychoanalysis, which significantly bridged the gap between the two rims of the Atlantic. From the European perspective, both in training and in clinical practice, the assumption that analysis is fundamentally a relational affair between two people talking in the analytic room (Freud), is a long-established matter of fact. I [Vincenzo Bonaminio] touch on this issue in my 2008 paper published in *The Psychoanalytic Quarterly*, "The person of the analyst" (chapter 5 of this volume). There, it is also specified that while this turn generated a school in the American psychoanalytic tradition, which defines itself as "relational psychoanalysis," the same has not occurred in Europe, for the reasons explained above, because the "relational" is integrated in the mainstream of European psychoanalysis, except for those relational schools subsequently imported from America.

4 In this sphere of literature, see in particular to the works of Winnicott (1969), Khan (1972, 1983), Aulagnier (1975), Abraham and Torok (1978), DeMijolla (1981), Faimberg (1981, 1985, 1988), Bollas (1989), Lebovici (1989), Cahn (1991), Eiguer (1991), Baranes (1991), Kafka (1992), Fonagy et al. (1992), and Kaës et al. (1993).

5 The Italian slang expressions are "pippe psicologiche," "pippe mentali." "Pippa" is the act of manual masturbation.

References

Abraham, N. & Torok, M. (1978). *L'écorce Et Le Noyau*. Paris: Aubier-Flammarion.

Aulagnier, P. (1975). *La Violence De l'interprétation*. Paris: Presses Universitaires de France, 1994.

Baranes, J. -J. (1991). *La Question Psychotique à l'adolescence: le Passage Du Cap Horn*. Paris: Dunod.

Baranger, M., Baranger, W. & Mom, J. M. (1987). Il trauma psichico infantile dai giorni nostri a freud: trauma puro, retroattività e ricostruzione. In: *La Situazione Psicoanalitica Come Campo Bipersonale*. Edited by M. Baranger & W. Baranger. Milano: Cortina, 1990.

Blos, P. (1967). The second individuation process of adolescence. *Psychoanal. Study Child*, 22:162–186.

Bollas, C. (1989). *Forces of Destiny: Psychoanalysis and Human Idiom*. London: Free Association Books.

Bonaminio, V. (1987). La pazzia della madre come "corpo estraneo." In *Un Sogno Di Un Ragazzo Tredicenne. Un Esempio Della Concezione*

Winnicottiana Dei "fattori Ego-Alieni" Nel Materiale Clinico. Edited by
P. M. Masciangelo, A. Limentani, et al. *La relazione aggressiva.* Roma:
Borla, 1988.

_____ (2008). The person of the analyst: Interpreting, not interpreting, and countertransference. *Psychoanal. Q.* 77:1105–1146.

Bonaminio, V., Carratelli, T. & Giannotti, A. (1989). Equilibrio e rot-
tura dell'equilibrio nella relazione fra fantasie inconsce dei genitori e
sviluppo normale e patologico del bambino. In: *Fantasie Dei Genitori e
Psicopatologia Dei Figli.* Edited by G. Masi & G. Ferretti Roma: Borla,
1991.

Bonaminio, V., Di Renzo, M. & Giannotti, A. (1993). Le fantasie inconsce
dei genitori come fattori ego-alieni nelle identificazioni del bambino. Qualche riflessione su identità e falso sé attraverso il materiale
clinico dell'analisi infantile. *Rivista di Psicoanalisi,* 39:4.

Bonaminio, V. & Di Renzo, M. (2000). Creativity, playing, dreaming:
overlapping circles in the work of Marion Milner and DW Winnicott.
In: Caldwell, L. (ed.) Art, Creativity, Living. Abingdon, Routledge,
2018.

Cahn, R. (1991). *Adolescence et folie: les déliaisons dangereuses.* Paris: Presses
Universitaires de France.

DeMijolla, A. (1981). *Les Visiteurs Du Moi.* Paris: Les Belles-Lettres.

Diatkine, G. (1984). Chasseurs de fantômes, inhibition intellectuelle, prob-
lemes d'equipe et secret de famille. *Psychiatrie de l'Enfant,* 27(1):223–248.

Eiguer, A. (1991). L'identification a l'object transgenerationnel. *Journal de
la Psychanalyse de l'Enfant,* 10.

Faimberg, H. (1981). Une des difficultés de l'analyse : la reconnaissance de
l'altérité. *Rev. Française de Psychanalyse,* 45 :1351–1368.

_____ (1985). The telescoping of generations. *Contemp. Psychoanal.,*
24 :99–118.

_____ (1988). A l'écoute du télescopage des générations : pertinence
psychanalytique du concept. In *Transmission De La Vie Psychique Entre
Générations.* Edited by R. Kaës, H. Faimberg, M. Enriquez & J. -J.
Baranes. Paris: Dunod, 1993.

_____ (1993). Il mito di edipo rivisitato. In *Trasmissione Della Vita
Psichica Tra Generazioni.* Edited by R. Kaës et al. Roma: Borla, 1995.

Fonagy, P., Steele, M., Moran, G., Steele, H. & Higgit, A.C. (1992). The
integration of psychoanalytic theory and work on attachment: the
issue of intergenerational psychic process. In: *Attaccamento e Psicoanalisi.*
Edited by D. Stern & M. Ammaniti. Bari, Italy: Laterza.

Freud, S. (1923). The ego and the id. S. E., 19:3–66.

_____ (1940). An outline of psycho-analysis. *Int. J. Psychoanal.,*
21:27–84.

Green, A. (1992). *La déliaison: psychanalyse, anthropologie et littérature*. Paris: Les Belles Lettres.

Kaës, R., Faimberg, H., Enriquez, M. & Baranes, J.-J. (1993). *Transmission De La Vie Psychique Entre Générations*. Paris: Dunod, 1993.

Kafka, E. (1992). The influence of parents' unconscious fantasies on children's adaptation as illustrated by transsexuality. *J. Clin. Psychoanal.*, 1:547–559.

Khan, M. M. R. (1972). Exorcism of the intrusive ego-alien factors in the analytic situation and process. In: *Tactics and Techniques in Psycho-Analytic Psychotherapy*. Edited by P. L. Giovacchini. London: Hogarth, 1972.

_____ (1983). *Hidden Selves*. London: Hogarth.

Kohut, H. (1977). *The Restoration of the Self.* Chicago and London: Chicago University Press.

Laplanche, J. & Pontalis, J. -B. (1964). *Fantasme Originaire: Fantasmes des Origines, Origines du Fantasme*. Hachette, 1998.

Lebovici, S. (1989). Fantasmatic interactions and intergenerational transmission. *Infant Mental Health J.*, 6:10–19.

Tripp, E. (1970). Pelops at Olympia. In: *Crowell's Handbook of Classical Mythology*. New York, NY: Thomas Crowell Company, 93–103.

Winnicott, C. (1977). *A Reflection Between Reality and Fantasy: Transitional Objects and Phenomena in Grolnick, S.A.* Edited by H. Grolnick. New York: J. Aronson, 1978.

Winnicott, D.W. (1947). Hate in the countertransference. In: *Collected Papers. Through Pediatrics to Psychoanalysis*. London: Tavistock.

_____ (1962) The aim of psychoanalytic treatment. *The Collected Works of Donald W. Winnicott. Volume 6.* Edited by Lesley Caldwell & Helen Taylor Robinson. Oxford: Oxford University Press, 2017.

_____ (1969). Mother's madness appearing in the clinical material as an ego-alien factor. In *Psychoanalytic Explorations*. Edited by C. Winnicott, R. Shepard & M. Davis. Cambridge, MA: Harvard University Press, 1989.

_____ (1988). *Human Nature*. New York, NY: Schocken Books, 1988.

Zemeckis, R. (1985). *Back to the Future*. Universal Pictures.

"A HUNDRED TIMES I DIED, AND A HUNDRED TIMES I WAS BORN AGAIN ..."

The long-term development of the clinical case of Bernard over 30 years, from three different perspectives: evaluation, supervision and analytic treatment.

Bernard came to see me again very recently for a single consultation after the end of his analysis, approximately six months following our last *on demand* consultation. He was briefly back in Rome, though now he lived in another European city, where he worked with some stability in a specific academic field. He seemed to have guessed that I was writing about him, and that maybe I was looking for a title to give my clinical presentation.

After going over the long and troubled phases of his analysis, and after my comment that he suffered much for his distress, but also showed a great capacity to withstand it, he replied: "yes, I think it is true: I am fragile, or, better, I discovered myself to be fragile, even though now I feel stronger and more integrated (the Italian term is *compatto*, i.e., *compact*), however, I always had on my side my stubbornness to go forward ... *a hundred times I died, and a hundred times I was born again* ... only my stubbornness helped me ... also analysis for God's sake ... now I feel a cycle is complete."

This statement "a hundred times I died, and a hundred times I was born again" seemed like a gift Bernard had given me, since it epitomized perfectly our mutual efforts in analysis: on the one side I supported him when he was "gasping" because of his panic anxieties, on the other side, he would jump over obstacles, with a totally absent sense of self-doubt, which just one week before had seemed like an impossible task.

 DOI: 10.4324/9781003228332-11

Introduction

In this chapter, I deliberately wish to interconnect, through a focus on clinical material, two levels of analysis. On one side, the perspective *of psychoanalytic developmental psychopathology;*[1] on the other side, the development of an analytic process with an unusual approach over a fairly long period of time.

I am well aware that in reporting this clinical case, I am using material from different clinical settings. We are all aware that from an epistemological perspective, this clashes against one of the pillars of our psychoanalytic clinical practice: clinical material coming from analysis has its own specificity, which allows it to be interpreted; that is, it allows the analyst to propose to the analysand an interpretation, that may be returned back elaborated, as the relationship between them is central, together with the free associations of the former, and the free floating attention of the latter, and the empathy and identification of the analyst with the patient's narration.

But material coming from different contexts, even if analytically oriented, cannot be compared, used to demonstrate, or integrated with that which is rightfully psychoanalytic.

This theme of epistemological correctness, i.e., avoiding the mixture of material from infant and adult analyses with *direct observations* of children, constituted an interesting debate during the first half of the '50s. In those days, the direct observations of Spitz and other authors, were 'interpreted' with concepts from rightfully analytic setting contexts. In order to be scientific, as epistemology teaches us, we know that 'correspondence rules' are required, to make material as homogeneous as possible. In clinical material, this implies specifying the origin of the material every time, and proceeding with caution in matching interpretative conclusions taken from psychoanalytic clinical material. For brevity's sake, I will not go into the details of this debate, but I wish to remind the reader how aware Anna Freud in particular, but also Kris and Hartman, were of this issue. The risk, in brief, is to draw conceptual and clinical conclusions susceptible to the charge of becoming a sort of wild analysis.

I wish to highlight Anna Freud's pioneering awareness of this topic in 'Pitfalls and Safeguards in Direct Observation' from her work *The Contribution of Direct Child Observation to Psychoanalysis* (1957), and the equally fundamental 'Child Observation and Prediction of Development. A Memorial Lecture in Honor of Ernst

Kris' (1958), which is a pillar of this topic and developmental psychoanalytic psychopathology. Being aware of this risk, I will try to consider the different origin of the clinical material in presenting it, and to exercise care in juxtaposing it, trying to avoid simplified and wild interpretations. However, I could not avoid putting together this material, because of the extreme interest I find in it, hoping the reader will share this view.

For clarity's sake, I will first summarize briefly the case and its course, then I will go into greater detail, in order to propose an argument and stimulate reflection in the reader.

My conceptual frame of reference

First, I would like to emphasize some clinical–theoretical concepts that constitute the background and rationale of my work, which, as I said, is essentially clinical.

I will use the concept of *continuity of being, going-on-being*, according to Winnicott (1960, 1963), who underlined the importance for every infant, after the *in utero* gestation, of being in a *facilitating environment*, and in *the presence* of the mother (or caregiver), able to ensure his *unity of being*, and to facilitate his developmental integration processes.

Presence of the mother, i.e., the analyst as other[2]: we will come back to this concept because it is important to underline the importance of *the mother being there* (and the analyst), more than her ability to offer adequate technical care. In the case of the analyst, a competent clinical ability is expected. The latter is important for both the mother and the analyst, but becomes pure technique[3] if not accompanied by the emotional presence, indeed, of the mother/analyst.

Limiting this concept only to the neonatal phase and the first year of life would be reductive. In fact, it can be related to the whole life span, and to the role and function of the analyst, even if the total dependence of the newborn is not replicated in the latency phase, or in the adolescent, young adult, or in general in the patient undergoing analysis. Of course, *ruptures in the continuity of being* in the first year of life have an aetio-psycho-pathogenic impact that is far more relevant than similar events occurring at a later age. However, we also know that these ruptures of the continuity of being can accumulate in the course of development. I am here introducing the second theoretical concept I mentioned previously, that of *cumulative trauma*, introduced as a revolutionary innovation by Khan (1963).

247

The importance of this concept, both in general and in particular, for the purposes of this argument, resides in the fact that ruptures may be reinforced or, on the contrary, revisited (*nachträglich, après-coup*), thus losing part of their pathogenic impact. Positive life events may reform the impact of early traumas and ruptures in *après-coup*. This is the heart and the innovative element of psychoanalytic developmental psychopathology, which in a way frees development from the restraint (repetition compulsion) of early pathogenic experiences – a bond that was in some way imposed by the classical psychoanalytic model, which we can trace back to the fixation-regression scheme first adopted by Freud in *Studies on Hysteria* (1895), and systematized by Abraham in 'A Short Study on the Development of the Libido' (1924).

Psychoanalytic developmental psychopathology considers the entanglement of the fundamental psychopathological organization of the individual (also dependent on environmental influences), but also the onset of the ailment, and obviously the concurrent *life events*. A choice aimed at picking the most adequate treatment can result only from an attempt to disentangle these elements. In this sense, our debt is to Anna Freud, who in 'Indications for Child Analysis' (1945) inaugurated, perhaps inadvertently, the developmental psychopathology approach.

In my personal experience this implies thinking in terms of *developmental risk*. It is somewhat like considering in the relational situation (patient-psychoanalyst) the patient's 'illness' with one eye to the past and with one eye to the future, and the ensuing developmental steps and problems which will confront the patient.

Adolescence as a specific, but not unique, developmental process

Adolescence is certainly the key phase where the early negative experiences can be overcome, but also the central factor of psychopathological risk.

In my experience of working with severe and neurotic psychopathologies from early childhood to pre-puberty and puberty – what Gutton (2003) calls *le pubertaire* – our goal is to evaluate the pre-adolescent phase determinants in latency and puberty that will shape the adolescent's disorder one way or another, both in terms of severity and possible outcome. This approach was already taken in a pioneering, fundamental paper by the Novicks (1994), where they

248

suggested the experiences of latency are like a "stamp on the passport." If the stamp is missing, those experiences have been skipped and the adolescent will start "on the wrong foot." This model combines *continuity* and *discontinuity* of development.

The third concept that lies behind my clinical presentation is that of *transformations* (Bion, 1965). Bernard's case is an *in vivo* example of developmental transformations, of the incessant reshaping of his anxieties and, as we will see later on, what Bion (1970) and his followers (Civitarese, 2015) called "transformation into hallucinosis."

The specifics of the case

As I already mentioned at the beginning of this clinical paper, the quite exceptional specificity of the presentation of Bernard's clinical history lies in the fact that, for various fortuitous circumstances, I had the chance to follow him directly (from diagnosis) and indirectly (in supervision and then, much later, in psychoanalytic therapy) the evolution of this case for approximately 30 years. This is an exceptionally precious opportunity for a child and adolescent psychoanalyst, that became accessible to me for totally serendipitous reasons.[4]

Where to start?

I have decided to choose a presentation that will place up front the psychoanalytic relationship he had with me from ages 17 to 24. This choice enabled me to highlight the specific traits of psychoanalysis in adolescence (Laufer & Laufer, 1984; Anderson, 1997; Cahn, 1997; Nicolò, 1997; Richard, 2011) and the transference/countertransference dynamic relationship between me and this patient. I wanted to show what I learned from the relationship with Bernard and its exceptionality, as in the evocative title of a chapter of a recent book by Richard (2011), 'What the meeting with the adolescent teaches the analyst'.

When he reappeared at age 17, I felt pretty cold towards him. I remember an early, negative countertransference reaction, which was quickly mitigated by a feeling of solidarity for the deep suffering that this boy was showing and that I felt as an emotional 'wave' coming from him. Since the case had been transferred to me by a colleague, I thought it would only require a brief psychotherapeutic consultation. I did not understand, at the time, the seriousness of the *silent psychotic breakdown* Bernard was portraying in the consultation, and I was expecting to conclude after a few sessions and then, if necessary, send him to another colleague.

It will be clear in the following exposition that I was confronted with the peak of my countertransference resistance towards what would become a very complex case. Evidently, I had intuited this complexity, but I was not ready to face it, and thus defensively I denied it. This resistance faded when the boy, whom I had first met when he was 5/6 years old, told me overtly, during one of our last consultations, "I do need to be helped by you!"

Compared with the child I had met when he was 5/6 years old, many elements combined in not giving me a positive attitude towards him: his heavy build, his being as tall as I, with a thick beard and muscular arms, obviously the result of a neurotic workout routine, large biceps where an aggressive tattoo could be half-seen, left incomplete but started "in order to be like my mates" (a sign of his ambivalence in belonging to his peer group), the hair already thinning, the scared stare, frequent blushing, and a sense of restlessness.

However, he almost 'intimated'[5] me to take him in analysis. He told me he felt he could go crazy, but as soon as he pronounced that word, he stepped back: "It's not that I'm crazy, I'm fine, I reason well ... it's that I always feel the anxiety coming from inside ... see? I'm *not* red, I'm *purple* in my face: this drives me crazy ... I mean it embarrasses me enormously with my mates and with girls. All this gives me incredible emotions. I feel full of holes where my emotions drain." Note how the term "go crazy" was uttered, reiterated and subsequently denied!

He described "scary" symptoms that instead were defined as "not so serious because they can happen to everybody." He heard *strange* voices, maybe noises, which always happened at sunset: "Maybe they are sounds coming from far away, but I am scared until going to bed. I have to go to sleep really tired, with the TV on, in order to cover the noises and the voices that may attack me."

I replied that what he was telling me must be really scary, just like it must be very embarrassing to blush suddenly for no reason, or to "sweat like a horse." I told him that now I understood that he was asking me in a very emphatic way to hold his hand in order to try to pull him out of the whirlpool in which he was drowning. I told him that he feels that he is going to pieces and that, contrary to what I said previously, I understand how bad he feels.

I offered to start right away three sessions per week, which reminds me of a book that Bollas (2013) wrote (which I would recommend to everyone) *Catch Them Before They Fall*. In those days, the book did not exist, but I had a long habit of working with and having supervisions with him, and I wonder if this quick proposal was inspired by what he and the Laufers (1984) told me: "Hold him before he breaks down … because once the breakdown has taken place, it's hard to put the pieces back together! Even more important, it's the patient that puts back together the pieces of his fragmented Self in a frankly psychotic way. You must act quickly, this is imperative" (personal communication).

This does not mean that our early countertransference reactions fade away, but clinical duty imposes to put aside for a while what may seem like a narcissistic countertransference defense. Later on we will be able to consider it.

After the analysis had started, I learned from Bernard that years ago his father had been dismissed for political reasons from a local council post that had made him and his family proud. A long legal battle had started and after 15 years the father was put back into the post, but ironically so much time had passed that he was now ready to retire! Bernard was hit heavily by the trauma of his father's retrocession. He tried to help him; he drove him around, but according to him, his father treated him with contempt and was always criticizing him.

The destitution of his father and the loss of family power caused a true *rupture of the continuity of being* for Bernard. It was a 'social castration' that not only put the family into economic trouble, but also caused in his father and mother to fall into depressive states that included episodes of alcoholism. "They go to bed drunk after drinking two bottles of wine," said a humiliated Bernard. Bernard was mortified in saying this, but his whole analysis at this stage was characterized by a sense of shame, sorrow for his condition, low self-esteem, exclusion, a sense of being "a loser," inept, and an idiot. He felt persecuted by his friends, even if it at times it seemed as if he did everything possible in order to be the targeted one. My interpretations did not diminish during this period of time, but I tried to support him emotionally, so that I felt my only contribution was to limit his almost delirious ideations.

The beginning: The diagnostic consultation

I saw Bernard for the first time when he was 5/6 years old. I was working full time in the Clinical Psychopathology Department of Child Psychiatry at the University of Rome, where I still work as a professor.

251

Bernard was assigned to me for a diagnostic evaluation, while the parents were assigned to two colleagues, according to our protocol. After the clinical evaluation, my hypothesis was of a phobic-obsessive disorder, a 'classical' child neurosis, strongly influenced by the mother's pre-Oedipal, symbiotic anxieties.

At 5–6, Bernard developed a fear of crossing a small forest that led into the center of a village where he could meet his friends. His mother had warned him of the danger of wounding himself with syringes from drug addicts residing in the area, and that they might leave on the ground their syringes infected with AIDS. Persecutory anxieties were therefore *subtly inoculated* into the child. The junkies were "waiting for him" and their syringes were extremely danger-ous. The mother decided to walk him, after homework, along that path. This route became a path full of dangers that strengthened the symbiotic pre-Oedipal grip on this child.

After the consultation, I leaned towards a diagnosis of a struc-tured phobic-obsessive neurosis, at this point no longer modifiable by interventions on the environment (Freud, 1965), and strongly influenced by the rampant, panicked anxieties of the mother. We decided on a psychotherapeutic intervention, which we believed should involve the child, and a couple therapy for the parents.

I will not go into further detail of the clinical evaluation. Bernard was sent to a female student in training ("the beautiful doctor," he says when in analysis and recalling that period of his childhood) who could take care of him at a reasonable rate. I advised three times a week psychotherapy and suggested the head of our unit supervise the case. Unfortunately, after a year and a half of analysis and supervision, the head of our unit died after a long struggle with cancer. We were all traumatized – the rupture involved the whole group – and the therapist asked me, since I knew the case, if I would become the supervisor.

For five years, during the latency period, via supervisory arrange-ment, I had indirect clinical contact with this boy. At 15 he con-tacted the therapist again. She could not take him back in therapy, for reasons that we will see, and sent him to me for an assessment. In reality, this became a 5–6 year, three-times a week, therapy.

During the time that Bernard's first therapist was supervised by me, perhaps due to a *natural evolution* (Winnicott, 1968) *of the analytic process* and the transference, an encysted trauma, or an "unthought known" (Bollas, 1978) surfaced. The little brother Bernard had insistently asked his parents for, so he had a playmate, and maybe, unconsciously, to subtract himself from what he already felt was his mother's strangling coils, was never to be born. When Bernard was eight, the mother underwent a hysterectomy due to a tumor. In analysis, through an obsessive repetitive game, Bernard portrayed his mother in the hospital having an abdominal surgery. These interpretive conjectures were subsequently confirmed by the colleagues who were working with the parents. However, Bernard was never realistically informed of this traumatic event, this catastrophic rupture that would push his mother into depression and despair.

In analysis, we only saw the effects of the mother's depression and Bernard's manic attempts to repair, to change her mood, exactly as Winnicott describes (1935, 1948). The child–not–born becomes a *ghost child* that haunts the house and the therapy sessions. He is Bernard's deathly *alter ego*. In the interpretations I suggest to the therapist – based on Bernard's playing, always characterized by attempts to 'revive the depressed object' – I think the child needs to be made aware of, to be informed that the little brother–not–born seems to have disappeared, and nobody talks about him anymore. The mate he wanted seemed to have vanished into nothing. Today perhaps, I would have interpreted differently.

The *gathering in the transference*, as Meltzer (1967) would say, of all these anxieties, and the child's developing ability to represent, correlated to a significant decrease in his anxieties in the social world. The child was calmer and more creative, even if he was still in the enveloping arms of his mother, who was also his schoolteacher in the only elementary school in the village. After a while his parents seemed to become tired of continuing the treatment that took them to Rome three times a week. Even Bernard protested when he had to interrupt his playing to come to therapy.

Together with the therapist, we considered that his claustroagoraphobic anxieties had significantly diminished. The child had passed through latency fairly well, 'protected by psychotherapy'; and we thought perhaps it was necessary, if not wise, to bring the treatment to a conclusion. We knew the work was not complete but we had to make the best of the situation. After 7/8 months of preparation, the analysis was concluded, with reasonable results. For a while the parents continued their relationship with the colleagues who had followed them to that point. However, I suggested that an individual psychotherapy be proposed to the mother. The offer seemed to arrive at the right time as she accepted it enthusiastically.

253

For a while, contacts with the family were scarce. The father respectfully sent gifts to the therapist during the holidays and kept her informed, grateful of the progress that had been made. However, later on, between the ages of 11 and 16, two serious ruptures occurred in the life of this boy.

While riding a bike in a competition with his friends, and worried about being the last one, he fell head over heels and seriously fractured his leg, and consequently was forced to stay in a hospital for four months, because he contracted a subsequent infection. In his narration he reported the time he spent in hospital as the time he "grew up." At night he listened to the dirty jokes of hospital personnel, and started to get in touch with his sexuality. It was also evident that he felt sad and depressed because he was confined inside the hospital's walls. He confessed that he started to masturbate, excited by the stories he heard in the hospital, but also that he needed to do this *to feel less alone.*

In the following analysis it was possible to infer – also through interpretation – that the narrations about sexuality and masturbation during hospitalization were perhaps a compromise formation for his unconscious identification with his mother's castration (hysterectomy), about which he consciously knew nothing, but nonetheless had absorbed as an 'unthought known' (Bollas, 1978). The child-not-born, his *alter ego*, so much desired and promised to him, became a persecutory object, due to his identification with his mother's female castration/amputation. The persecution of the drug addicts' syringes that threatened his life now resurfaced in other forms, expressed by his hypochondriac anxieties, started by the infection he contracted in the hospital.

Here two interpretations were possible. To take a Freudian approach, it may have been the unconscious identification with the castrated mother (psychic reality) that caused the auto-sabotage in the external reality of the patient. However, I believe that the expulsion from the real environment, the external trauma, caused the fracture in his *continuity of being*. It's interesting to note here how external and internal events merge into one; we may say this always happens. Indeed, this is the eternal discussion about whether psychic reality prevails on the external or social, or vice versa. The prevailing of psychic reality is what our being psychoanalysts considers the supremacy of the psychic. Conversely, being schematic, even among psychoanalysts, some believe that external reality triggers processes that otherwise would not have started. An abandoned child in an orphanage shapes his internal reality on the basis of an external traumatic event in order to survive. But I am not so interested in this discussion here. Freud already solved the problem by introducing the concept of "complementary series".

An even more serious rupture was awaiting Bernard, approximately two years after leaving the hospital. Just like his mother, the father too suffered a serious narcissistic collapse. All three were castrated, saddened, and depressed.

The son of a parent fallen into disgrace is at risk of strong professional inhibitions, because of the ambivalent wish to surpass/not surpass his father. Bernard had always dreamed of entering the Air Force and at this stage he began training to become a pilot. Bernard constructed an unconscious ghost of power (joining the military, wearing the uniform like his father) through desires that were only partially authentic but mostly restorative and compensating. These desires and fantasies were mainly 'super-hero' ideals having the purpose of avenging the father and re-establishing justice.

However, I believe they were also auto-sabotages that revealed the ambivalence of his wishes: on the one hand, Bernard would have liked to win back his father's honor, by occupying the most elevated place from where he could allegorically bomb the city hall that demoted his father and destroyed him. On the other hand, because of his Oedipal rivalry, he would have liked to participate in his father's destruction. He must have felt, more or less unconsciously, that this desire to become a military pilot was childish, a borrowed ideal created to satisfy an omnipotent and vindictive ego.

This further rupture threw Bernard into a depressive state to which he reacted manically. He became aggressive with everybody in his small town; he became hyperactive, the "clown of the village," getting involved in fights, surely as a reaction to his father's destitution, which mortified him.

The core of the psychotherapy in Bernard's adolescence

When Bernard was 16/17, his parents, facing his restless, complaining, unsatisfied, clown of the village attitude, decided again to contact his old psychotherapist. But they faced an unexpected event: the psychotherapist, a person at the end of her training, intelligent and clinically able, replied that she could not take Bernard back in therapy because she had decided to quit the profession due to the sudden and tragic death of a close family member. She also advised them, in the presence of Bernard, to ask me to replace her. She told them that I was her tutor, and thus I knew the vicissitudes of Bernard's case well, since she often spoke with me about the case. It may be debated how appropriate this was, both from a technical and transference perspective, but it must also be considered that this therapist was severely traumatized by the accidental death of her family member.

When I met Bernard, he immediately informed me that "his therapist" did not work anymore because of a recent loss, that she could not help him, but that he needed help. "You see, I don't become red, but purple, right now I feel purple with emotion, I would get undressed because, due to the emotion I sweat like ... like a horse, like an animal." He mentioned not feeling part of the group of his old friends, and being mocked for his blushing, then he told me of another great pain that he suffered, another fracture, as it were.

He told me that he decided to apply to enter the Air Force and take the admission exam, but it was a disaster. He realized he was giving the wrong answers, but because he was in a rush, he finished in a panic, aware of the disaster but unable to do anything about it. He just wanted to run away. His "suspect" answers, that he gave intentionally, were immediately detected by the examiners, who called him in for a further discussion. He replied "yes" to the question, "Do you feel like a woman?" although he wanted to reply "no." He also replied "yes" to the question, "Do you hear voices?" He was sent for a psychiatric examination, which he took although he was terrified of being considered mad. He told me that he replied randomly to the questions and talked about his blushing. "I do anything possible to make my situation worse," he said.

Flunking this exam threw him into the deepest desperation: he told me that his father attacked him as inept, told him he was a real "asshole," and that he would not achieve anything in life. His mother tried to support him but he reacted manically: "I don't care at all about not having been accepted; actually, it's better like this." His mother tried to stimulate him but always in an obtrusive, entangling manner. She brought him breakfast in bed as soon as the father left the house to support him with what she felt was an "anti-depressive" solution.

Afterwards, during the consultations with me, before we began the psychotherapy, he said, almost talking off-hand: "but the story of the voices was true ... the rest was bullshit that I said because of the anxiety, but I really hear the voices."

This was a severe blow to my countertransference: I asked myself in rage and with anxiety, "Why the hell did the therapist send me this psychotic adolescent?"

Bernard told me that at night, mostly at dusk, he "hears voices," maybe coming from far away or nearby. He said he felt confused and scared, that they called him, or he was under the impression of being called, or he heard conversations, fragments of conversations, sometimes about him, sometimes not. He said he needed to leave the TV on all night so that "the voices from the TV mix with those I hear or believe I hear." This method relaxed him and allowed him to slowly fall asleep. He complained that his long psychotherapy that had worked well for a long time, even after it was over, "now doesn't work anymore." He felt invaded by all sorts of anxieties, by hypochondriac fears, so much that he avoided going to the doctor, "in order not to know." He was a passionate reader of the health section of the newspaper *La Repubblica*. Just like a medical school student, he "gets sick," or feared that he would get sick, with all the illnesses mentioned in this section, that ironically he called the "illness section."

In our consultations, he kept telling me about failing the admission exam for the military academy. He did so in a light tone, perhaps eased by my progressive attunement with his anxieties, after my early 'not accepting' countertransference. I told him that this was not a minor defeat, even though he seemed to present it like this; but instead it was a severe blow to his lifelong ambition, considering his passion for airplanes that I remembered from when I had first seen him. Ten years earlier he had pretended to be a sort of a Red Baron. Intentionally, trying to link past and present, I added, "When you were afraid to sting yourself with the syringes of the drug addicts." He smiled, almost with nostalgia, and said, "If you only knew how much we talked about it with my therapist who now can't take me back, because she had a terrible death in the family, her husband died."

I think silently that he was told too much, that he was overloaded with news of mourning and loss. I said that maybe the death of his therapist's husband served the purpose, in the sense that it prevented him thinking about how serious the death of his ambition was.

He blushed: "Yes, it was a serious blow, I don't think those assh ... that my parents understood it ... my father, who spends his time criticizing me. He's only able to tell me I'm a loser, that I will achieve nothing in life ..."

I told him that his father's bitter words were also caused by his own frustrations, and that they had placed hope in him. Surely those comments hurt, and were not necessary, when he only wanted to be understood." He replied, "It's my father's hobby, he always attacks me, since I was a child ... he knows how to do everything and I know nothing ... he hates me, I feel it, because I don't achieve what he wants."

I felt I was on the right track in this consultation because Bernard reacted to my interpretations; however, I was still cautious and hesitant, since I had originally intended to send him to a colleague. Another factor made me hesitate, the masochistic component of his narration, which seemed like a well-rehearsed act, repeating the masochistic mess he had made when applying for the military academy, in order to be expelled and despised by his father, perhaps as a punishment-revenge against his disdainful attitude. I wondered whether this dramatic narration was a way to be expelled by me, just like the military school episode, or if he wanted to upset me, to make me worry, so that I would try to keep him.

As I mentioned, he came to the fourth consultation very anxious and practically intimated me to take him into analysis. I *must* take him, he said. He said he was so anxious that even when he had sex with his girlfriend in his car, he had to find a spot where he could tap his finger, in order to cover the noise of his raging heartbeat. He couldn't wait to finish because he was afraid of having a heart attack. His girlfriend Lucia complained that he was distracted and accused him of having sex only to come, not because he really liked her. Sadly, he said this was not true. He liked Lucia, but he couldn't control his fear. He had to rush, be quick. It was a kind of a compulsion. Even when he was with friends in the pub, after a while he had to get out, catch some air. And when this happens, when he goes back inside, his friends have taken the best seats, so he has to sit at the end of the table, where he thinks nobody pays attention to him or cares about him.

During our first sessions, he often looked at the couch. I asked him if he was interested, and told him, if he wanted to, he was free to talk, and he was not forced to make eye contact. He replied that he would never go on the couch, that he must be able to see my face. He said if he did, after a second he would jump up, or faint, or explode because of all the anxiety that was inside.

In the following sessions he told me in a flood of information the extent of his claustro-agoraphobic symptoms, his anxiety and panic attacks, his hypochondriacal anguish, all factors that were progressively related to the relationship with me.

Analysis, he said, was a relief, but also the cause of his terrible symptoms. "Last time I came to analysis I felt terrible until today's meeting, then this morning I felt a little better because I knew I was coming here ... during the session I felt relieved by being able to say everything about me, even the worst things ... but I can't spend my whole life in analysis ... I will never be like the other ones ... the voices, they never stop, but I fear them less now."

I told him that maybe being able to talk about the voices and his fears, even the worst ones, relieved his anxiety a little, because he felt there was somebody really listening to him. But when he left, what he had said to me became like facts, real things, that persecuted him. In the room they had a sense that we could attribute to them together, but when he was alone they became "objects." He accepted this interpretation.

Analyzing the transference, it seemed more and more obvious that his depression, triggered by his disappointments and the despotic attitude of his father, was contrasted with a manic defense that made him the bully of his town, always ready to get into a fight, especially if he feared being excluded from something. Here, interpretation was particularly complex. It was difficult to convey, even through the transference, that he had to become the "clown of the village" to defend himself from depressive feelings, from the fear of being "a nothing." Everybody always expected something bizarre from him. Sometimes, even in therapy, his manic arrogance surfaced, when my interpretations were not pitched right: "you analysts only see how the patient reacts," he said, "but come, come to my town and look, perhaps hidden, at how the others treat me. I'm tired of hearing the bullshit that it's all my fault."

I told him that he was being unfair: I never said it was his fault; quite the contrary, I wondered how he could stand his father's disdain, why he did not have the courage to revolt against him. My comments were aimed at showing him that if he felt weak in front of his friends, because of his low self-esteem, it was obvious they would target him.

When it came time for Bernard to register with a university he decided to study psychology: "Even if it's almost an all-female department, I want to take Psychology," he said, "maybe it's a chance to pick a few of them up." He passed his tests, and I told him that he was thinking omnipotently that if he became like me, if he wore my clothes, he thought his problems would disappear and his anxieties dissolve (projective identification). Notwithstanding my interpretations, he was determined to enroll. However, after six months, because of conflicts with "girls," the students he was supposed to pick up, he changed department and enrolled in the law school with a group of male friends: "Those guys fuck all day," he said.

His parents were fiercely against it, but I silently appreciated his unsuspected ability to rebel against their orders. He said, "Law school is my way." After a few months, I understood that this too was an imitative choice, where he wanted to dissolve in the male group, in the hope of taking from them the self-confidence he was missing—a legitimate solution, which, however, triggered homosexual anxieties. He felt he was the weakest of the males, whose phallic power he wished to take away. However, it seemed that for him there was no other way to take this power, other than through passivity, incorporating the penises of these more powerful males. Surprisingly, he accepted this – we might say – strong interpretation and replied that maybe I was right, because he would like to be active and masculine, since he always felt he was the last one.

He seemed to offer me an opportunity for a transference interpretation: "Then, also accepting my point of view is becoming passive, submitting to me," I said. "It seems that you don't have the courage to take a decision by yourself." This interpretation, given before the summer break, continued to 'work underground,' and after the summer vacation, he came back with the decision of enrolling in architecture: "That's where all the daddy's boys from the rich families go, the sons of the architects ... I'm a country boy coming from the village, you can hear it from my accent too, but it's a challenge I want to take." I endorsed this decision, and this new challenging approach, which I also saw as an Oedipal challenge to me. But what more could I expect from such a disturbed and suffering young man?

Even greater anxieties were waiting for me around the corner, filling the last years of analysis. Not only did he feel like he was the excluded one, that "others avoid," who ask him "with an ironic tone if I come from the countryside," but his anxieties progressively turned into panic. I felt desperate. Usually he came to therapy on the "safe and reassuring" train. Sometimes, feeling more masculine, he

260

came on a Yamaha Maxi motorcycle. But one day this threw him into a panic: he called me from a gas pump, told me that he saw with horror his arms detached from his body, and attached to the motorcycle's handles. I told him to go to the bathroom, cool down, dry his sweat. I said I would wait for him until the last minute of the session.

Bernard arrived, even though there was a long delay, thus we had a chance to talk about the terrible sensations. I took this as a "symptom of hope," in Winnicott's style, that Bernard was able to take things from the past environment, which evidently included some good experiences, among so many disastrous ones, but also from the current analytic environment, from the person of the analyst.

"This time I really felt it was the end, time for my funeral," he said.

With a friendly irony, I said that I would not have missed it, after so many years of knowing him. "Poor Bernard," I would have said next to the grave, "you fought so much but in the end you had to give up."

"Never!" he replied immediately. "I don't give up, even if I had to come here on my hands and feet ... anyway, it's more likely that I come to your funeral, crying about my poor analyst who I tormented so much! I will come to your funeral, not you to mine!"

I told him that this was one of the first times that I heard him talk like a man, not like a scared child! "You had the guts to *kill your father without killing him in reality,*" I said. *"You killed me. Now we are more equal, we are peers!"*

Analysis continued for approximately a year and a half, but this was surely a turning point. A series of symptoms persisted, but their intensity and frequency declined, and were not comparable to precedent peaks.

He found himself a new girlfriend, very beautiful and desired by his friends, but before that he had several less important relationships. With this girl, he had a more mature relationship, but every now and then suffered from sexual difficulties that threw him into a panic.

Conclusions

Thinking over the whole story of this case *a posteriori* (perhaps here the term *après-coup* is not appropriate), I understand that the psychopathological organisation I defined as claustro–agoraphobic,

261

phobic-obsessive and neurotic in structure, was really a defensive structure relating to much deeper psychotic anxieties, perhaps to the mother's 'abortion' of the promised brother.

If this is the case, or close to being the case, the question is whether a child analyst could have seen beyond the psychopathological defensive structure in a 4/5-year-old child. I would say, without excusing myself from not having been able to grasp the primary psychotic anxieties,[6] that we should consider, as Winnicott says, that these primitive states cannot be seen clinically before they develop. Is it possible to grasp them *in statu nascendi*? Not really, not only because they have not developed yet, but also because they may not have developed in the particular direction the present if various life events had not surfaced (in this case, the broken leg, the feeling of being rejected, and the self-disdain, the fracture in the continuity of being that was related to rejection by the military academy, and the therapy denied by his therapist, who probably, in her circumstances, conveyed a sense of death).

Without those life events, I wonder if these depersonalization symptoms, together with the alteration of the body scheme, the very same symptoms that induced me to take this young man into therapy, would have manifested themselves.

This case offers a rare opportunity to see the interconnection between developmental processes, while these connections are being made and unmade, and how trauma influences such processes, increasing their psychopathological intensity. In this case the effect was a cumulative increase. In addition, in adolescence or post-adolescence, it was possible to see in *après-coup* (and this, as child and adolescent analysts, is useful) psychopathological episodes whose true gravity had not been assessed completely. This happens because, as Winnicott said, around the psychotic fundamental structure a highly sophisticated, neurotic structure is subsequently created, in order to protect it. Thus, an analysis that went straight to the psychotic anxieties would have been an additional trauma to this young man. His destiny was inextricably linked to these permanent transformations (this is why I refer to Bion's transformation concept) and his fundamentally constant symptoms, that nevertheless developed into panic attacks, where he felt a deep alteration of his body perception, and in the symptoms of depersonalization, where the strong anxieties put his identity at risk.

In time, it became possible to relate all of this to the relationship with his mother; some forgotten memories surfaced again, like that of his promised little brother, who would have kept him company but was never born. It is possible that the symptoms of depersonalization, the arms detached from the body, may be related to a 10-year-old boy's perception of his mother's hysterectomy.

Also, thanks to the analytic work, he started to think about his clownish attitude, his revenge against his mother, who denied him a little brother, and put death anxieties into him without explanation. Progressively, he understood how his clownish attitude, that always made him ridiculous, was aimed at repeating the feeling of exclusion that originated in the trauma of his father's exclusion. In the second part of this analysis we worked a lot on this. What at the beginning was only presented in the transference, almost acted out, slowly became representable. We started to reconstruct a developmental history, a narration that belonged equally to both of us, and some life events began to take on a new meaning. We went back to the broken leg trauma, to the failure with the military academy. A new integration process started. In the most intense negative transference moment, he seemed to fragment and make a persecutory object of me. Obviously, his anxious structure persisted, but he made significant progress. The psychotherapy was concluded, even though it was interrupted by stays abroad, during his architecture studies, since it is customary in Europe for university students to spend a year abroad. Bernard could not accept anything less than the others, but at the same time he had to work much more than the others in order to achieve this.

His saying, "a hundred times I died, and a hundred times I was born again," epitomizes this struggle. He was happy with his degree, but not too much, while in my eyes it was an unbelievable success. Also, his parents had made so many sacrifices in order for him to enter an architecture academy, one of the most expensive and prestigious schools in a European capital. But again, once he was there, all sorts of symptoms surfaced: "I feel excluded, the others are always better than me, the professors don't consider me as they should." There was always a vaguely persecutory atmosphere. In the meantime, we would have Skype therapy sessions, or he would come to Rome frequently and I would see him at his request, in order for him to feel heard and supported. I had suggested a psychotherapy with a British colleague, but he wanted to speak Italian.

Today, he lives in a capital city, works in a prestigious architecture firm, earns a very good salary, and wonders if he wants his girlfriend to travel around the world with him, since he has always felt that there is an unlived part of his life, in the sense that he always wants new experiences, even though he has some difficulties in establishing new relationships. Thus, it depends on him whether he will make this long-time girlfriend travel or not, and here all sorts of projection mechanisms are activated. He is not dependent on the girl; it is she who is dependent on him. However, in the end his symptoms have improved and he is getting along well in his work.

Notes

1 Started by Anna Freud (1936); her pioneering role on this topic is not acknowledged as it should be.

2 "In the early stages in which the mother's continued presence has a specific value for the infant" (Winnicott, 1965a, p. 77). "This unrewarding work ... a complex test of the analyst's capacity to meet the various communicating techniques ... that is in fact based on the analyst's (mother's) ability to identify with the patient" (Winnicott, 1965b).

3 "It cannot be overemphasized—" Winnicott writes in a more famous and meaningful declaration "—that being is the beginning, without which doing and being done to have no significance" (Winnicott, 1966, p. 111–2).

4 And is too instructive to be put aside for these reasons.

5 It is worth noting that the term 'intimate' can have a double meaning due to the sound of the word. On one hand its meaning is to be a 'close acquaintance' and suggests 'intimacy' in the psychoanalytic situation. On the other hand, as a verb, to 'intimate' also means 'to summon,' 'to order,' 'to command,' and is close to 'intimidate.' This second meaning derives from the Latin root *timeo*, 'to fear,' i.e., to intimidate a person by threats or blackmail. We can say that Bernard wanted both to order me, or impose to me and become intimate with me.

6 I am not saying this out of false modesty, but to emphasise the omnipotence of the child analyst who thinks he is able to take a picture of a psychopathological state, while the psychopathology of development tells us that the being, the psyche, is permanently modified by its interaction with the environment.

References

Abraham, K. (1924). A short study on the history of the libido. In: *Essential Papers on Object Loss*. Edited by R. V. Frankiel. New York: New York University Press, 1994.

Anderson, R., (1997). Esigenze della formazione al lavoro psicoanalitico con gli adolescent. Richard e Piggle.

Bion, W. R. (1965). *Transformations; Change from Learning to Growth*. London: Tavistock Publications.

_____ (1970). *Attention and Interpretation. A Scientific Approach to Insight in Psycho-Analysis and Groups*. London: Tavistock Publications.

Bollas, C. (1978). *The Shadow of the Object*. London: Free Associations Publishing.

_____ (2013). *Catch Them Before They Fall. The Psychoanalysis of Breakdown*. London: Routledge.

Cahn, R. (1997). Specificità nella formazione al lavoro psicoanalitico con gli adolescenti. *Richard e Piggle.*

Civitarese, G. (2015). Transformations in hallucinosis and the analyst's receptivity. *Int. J. Psychoanal.*, 96:1091–1116.

Freud, A. (1936). *The Ego and the Mechanism of Defense*. London: The Hogarth Press and the Institute of Psychoanalysis, 1961.

_____ (1945). Indication for child analysis. *Psychoanal. Study Child*, 1:127.

_____ (1957). The contribution of direct child observation to psycho-analysis (1957). In: *The Writings of Anna Freud*, volume V. London: The Hogarth Press and the Institute of Psychoanalysis, 1970.

_____ (1958[1957]). Child observation and prediction of development. A memorial lecture in honor of Ernst Kris. In: *The Writings of Anna Freud*, volume V. London: The Hogarth Press and the Institute of Psychoanalysis, 1970.

_____ (1965). *Normality and Pathology in Childhood*. London: The Hogarth Press and the Institute of Psychoanalysis.

Freud, S. (1895). Studies on hysteria. *S. E.*, 1.

Gutton, P. (2003). *Le Pubertaire*. Presses Universitaires de France.

Khan, M. M. R. (1963). The concept of cumulative trauma. In *The Privacy of the Self*. London: The Hogarth Press and the Institute of Psychoanalysis, 1974.

Laufer, M. & Laufer, E. (1984). *Adolescence and Developmental Breakdown*. London: Karnac.

Meltzer, D. (1967). *The Psychoanalytic Process*. London: Heinemann.

Nicolò, A. M. (1997). Esiste una specificità nella formazione al lavoro psicoanalitico con gli adolescenti Richard e Piggle, 1997.

Novick, K. K. & Novick, J. (1994). Post-oedipal transformations: latency, adolescence, and pathogenesis. *J. Amer. Psychoanal. Assn.*, 42:143–169.

Richard, F. (2011). *Le Rencontre Psycanalitique*. Paris: Dunod.

Winnicott, D. W. (1935). The manic defense. In: *Collected Papers: Through Paediatrics to Psychoanalysis*. London: Tavistock Publications, 1975.

_____ (1948) Reparation in the function of the organized maternal defense against depression. In: *Collected Papers: Through Paediatrics to Psychoanalysis*. London: Tavistock Publications, 1975.

_____ (1960). The theory of parent–infant relationship. In: *The Maturational Processes and the Facilitating Environment*. London: Hogarth, 1965.

_____ (1963). Communicating and not communicating leading to a study of certain opposites. In: *The Maturational Processes and the Facilitating Environment*. London: Hogarth, 1965.

_____ (1965). *The Maturational Processes and the Facilitating Environment*. London: Hogarth.

_____ (1968). The use of an object and relating through identification. In: *Psychoanalytic Explorations*. Edited by C. Winnicott, R. Shepherd & M. Davis. London: Karnac, 1968.

"NOTICING, UNDERSTANDING AND INTERPRETING"

'The Mother's Madness Appearing in the Clinical Material as an Ego-Alien Factor' (1969)

Winnicott starts his paper at lightning speed, revealing a method-ological certainty in his argument, typical of his style as a consum-mate clinician. "In a recent case of mine, the sudden intrusion of 'foreign' material needed to be *noticed, understood* and *interpreted*" (Winnicott, 1989, p. 375, my italics).[1]

Let's begin at the beginning with "sudden intrusion" and "for-eign material."

Winnicott starts his paper at lightning speed, revealing a meth-odological certainty in his argument, typical of his style as a con-summate clinician. And let's immediately note the epistemological, rather than technical, significance of the sequence "noticed, under-stood and interpreted." The speed with which Winnicott distils the cognitive (epistemological) processes passing through the analyst as he moves towards an interpretation in order to reach the patient, sums up – wonderfully, for me – the essence of the psychoanalytic process observed from the epistemological vertex.

To these observations, I would add the insistence, not on the opta-tive mood of the verb, but the "imperative," which in my opinion tells us much about the "analyst's task and responsibility to the patient."

Here Winnicott uses a terminology free of psychoanalytic jargon, and I suggest that in doing so he wants the case to have the same impact on his readers as it initially did on him. We value the way that Winnicott often writes what he feels or has felt, and tries to convey the same feeling to the reader.

To clarify: "foreign material" and "sudden intrusion" are two expressions, especially the first, which capture the reader's attention and stimulate his/her curiosity. Have you ever have heard these expressions being used in psychoanalytic case reports before Winnicott? It is as though he is privately reflecting on this "eccentric" material while at the same time conveying it to the reader in the way he speaks, muses, to himself.

'Mother's Madness Appearing in the Clinical Material as an Ego-Alien Factor' is a striking short case narrative, striking both in the author's bold clinical understanding of the child's anxieties, and in the rich and complex conceptual model underlying an apparently simple presentation.

Here an implicit epistemological background is revealed in the way Winnicott proceeds through *noticing, understanding,* and, before that, *apperceiving* the clinical material. The richness of 'apperception' (as opposed to simple 'perception') is hinted at in the choice of the verb *appearing,* which, in my view shows, Winnicott's surprise at something *that is coming into sight, becoming visible, especially without apparent cause.*

This material deals with a subject that when I read it – almost by accident 25 years ago – left me literally breathless, and since then it has been an indispensable point of reference for my clinical practice with children and adults, and in my writings, whether I mention it explicitly or not.

Now let's see how the story of Mark, a boy of six, appears in front of Winnicott, how a coherent hypothesis is immediately formulated, and how it progressively becomes plausible enough to be presented verbally to the child at the end of one consultation.

So we become the privileged observers of a clinical process in the making, where the psychic reality of the child, the psychic reality of the mother who impinges on him (the external reality of which he has just witnessed at the station), the internal processes, and the analyst's intuition mingle into a single, surprising, plausible hypothesis which finds support in the progressive presentation of clinical evidence.

This is a single session and a single interpretation which Winnicott grasped by trial and error, simply and honestly unveiling his temporarily misguided hypotheses, which were nevertheless close enough to the core of his initial – perhaps blurred, vague – intuition.

We are witnessing the agility of one who knows how to step back and change direction when – through understanding the child's signals in the transference/countertransference – he realizes he is not on the right path towards discovering the core of Mark's problem, "who feels a nothing" and who is sporadically invaded by his mother's madness.

> The patient was a boy of 6 years who was referred to me on account of his being unable to make use of his good intelligence; instead, he would bite holes in his gloves, coat, tie, and jersey, and he would only defecate in a chamber pot near one of the parents. Further, he demanded routine that was strict in many details, and he was restricted in the foods he could eat.
>
> There is no need for a detailed description of the case here, where I have the limited aim to describe the psychotherapeutic interview that he had with me on the only occasion that I saw him. The interview had a good effect because I was able to sort out the muddle in the boy's mind from the muddle introduced into his life by certain characteristics of the mother. It can be taken for granted by the reader that this only child was loved by his parents and that the family was in no danger of breaking up. The father was of professional class, and the mother had had her own training as a teacher.
>
> In order to give a useful picture of the session I must ask the reader to follow many details which need to be reported simply because they give continuity to the material.
>
> (Winnicott, 1989, p. 375. All subsequent quotations and drawings from the session with Mark are taken from this paper.)

Though he declines to describe the case in full, the "details which ... give continuity to the material" are the soul of the clinical work and its narration, and Winnicott does not neglect their importance. Indeed, he elevates their cognitive significance, both for the reader who is outside the clinical relationship and therefore "does not know" what the analyst knows, but also for the analyst himself who is not only immersed in the relationship with the patient but simultaneously outside it, constantly looking for those individual details that may give meaning to the "material." The word "material" returns here in Winnicott's terminological repertoire with a distinctive semantic density, as is happily illustrated in a chapter of his posthumous book *Human Nature* which I think may be unique in all of psychoanalytic literature in dealing with and distinguishing "the various types of psychotherapeutic material." I do not have time to dwell further on this particularly original Winnicottian theme that is so densely packed with meanings.

He and I played the Squiggle Game together, and it was easy for me to find his capacity to enjoy playing and to play along with him. This is what happened alongside the drawings: after a desultory discussion of his home and his family situation, we prepared the paper and two pencils, and I started with the first squiggle.

1. Mine, which he made into a donkey, giving alternatives: pig, cow, horse, dog. "It has a funny eye." Here in the "funny eye," we already had a reference to the unpredictable.

11.1

2. His, which he said was a head, and I gave it a girl's body.
3. Mine, which he turned into a funny head. Note the recurrence of the theme of "funny," indicating its significance. He made a reference to me which belonged to the mother's assessment of me. Apparently, she possesses a book by me and he had seen this, and he said: "You do good head writing." I think the elaborate scribble on the forehead referred to brains, as if it were a portrait of me seen through the mother's eyes. "The man has a funny nose with three nostrils. His ears are behind so that you do not see them."

11.2

He told me about other things he could draw, including a bus, and he was very keen to get coloured crayons. He had already used me *to talk about the idea of something funny about the mind. I, of course, made no interpretations.* The three nostrils could be thought of as mad, but within the area of the boy's play activities.

(Ibid., pp. 375–376, my italics)

Note Winnicott's impressive progression in identifying, step by step as the squiggles are made, the emergence of a "funny" element, both comical and strange. This is naturally an example of that pre-conceptual determinant which orients clinical observation but also, on the epistemological level, clearly reveals what Bollas calls the

271

perceptual nature of theories, which I earlier defined in terms of their "clinical derivation."

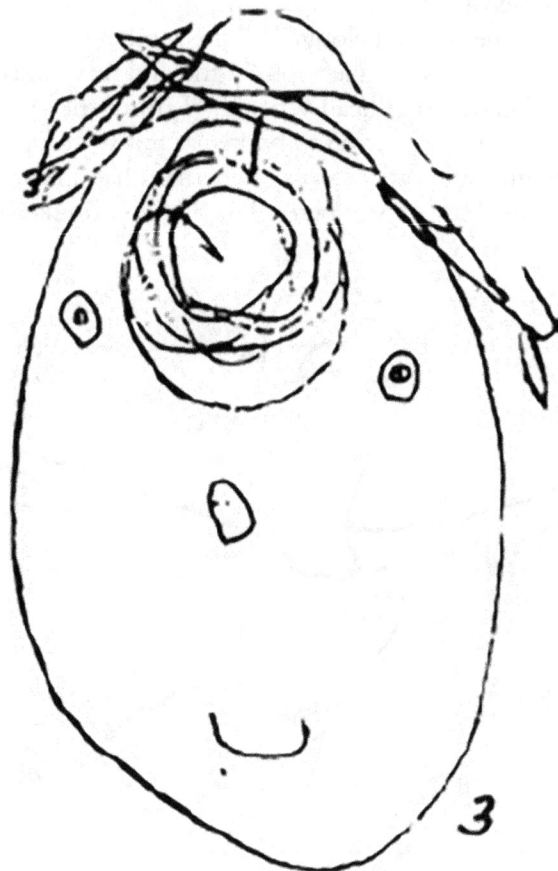

11.3

4. Here the paper got torn in the process of vigorous drawing. He did not manage to draw anything at first.

With hindsight we could say that it is here that the 'alien' material, pressing from the unconscious, starts preparing the way to 'come through.'

5. This has some sort of mystery to it. It was his and up in the corner he made a mark. This mark was also part of an M. There is a pun on his name here. He said, "It's a nothing." He had reached an extreme defense, for if he is a nothing then he cannot be killed or hurt by the worst trauma imaginable

11.4

11.5

Figure 11.1d1 and 11.1d2 Winnicott's cognitive process begins to take shape: from the clinical viewpoint it is exemplary in the way he allows himself to be guided by that incomprehensible little mark to the side of the squiggle, which leads him to ask the boy what it is. "It's a nothing," says the boy. Mark feels "he is a nothing," like that negligible mark. A first interpretative hypothesis, a first gestalt, has already taken shape, but various changes of direction will be needed

273

before Winnicott can find his way onto the correct path; a first interpretative hypothesis has taken form but is awaiting other clinical developments, other transformations, in order to be understood and interpreted.

> I followed up the theme in talking to him here of drawing as a way of getting something out of his head onto the paper. He talked about the way in which the train sometimes has to stop to allow an express train to come through. He said, "Our train gets blocked because they have to change the points and then we can come back again."
> Here he just saved the pencil from falling onto the floor, and these and other small things seemed significant, indicating that there was chaos rather than order in his immediate experiences.
>
> (Ibid., p. 376)

To Winnicott's insight about the "blocked train" is added a further insight which shows almost in real time the epistemology of the case: chaos instead of order, another building block to be added to the funniness of the eye, the mark that is "a nothing," and the blocked train.

> We had an interlude here. I used the pause to ask him about dreams. He said, "I don't know." Now he was back doing no. 4. "It is an engine. That is a good window. It is like a real engine's window, a steam train."
>
> (Ibid.)

Winnicott has prepared the ground – "dug the tunnel" we could say, to use the language of railways – so that the "ego-alien" element can get through. In doing so, he has transformed something, "given form" to something chaotic, not fully representable, and not represented in the boy.

> He was getting towards the traumatic express train, which evidently reminded him of Mother. "In Battersea Park there is a train that looks like a stream train but really it is a diesel. Mummy thinks it is a stream train!" He went on about steam trains that he sees on the underground. He watches real shunting and he has seen it a lot of times on various trips to Victoria Station; backwards and forwards. "I have seen in the paper something on the

274

other side of the world that was on fire. People weren't killed; well not while it was a little fire."

(Ibid., pp. 377–378)

Winnicott does not mention this, but let me hypothesize that "the other side of the world" is mother's madness which turns his mind upside-down. In saying that "people weren't killed: well not while it was a little fire," Mark means – if I am allowed to suppose this – when mother madness was circumscribed, not invasive.

We could say that, in terms of the case's epistemology, Winnicott is pushing ahead, putting together more things than the child is saying. If until this moment he has proceeded with caution, respecting the child's rather measured rhythm, here it seems he hits the accelerator, as if he himself was in a hurry to give shape to what has not yet been formulated. As analysts we cannot deny that we are constantly subjected to changes of speed along the way to understanding: a more linear flow, sudden accelerations, changes of gear.

> The immense potentialities of the danger are indicated – a comment on the fire in the steam engine "Oh, we forgot the coal tender." He started to try to add it onto the back of the engine; many further details got lost at this point, and then he suddenly manifested something quite new and out of the general trend of the material.

(Ibid.)

Winnicott detects a fracture in the continuity of the clinical material. Indeed, the next section of the paper is entitled 'The Traumatic Agent Arrives.'

> At this point he started to behave quite out of character. I could hardly recognize him as the same boy. A new thing had come and had taken hold of him. This that was new had to do with hearing a funny noise.

(Ibid.)

"Funny" appears again, as at the beginning of the case description.

> It was a booming sound. It might come from the gas fire, a sort of sound when it is leaking. He went over to examine the gas fire, but there was no smell to it, so it wasn't leaking

275

It was not possible to be sure whether he was hallucinating or remembering in auditory terms. *I fished around* by making an interpretation about hearing the parents in the other room, to which he gave a strong No, and he said: "It was very high up on the hills or perhaps right away at the source of the Thames."

(Ibid., my italics)

The striking sentence is "a new thing had come and had taken hold of him": another step forward in Winnicott's hypothesis, but still being mulled over in the countertransference. Although there are now many clues, this is the most decisive one so far. "Taken hold of him" is like saying "it had taken possession of him." The ghost of the mad mother appears here clearly for the first time.

The register of the session has been suddenly transformed. The boy has changed direction. From the epistemological viewpoint we might wonder if what Winnicott calls the arrival of the traumatic agent may not be the result of that pre-formulation by the analyst which the boy must in some way have detected, from unconscious to unconscious: "there is room" – we could say Mark is considering – to bring out "the thing" on the basis of the ground that Winnicott has prepared, that listening environment which from the beginning, through the analyst's noticing what is "funny" and the mark that is "a nothing," has given Mark the feeling that this dimension of the bizarre has been *noticed, understood, welcomed.* Just as when the arrival of the metro, even when it is still far from the station, is anticipated by a warm gust of wind whipping up scraps of paper and disturbing the waiting passengers' hair, the arrival of the traumatic agent is foretold by this disorganizing of the session, this sudden loss of sequential coherence.

However, reversing the direction of the vector which has accelerated Winnicott's internal interpretation, it could also be inferred that he needs to give form to something that was coming together, to have identified the boy's defense against chaos.

Before going on with my narrative of the session's development, I think it is useful to focus the reader's attention on Winnicott's diction: "I fished around." Have you ever read a psychoanalyst being so honest as to use this expression "I fished around" to convey to the reader that he does not fully comprehend the situation? In my opinion it is Winnicott himself who is not fully convinced. We can suppose that, not really understanding the communication that is going on, he tries a vague and tentative interpretation just to maintain a connection with the child.

Let's listen once again to what Winnicott says about his "fishing around":

> *I fished around* by making an interpretation about hearing the parents in the other room, to which he gave a strong No, and he said: "It was very high up on the hills or perhaps right away at the source of the Thames."
>
> (Ibid.)

This passage and what follows deserves to be read in full because it gives us a view in real time of the constant errors to which the analyst is exposed, and the constant readjustments you have to make, even going into reverse, if you want to stay in touch with the clinical material you yourself have contributed to transforming.

> I continued with my theme, saying "Like it might be the beginning of Mark, something happening between mother and father."
>
> He followed up my theme in an effort to comply by saying, "I started inside Mummy and I ended up out of Mummy at the hospital. There was no noise, babies crying."
>
> I said, "I wonder if there was noise inside Mummy," and he said he had his eyes closed so that he could not hear. I myself was bewildered and I seem to have persevered with this primal scene interpretation as if at a loss.
>
> It was difficult to take notes of the chaotic way the material was appearing. He made noises illustrative of the sort that he was hearing or remembering, and they seemed to include the word "No," and this sort of thing repeated itself many times. It was all frenzied or hectic. He interrupted this by saying, "What are you doing? – writing more books?" referring to the notes that I was taking. So I wrote "Mark" very big, and in several different ways. He said, "It's not good writing, it's scribbling."
>
> I think it was here that no. 4 was torn apart by Mark making his mark more and more vigorously. Here he found he had completely lost his pencil.
>
> (Ibid., p. 379)

This passage is worth commenting on in detail because of its epistemological outcomes in the context of the argument I am proposing.

In this respect, among the many other observations that come to mind after reading this text, we could highlight the way Winnicott offers the boy his interpretation, preparing it privately in step with the way the relationship is proceeding, mentally correcting it if new material leads in another direction, giving up an explicit statement if he notices that the boy is not yet ready to receive it: a matter of timing. And even when the boy is offered the interpretation, Winnicott is no less aware of making a suggestion, the most important aspect of which is certainly not the unveiling of an unconscious fantasy enclosed *inside* the patient, but the amplification of emotional and relational meanings that it generates in the boy who, in turn, refers them back to the analyst in a semantic circle. And so Winnicott uses the idiomatic expression "I fished around" which emphasizes the discreet attempt to reach the boy by referring to the primal scene after the "mad" experience's sudden irruption into the session.

And he points out to us the significance of Mark's referring back to his interpretation when he says the boy "followed up my theme in an effort to comply": a live example in transference terms of the False Self whose function is to protect the True Self from exploitation and annihilation.

I think it was here that no. 4 got torn by Mark making his mark more and more vigorously. Here he found he had completely lost his pencil. This seemed significant, although for a time he went over to an interest in an old penknife in the pencil box. Together we explored this and he said: "I am allowed a knife." With the knife he jabbed the paper and sometimes jabbed the table and it was at this point that most of the damage to no. 4 was done. Several times the sheet got new damage, and I think he was showing why he had to be nothing if he was to let the traumatic "thing" arrive. Here, too, was the penetration theme that we had already obtained of the origin of Mark.

He was then exploring the tin containing pencils and crayons. Have I got a "rubber"? (I haven't.) "My goodness." And so on. The game was now at the end and he began walking around starting some new theme. He took something from his right and left pockets and stuffed them in his right and left ears, and it seemed legitimate to suppose that he had come prepared to deal with them, and had brought right and left bits of paper for use in this respect.

He was manifesting a confused state, but he quickly changed the subject and referred to my roof garden which he could see from the window. He referred to a story in a comic and he wondered where the comic might be. Probably mother had it in the waiting room, he thought. In this way the actual Mother came back into his mind, and I was able to see that *the express train had been a mad Mother.* I was still unsure of my ground, however, and postponed making the main interpretation.

(Ibid., italics in original)

Again with apparent ingenuousness, Winnicott allows us to enter the temporary stalemate in his countertransference or, rather in his "bewildered" musing about the material. Such an impasse is a frequent occurrence in analytic work, but how many case reports are so open about this?

I certainly do not intend to reactivate here a technical controversy from the past that would no longer make sense today. However, with regard to the semantic and epistemological features of the session, while the classical Kleinian approach would be to make deep and premature interpretations, at the point where the anxiety emerged, in order to eradicate the supposed unconscious fantasy *inside* the child (or the adult patient), Winnicott is engrossed in following the course of the session and continually wondering whether the moment for interpretation has arrived, because he is so aware that an untimely interpretation is disruptive for the child and interrupts the sequence of the clinical process.

The register of the session changes again, perhaps we could say because of Winnicott's "stereotyped" interpretation of the primal scene, an error he is aware of and abandons as an inauthentic way forward. And yet, even though Winnicott decides not to follow this path, the boy becomes more disorganized.

Nevertheless, this disorganization is also representative of the "madness" that shortly makes its verbal entrance into the room. I think it is a uniquely astonishing moment when Winnicott observes that he "was able to see that the express train had been a mad mother," but was still unsure of his ground and therefore decided to delay the interpretation. Here the analyst's internal processes are evident, especially the preconscious and conscious ones, which are of course organized under internal unconscious pressure; but what is especially evident is the distinction between *interpreting and doing interpretations* which represents one of Winnicott's most exceptional contributions to the theory of technique. In essence, by abandoning or deferring interpretation, Winnicott once again tells us that we must go back to the patient in order to be sure enough that what we say will be sufficiently precise and pregnant: above all, *plausible*, even if it is not definitely true. In other words, the interpretation of the case must be given not only when the cognitive process has almost reached that epistemological point, but "at the right time" and in the appropriate *state of the self*, so that the boy, the patient, can take it, however troubling the analyst's interpretation may be. This is how Winnicott continues:

> Anxiety showed still further by his saying, "I might be going home soon, or now." He referred to fear of the noises, and there was some fun about the chair walking away and behaving as if it would kick Mother or get knocked over.
>
> I made a reference to the madness that his represented. Either he or I said, "Everything's gone mad," and there was some laughing. I said, about the head, "It's got eyes, but no ears," and he said, "Yes it has, but it fell over and now it's upside down."

In my view, there are two relevant remarks to be made here. The first refers to "either I or he said." Winnicott doesn't care to specify obsessively who it was who spoke. *Naïvely* he asserts the authenticity of his lack of a precise memory; secondly, and more importantly, the two partners of the interaction were mingled, so to speak. The sentence was a product of both of them.

> There was a moment of a mad world and some kind of sound like "Woof, woof" inside the mad chair, and then this noise went out on the other side of the chair. I made a remark about a mad place inside his head or possible inside his mother, and I began to have a conviction that this boy was bringing me a picture of his mother as an ill person.
>
> Continuing the primal scene theme, I said, "And then Mummy did a big noise and it was called Mark." Eventually I definitely stated, *"Mummy sometimes goes mad when you are there. This is what you are showing me."*
>
> He was distracting himself by talking about the care that you have to take with electric gadgets. He said, "I was born a boy."

I said, "You were born a big noise!" And he said, "I didn't!"

He was now wanting to go but saying that he was not scared, simply that he wanted to see his mother, so we went together to collect her.

(Ibid., p. 380., italics in original)

Before concluding with the comments of Winnicott himself I want to emphasize two relevant points. The session acquires a sort of circularity when Winnicott reconnects to the head of the third squiggle, i.e., "It's got eyes but no ears," and Mark replies, "Yes it has, but it fell over and now it's upside down." Secondly, Winnicott is at last almost sure about his cautiously constructed interpretation when he eventually releases it to the boy as a result of an intense inner work of imaginative elaboration.

Comment

When I had a new look at the mother, I realised that she does carry with her a severe personal problem, and when I spoke to her about this she was very willing to admit that she was often an ill person.

Later the mother said she was so very glad that I had seen in the way the boy behaved that she does go mad in front of the child, and she knew that it was this that was disturbing him. She is herself having treatment for her mental condition.

(Ibid.)

It is in this surprising comment that Winnicott sums up, step by step, the crucial moments of the internal process and the epistemology of the case which have finally led to the interpretation. In this way he sums up what has happened for the reader, or rather he interprets, deciphers what has happened, but in this summary he also adds something more: he offers us a coherent model that underpins the interpretation he has finally been able to offer the boy. With the metaphor of the small local train that has to stand still on a siding while the express train, the mother's madness, rushes through, he offers us a model which, as Bollas would say, has a "perceptual" meaning. It is not clear whether Winnicott is presenting the boy with this interpretation as a whole, but it is certain that the metaphor he uses for his model really transports a meaning from one place

281

to another, transforming it. I conclude by leaving the last word to Winnicott:

> In this example of a therapeutic consultation, it is possible to watch a boy of six years communicating a complex and dynamic personality pattern, not a profile but a representation in depth, integrated in a space-time continuum.
>
> He quickly senses the special conditions of the professional situation and develops the necessary trust in myself. On this premise he plays around with personal madness, testing out whether I can stand the 'funny' eyes and the triple nostrils. Then he shows the way he has learned to adopt the extreme defences of nothingness or invulnerability. He is no more than a mark, a mark that can be easily unnoticed. He happens to have the name Mark and he uses this in a playful way.
>
> Now the stage is set. He is there playing with me, and all is well. He warns me of the trains that have to go into a sideline to let through the express. In terms of the details of the steam train, he tells me about an immense potentiality for destruction: fire on the other side of the world.
>
> Then suddenly he goes mad, but it is more true to say that he is possessed by madness. It is no longer him, but it is a mad person that I watch – one who is completely unpredictable. The express train is rushing through the station while the local train is standing still in a siding.

Winnicott acutely notices that "'Nothing' is not being destroyed by the mad 'something.'"

> Then the mother's madness passes and the boy begins to want to use his mother as a mother who cares for him and whom he needs in order to get home. The boy leaves my house in a happy state. He is confident in this mother whose going mad is now been shown to me, whose going mad has been objectified and limited by its own boundaries. *Mark has become something instead of nothing* and he can play again, even play at absurdities which, being part of his own madness, are not traumatic so much as comical and laughable.
>
> (Ibid., pp. 380–381, my italics)

"Where is he when he is nothing?"

With this question, which he does not leave unanswered, Winnicott concludes this fascinating case, not for an instant losing his clinical grip on the material. As he says:

I think that in the consultation he relied on my having a mental image of him in my head which he could recall after the express train had gone through and the local train could come out of the siding.

The translation of this chapter was carried out by Gina Atkinson with the support of Adam Elgar.

Note

1   *Psycho-Analytic Explorations* (London: Karnac, 1989) includes this paper by Winnicott, dated 1969 but as the editors remark, it was published for the first time in *Tactics and Techniques in Psychoanalytic Therapy*, ed. Peter L. Giovacchini, (London: Hogarth Press; New York. Jason Aronson, 1972). Quotations and images from Winnicott's paper reproduced by permission of The Marsh Agency Ltd., on behalf of The Winnicott Trust CIO 1174533.

Reference

Winnicott, D. W. (1989). *Psychoanalytic Explorations*. Edited by C. Winnicott, R. Shepherd & M. Davis M. Cambridge MA: Harvard University Press.

THE BURDEN AND ENCUMBRANCE OF THE ANALYST AND THE ANALYSAND'S BODIES WITHIN THE CONFINES OF THE CONSULTING ROOM

Introduction

In this paper I would like to make a few points about the nature of the virtual relationship between the analyst and analysand's bodies in the consulting room. Although these bodies do not actually touch, fantasies of bodily contact may hinder the possibility of meaningful communication and may lead to the arousal of primitive persecutory anxieties relating to the destruction, dissolution, or fragmentation of the self.

I don't think it is *hyperbolic* to say that psychoanalysis was born with the body. The bodies of those young hysterical women, who at the end of the 1800s would rush to the most famous neuro-pathologists of the day with their fainting, mysterious paralyses, and temporary blindness often escaped understanding. I will not go further into this topic because it is a well-known part of psychoanalytic history, the close connection between the birth of our discipline, hysteria, the body, and the revolutionary role of women, who challenged conventions through their symptoms.

Freud's expression, *Organsprache* (1915), meaning the "language of the organ," is revolutionary because it captures the essence of

DOI: 10.4324/9781003228332-13   284

the thing that cannot be said, but at the same time finds a way of suggesting that communication can occur through the body. Let us consider the *inner semantics* of this expression, which amounts to a kind of *oxymoron,* since language was born precisely to elucidate what organs alone could not express. Here, Freud is confronting the paradox at the essence of hysteria: where the body, violated by real abuse or hyper-cathected by infantile sexual fantasies, carries scars that cannot be spoken about but search for a way of being expressed.

I would like to focus on this topic because I am interested in the dynamics between the bodies of the analysand and the analyst in the consulting room, of the fact that they are always on the verge of touching without ever physically touching, of the potential rather than the actual phenomenon. I wonder how it is possible that along the evolutionary path of psychoanalytic theorizing, up to and including today's significant subtleties, the body has almost disappeared from the psychoanalyst's horizon, except for some valuable recent contributions like Alessandra Lemma's (2014a, 2014b) and a few others. Recently, Lemma has brought the body back to the forefront of the analytic scene, especially as far as adolescents are concerned, in line with the Laufers' (1984) contributions and those of many French psychoanalysts on the subject of the pubertal body (Gutton, 2013).

Despite these contributions one may wonder if André Green's (1995) statement 'Has Psychoanalysis Anything to Do with Sexuality?' provocatively delivered as the 'Sigmund Freud Birthday Lecture' at The Anna Freud Centre in London, is true also for the body. Green's astute realization was that the central element of psychoanalysis, infantile sexuality (also – not by chance – connected to the body), had become progressively diluted, as if analysts themselves had towards sexuality the same resistance Freud had identified in his patients and educated audience (Freud, 1913).

The analysand and the analyst's bodies as "heavy presences" in the consulting room

I will try to discuss this topic from a clinical point of view, with a specific focus on the analyst/analysand relationship. By 'relationship' I do not mean only transference-countertransference dynamics, but also everything else that is, so to speak, 'behind the scenes,' and about which we are becoming increasingly aware today.

285

I mean, for example, the stomach gurgle of the silent patient or the analyst (who is often troubled by not knowing whose stomach is gurgling!), or the stripping of cuticles while a patient is thinking, or the biting of the inside of the cheeks, or the sudden request to go to the bathroom (Lemma, 2014a). As far as the analyst is concerned, there is also his transitory physical malaise, his adjustments on the seat, looking for a better listening position, the weight on his stomach if he had to eat in a rush, or, on the contrary, the craving for food if he had to skip lunch.

In my opinion, all of these phenomena relate to two bodies in the analytic room, which never touch but are in a continuous relationship. They could inadvertently touch, brushing against unintentionally, which is as important as the fact that they do not.

A young patient speaks with haste of a problem that surfaced the night before with her partner. She is so immersed in her narrative that she almost forgets the analyst, listening behind her. At some point, in the haste of her narration, she points her elbows on the couch and raises her torso. *Organsprache*: the patient puts herself in a premature Ego position (clinically related to premature ego development, which Winnicott refers to in his theory of the early parent–infant interaction (1960).[1] She refuses regression because she needs to underline her particular anger, or a particularly intense affect that could not otherwise be expressed. Then, lying down, she starts speaking in a calmer but still hasty way. I don't think anybody would consider interpreting this behavior until it became semantically meaningful. The beginning of Winnicott's paper 'Interpretation in Psychoanalysis' (1968) deals specifically with this topic:

> It is important from time to time to look at the basic principles of the psycho-analytic technique and to attempt to reassess the importance of the various elements that the classical technique comprises. It would be generally conceded that an important part of psychoanalytic technique is interpretation, and it is my purpose here to study once more this particular part of what we do. The word "interpretation" implies that we are using words, and there is an implication, which is that material supplied by the patient is verbalized. In its simplest form there is the basic rule, which still has force, although many analysts never instruct their patients even on this detail. By this time, after more than half a century of psychoanalysis, patients know that they are expected to say what comes

to their minds and not to withhold. It is also generally recognized now that a great deal of communication takes place from patient to analyst that is not verbalized. This may have been noticed first in terms of the nuances of speech and the various ways in which speech certainly involved a great deal more than the meaning of the words used. Gradually analysts found themselves interpreting silences and movements and a whole host of behavioral details, which were outside the realm of verbalization. Nevertheless there were always analysts who very much preferred to stick to the verbalized material offered by the patient. When this works it has obvious advantages in that the patient does not feel persecuted by the observer's eyes. With a silent patient, a man of 25 years, I once interpreted the movement of his fingers, as his hands lay clasped across his chest. He said to me: "If you start interpreting that sort of thing then I shall have to transfer that sort of activity to something else which does not show." In other words, he was pointing out to me that unless he had verbalized his communication it was not for me to make comment. (p. 207)

This 'mistake' helps Winnicott with another work, 'A Point in Technique' (*undated*), in my view a true pearl of Winnicott's clinical intuition (the editors of the posthumous volume *Psychoanalytic Explorations* (1989) were not able to date it).

I have learned recently to adopt the following procedure in analytic practice. When the fantasy that is represented in the transference material is revealed I ask myself: what and where is the accompanying orgastic bodily function? And, per contra, when in the analytic situation there is orgastic bodily functioning I asked myself: what fantasy material is the patient telling me about by this functioning.

(Winnicott, 1989, p. 26)

A first "early" countertransference nightmare

Let us get closer to the analyst's body through two countertransference dreams that *après-coup*, seem to be related, in the sense that one explains and gives meaning to the other. If what I have just defined as *A first "early" countertransference nightmare* is not really a countertransference dream, it becomes in my view a countertransference dream after the real countertransference for the similarity of the structure of the nightmare and the position of the bodies of the two persons. Approximately 10 years ago, during a long road trip in the US with a large group of friends, I extended the vacation for an extra week, which was to be spent in Hawaii. The 'Hawaiian group' was made up of two couples without children, plus myself and my younger daughter, who was in those days an early adolescent. I was Oedipally proud of this trip, mostly of being able to offer it to my 'beloved girl' who was enthusiastic about it.

It was the first time that my family (my wife, my older son, my daughter, and myself) would be separated on vacation. I was happy to have this opportunity but I felt I should be additionally vigilant, both because it was the first time I was taking a vacation alone with my daughter, and because the islands did present some real dangers. My daughter attended a brief surfing course and I remember waiting anxiously on the shore, trying in vain to see her head in the water. My anxiety was increased by daily news of surfers drowning. One could often hear rescue helicopters searching for surfers. Swimming was possible only in secluded bays but that too, although fun, was very different to swimming in the Mediterranean. There were many yellow warning signs. For example, in apparently calm and flat waters, all of a sudden, a long wave would come in, causing, on its way back of the bay, a strong suction towards the bottom. This suction was so strong it would give the feeling of the blood being sucked out of one's veins. This was also entertaining and exciting for all of the children and swimmers.

After the holidays, going back to work and having dinner with friends, I would often speak of this episode, which seemed interesting to many. During this time I had the following dream.

I was in the water with my daughter, waiting for the suction towards the bottom, but this time it was so strong I lost sight of her. I was waiting anxiously for her to surface again. After a while I became very worried, screaming for help and diving underwater to search for her. In the murky water mixed with sand, I could barely see the color of her swimming suit. I tried to get close to her which was very difficult and required enormous effort. In the end I managed to grab her and pull her out, but she was unconscious. I was hoping she had just lost her bearings, but I woke up from the nightmare sweaty, worried that she had lost all the blood in her veins, because of her pallor. The feeling of having the blood sucked out of my veins had become reality. I thought *the ocean was like a vampire that had killed her.*

I would like to highlight the significance in this countertransference dream of the terrible sense of having the blood sucked out me, a specific element that becomes meaningful only in *après-coup*, or in *imaginative elaboration* (Bonaminio, 2014), which acts as a bridge between the two following dreams. As I pointed out in a paper (Bonaminio, 2015) on Anna Freud's work 'Notes on a Connection Between the States of Negativism and of Emotional Surrender' (1952), the emotional surrender of the object, the state of total passivity, the terror of being sucked in and included in the love object, is an anxiety so profound and primary that it compels the Ego to raise very early defenses, equally primitive, such as negativism.

A clinical presentation: Giuseppe

Giuseppe is a 31-year-old patient who appears to be very clumsy. He was embarrassed in his first few sessions, apparently attempting to hide or minimize a brilliant intelligence. He would seem passive or negativistic, always at the point of surrendering to the object, both in his affectionate relations and in the transference, then withdrawing for periods of variable length into autistic-like psychic retreats, like those described by many authors from different perspectives (Winnicott, 1954; Tustin, 1990; O'Shaughnessy, 1992; Steiner, 1993).

When the patient entered these retreats, his analysis revolved around significant self-criticism and self-loathing, which he believed was evident to everybody. These, of course, were accusations leveled at the analyst. He was indeed a very complex patient who began analysis as a university student, in the '70s, having taken some 'group exams.' In those days, the outcome of these exams would invariably be an "A" for everybody, thus most had only a superficial knowledge of the topics. He was the organizer of these farcical exams for a complacent but admiring professor. Giuseppe was part of a radical Bionian group and this led him to say that it was not the individual, but *the group who produced thoughts searching for a thinker,* paraphrasing Bion (1977), a senseless *mantra* that I was soon to understand. There was a strong aggressive dimension to this, as if he was saying, "Fuck the professors and the analyst too," which, on the other hand, hid a bottomless self-loathing.

289

I had been immediately impressed by Giuseppe's body, by his heavy build, although not fat, his thick beard, his way of occupying the room: when he would lie on the couch he "fell, even as a dead body falls."[2] Sometimes his narrative would allow me to make an interpretation; more often, he would be locked in an aggressive, inviolable silence, apparently against the analyst, but in fact against himself.

A session halfway through the first year of his analysis: he looks sullen as he comes into the room, self-critical. He drops his jacket with apparent care on the chair facing the table. His jacket is made of a slippery fabric. While he passes, I look at him, at his overwhelming body, and the jacket. Before he lies down, the jacket slowly slips onto the floor. He hears it falling, turns around and sees it on the floor, shrugs his shoulders as if to say, 'Who cares?' and lies down.

My countertransference feelings flare up. I feel a strong anger that is difficult to contain, caused by the way this patient treats himself. I am compelled to an enactment, probably activated by his shrugging of his shoulders. I try to stop myself but I stand up while he is still lying down. He stares at me, surprised, as I pick up the jacket. I position it with care on the chair and say: "If this is your way of letting me know how much you despise yourself, your body, and myself too, well, I don't accept it, I won't collude with you. For me your body is important, it's not an old rug." The patient laughs nervously and, almost with a challenging tone, says, "Yes, but I would have picked it up later." I said, "But in the meantime your cadaver would have lain here between us." He replies, "Cadaver! You exaggerate as usual!" I say, "Despising my words is useless, since they have the same dignity as yours, the only difference is that I'm here to help you."

He shrugs his shoulders again, as if to strengthen his hatred. He remains silent for a long time. With a hesitant voice he says: "*This is not the important thing of today. It's a dream that I had one or two nights ago, a nightmare, yet which still leaves me indifferent, like everything nowadays.*" My heart starts accelerating, as if I were forecasting in a delirious way something that could not be said.

A traumatic event in the life of Giuseppe

Before reporting the dream, I have to point out that this patient had told me of a *traumatic episode* that left a permanent mark on his family. He has seven brothers, all of whom worked actively as farmers from ages 12 to 18. This was not an idyllic situation, but one of significant conflict inside the family, both among the brothers and with the parents. He was the second to last, thus the most privileged and most loved by his mother. She had planned for him to graduate, with the hope of changing the family's destiny, while the other brothers had taken menial jobs, married, and had children. He is very successful with the women from his university department, a kind of boyfriend to all of them *("il fidanzato di tutte")*. He spends one or two weeks with an idealized mate, then feels oppressed and interrupts the relationship.

The traumatic episode I learned about is truly upsetting. There was a harsh discussion between his mother (his father is always silent) and the youngest son, who was perhaps expected to be a girl. This discussion was so violent that the boy, at the time 16, left the dinner table, a true challenge to his parents' authority in the eyes of a rural family. He ran outside, downhill, along the cliff surrounding the south side of the house. According to my patient's story, it was as if time had stopped. His father said nothing, one could only hear the nervous clinking of spoons against soup dishes. Then, the mother spoke to my patient in dialect, using vulgar terms, "What the fuck are you waiting for? Go get him, he's hot-headed. Go see where he's gone." My patient says he heard his mother's order, but was paralyzed, fearful of making things more complicated. Then he jumped from his chair, ran down the hill, all the way to a torrential river. He screamed, calling for his brother, but received no answer. An uncontainable anxiety started building up in his chest, his heart beating fast. Finally, going down the river, he saw in the water the limp body of his brother, still hanging onto a tree trunk, with a large wound on the head, probably caused by hitting another tree trunk. He dived in and dragged him out of the water. He saw blood coming out of the occipital area, but still hoped to save him. He alternated screaming for help with attempts to resuscitate him, trying everything, until he saw in a bend of the river a large pool of blood. Then he understood there was nothing more to do. At that point, all the family members arrived. There were screams, accusations, and his mother's dreadful phrase: "Giuseppe, you killed *my* son ... You are not my son any more ..."

All that follows is quite dramatic, but space does not allow me to go on. All I can say is that his adoring mother's phrase transformed the situation into its exact opposite. Basically, he is now perceived only as his brother's killer. This mark will stay with him until college, not allowing him to excel precisely because it would be a challenge to his mother's curse. All this is interpreted in the transference from several perspectives, for example, when he asks in a despising manner: "You are so good and famous, what would it take for you to write my thesis? Instead of leaving me drowning in my difficulties. If this is psychoanalysis, then it's fucking useless."

Going back to the dream that, according to my patient, would put into perspective the jacket episode, here is what he tells me.

Giuseppe's dream

I was in a kind of third-class hospital with flaking walls and a bad smell suggesting poor hygiene. I look around, awakened by the busy movements of the hospital's personnel, wearing dirty white coats. I raise my head and I realize I'm in a low stretcher, next to my mother's bed. Out of my arm I see a disproportionately large tube that I follow with my eyes. I notice it goes under my mother's sheets. While the nurses check that everything is fine, I realize something horrific. It is a blood transfusion, from me to my mother.

I have to donate blood to my mother, who has lost plenty of it, but what is monstrous is that the tube really is some kind of umbilical cord, going up my mother's vagina. I assume my mother had a large uterine hemorrhage, but I don't understand how her blood can be restored in this manner.

It is not possible to get into the details of this dream, but roughly speaking, as it was interpreted to him extremely cautiously, the patient felt it was his duty is to revive, to give back life, to his dying mother, although she was still angry at him as responsible for his youngest brother's death. In other words, he has to give himself to his mother in order to make her live, but by doing this he becomes bloodless, that jacket/rag that fell from the chair.

While I listen to this terrible, anxiety-provoking dream, my countertransference is bombarded by a series of associations and violent emotions that I have a hard time containing. My mind is focused on the image of myself, carrying my dead, bloodless child out of the water, desperately screaming for help that nobody would give me.

The second countertransference dream

I believe this dream was a sort of a *countertransference forecast* of something unconscious that captured the essence of the relationship between myself and my patient, of which I had only a vague impression at the time.

I find myself in an incredibly crowded festival, the so-called "Roman Summer" similar to Oktoberfest. I feel lost in the disorderly crowd that runs wildly among the stands of food and sweets, among people who are drunk and invite me to dance. At a certain point, the crowd parts, as when Moses parted the Red Sea to rescue the Hebrews from the Egyptian oppressors. I see, from a distance, a man coming towards me, a man of large size, and a hand approaching. It seems to me to be my patient. In recognizing me he speeds up as if he were searching in the chaos all around me. I stiffen, but at the same time I am trying to be friendly and containing. I throw my arms around him. I smell the strong and acrid smell of alcohol. He pronounces words disjointedly, like "dehydrated" … "I have no more blood." Clearly he is asking me for mouth to mouth resuscitation. I wake up from the nightmare sweaty and panting.

The transformative experience of hearing my patient's dream, forecast, so to speak, by my two countertransference dreams, sheds light on the reciprocal quality of the relationship between this patient and myself. Even though in previous phases I had understood the quality of this relationship to lie in the pre-Oedipal realm (i.e., "you are so good…" equivalent to "Mummy, you do it"), I had not yet become aware of the symbiotic *transfusive* quality of our relationship. Perhaps this meaning hovered on the edge of my awareness while I was awaiting this passage. Perhaps a blind spot prevented my seeing it.

In effect, in his treatment with me, Giuseppe would always feel like a dependent child trying to recover the privileged relationship with his mother. But since I had not perceived this level of meaning, my interpretations were always aimed above this primary fusional (or *trans-fusional*) need.

For a while, looking at the various phases of his analysis as flashbacks, it seemed to me that I had systematically missed this level, making my patient always more demanding and more dissatisfied with my contributions. In brief, it was as if he was saying, "I come here, I give you my blood, and you ignore my sacrifice?" All of a sudden, I realized that his dream (and my countertransference dreams of which he knows nothing) belonged to that transformative dream category that, as Freud said, *turn the page* (Cfr. Quinodoz, 2002) After this, everything became clear.

Obviously, this hypothetical clarity – I am reminded of Meltzer (1973) – did not make things easier for me. On the contrary, it made my task more demanding. Inspired insight (Meltzer, 1973) can contain an omnipotent, delirious, omniscient element. The analyst who thinks he is finally on the right track arrogantly yields to unilateral interpretations, while true analytic work is always made up of blood, sweat, and tears, regardless of insight, and can only have as confirmation the circular feedback of the patient. I have called this the *spiral circularity of interpretation* (Bonaminio, 2001). Secondly, if before I felt the physical presence of this patient as bulky, now, in moments of silence, breathing at the same time, seeing his belly movements and hearing his small coughs, I felt we had been brought even closer together, which is what Little calls basic unity (1960).

This turn of events did not please me. My patient, as I had pictured him up to that point, needed to be brought to an Oedipal level, so he could recognize me as a separate figure. But I began to realize that our relationship was at a much more primitive level than I had imagined, and that the road I had taken was only the beginning of a long, complex trek in the woods.

This framework of the analysand feeding the mother/analyst by giving up parts of himself is certainly not new to us, and was described in Winnicott's 'Reparation in Respect of Mother's Organized Defense against Depression' (1948). In essence, the child listening carefully to his mother's emotional movements is some kind of detector, identifying her deepest feelings. When her depressed moods surface, he sacrifices himself, trying to make her happy. In this way, the child works to create a supportive environment that he cannot take for granted, but that is fundamental for his growth. The child and the patient in analysis renounce substantial parts of themselves in the hope they will reappear in the form of a smile on the face of the mother/analyst with whom he can identify.

In other words, the child is on his own attempting to repair the situation. It is not by accident that in the article cited above Winnicott calls this "false reparation," as opposed to the *autochthonous reparative elements* described by Melanie Klein (1946). As we know, Green (1980) writes one of his most interesting papers on this configuration, *the dead mother complex,* although he fails to give full credit to Winnicott for the origins of this idea. This configuration can be called "psychic work done for the other" (Bonaminio & Di Renzo, 2000).

Even though I must admit this is not the patient I wanted and that – to use Winnicott's words – I had conducted a "false analysis" (Bollas, 1987), several aspects were clarified and almost spontaneously I was able to direct my interpreting in a more benevolent direction. For example, on one occasion I interpreted what previously I did not have the courage to interpret, when I was locked in a trans-fusional situation I failed to fully understand. I said that he did not feel ready to graduate, so he demeaned his intelligence, as he had with his jacket, by allowing everything to drop. He did not feel "whole but in fragments, badly put together." He expected me to put him together properly, in a functioning single component that would allow him to write his thesis.

In other words, his self-devaluation resulted in him believing that only I could write his thesis, and that the exams he had passed were pre-digested pieces of culture, waiting for his mother (and in the transference, his analyst) to complete digesting them. In the same way, the many relationships he had with girls could only be brief because he could not support a genuine intimacy: his mission was only to give pleasure to these girls. Nothing was left for him.

I will come back to this analysis, but what I wish to stress here is that I see this "catastrophic change" (Bion, 1977) as a transition from a reciprocal projective identification between the patient and myself, which only reinforced our reciprocal defenses, to a primary identification, where the identification acts like a soothing agent between my patient and myself.

In his last fundamental contribution, 'Impasse and Interpretation' (1987), Rosenfeld recognized that with traumatized patients, interpretation should pass from the analyst to the patient osmotically, somewhat like the mother's contents passing osmotically to the child. This is contrasted with transference interpretation, (strongly favored in his 1953 book and based on projective identification) which in the transference reproduces the trauma, often somatic, that the child suffered in his early separation from his mother.

As far as Giuseppe is concerned, one may say that through my somewhat nervous and vaguely punitive enactment of picking up his jacket, he began to allow me to get closer at a physical level to the trans-fusional bond between his mother and himself, and in the transference between myself and him.

In avoiding generalizations or emphasizing one element over the others (since the analytic relationship is always multifaceted and existing at various levels), the physical level, even if undetected, is the one that guides emotional exchanges between analyst and analysand. I believe that what we have to do is re-evaluate the central role of the body of the analysand and the analyst in the analytic process.

How the presence of the body and its specificity affect the relationship between the analyst and the adolescent's relationship in the consulting room

I would like to refer now to a different category of patients, mostly 'confrontational' adolescents (Lemma, 2010), who seem to convey an attitude of 'I am doing you a favor and I only come because my father who is the crazy one sends me, but it should be him coming.' They attack the analyst at various levels, despising and devaluing him, as if they were on a mission to make him explode. Not only adolescents, but also traumatized, schizoid patients, those defined by Rosenfeld as "thick-skinned" (Rosenfeld, 1987) and apparently impermeable to the analyst's work are similarly provocative.

The movie 'Crash,' directed by Paul Haggis (2004), well exemplifies the friction these patients bring into the transference. The movie focuses on the fact that in contemporary postmodern society, relationships between individuals are possible only through a crash; maybe in some cases something relational can happen only after the crash has been absorbed. The movie begins with a police officer arriving at a Los Angeles highway car crash, where a violent discussion is taking place between two drivers (a second crash). This movie basically points to the intrinsic conflict-laden nature of coexistence in a city like Los Angeles, but it could be set in any metropolitan city. This condition of conflict is acted out by a series of fights, both interracial and between social classes. In the end, everything connects in a sort of circular puzzle.

The dialogue which opens the film makes clear the lack of physical contact in LA, where everyone lives behind glass and metal, and no one brushes against a passerby. The only way to feel the other's presence is by crashing into them.

What follows are two scenes from the movie that I find particularly meaningful.

An American upper class black couple (he is a TV director) is returning home from an award ceremony and behaves in a blatantly transgressive way, taking for granted privilege and freedom based on his social class. His wife gives him oral sex while he is driving. Two white police officers see them and stop them, taking the opportunity to confront and overturn the class difference between them. They use the power inherent in their uniforms to humiliate the couple, even to the point of searching the wife in a sexually violent, intrusive and abusing way while the husband is held with his hands tied behind his back. They are then released in a condescending and humiliating way.

In another scene, the police officer from this scene returns to his sordid home where he cares for his father, ill with prostate cancer. He helps his father urinate and is obliged to clean up his urine and feces. The emotional atmosphere around this 'rapist' cop changes completely. Now he is pitied by the spectator: activity and passivity, sympathy and loathing seem to be merely two sides of the same coin.

Due to time constraints, I can only provide brief sketches of what I call the secret intertwining of bodies in the analytic setting, even in the absence of physical contact. Previously, I have discussed the Osvaldo case (Bonaminio & Di Renzo, 2014), and I will only make brief mention of it here. Persecuted by paranoid anxieties, and by being the subject of bullying at school, my patient Osvaldo felt neither male nor female, but some kind of non-gendered monster. However, he did feel persecutory physical sensations coming from his erogenous zones. He is the boy who told me in our first session, "You can't help me because my problems are physical, not psychological." The early phases of the analysis were conducted, of course, face to face (his refusal to use the couch was an attempt to ward off further persecutory anxieties). Osvaldo carefully inspected my body, attentive to even the smallest movement, to which he would attribute imaginative sexual signals. These first sessions were very unpleasant for me because he managed to paralyze and control me. Only when I understood, not intellectually, but through a flesh and blood experience, that what he was doing in the transference was like a reversal of his mother's continuous exploration of his body, did the pressure lift somewhat. Osvaldo continued to fantasize about my body, but now these fantasies could be put into words and elaborated. His main anxiety and desire was to be sodomized (he would walk past the long line of showers at the gym, looking stealthily at the athletes showering, which excited him and caused compulsive masturbation at night). Eventually this fantasy came into the room, when he said: "I had the thought that all of these fantasies of being penetrated are directed at Dr. Bonaminio. Now it's all over, I am hopeless."

I present this brief summary to emphasize that the body-crash can only be mitigated after the analyst's words reach the patient. This can occur only after a long period of elaboration and can transform a concrete bodily experience into feeling states that can be shared.

It is more difficult to talk about my countertransference feelings, due to the extreme passivity of Osvaldo, even if disguised by a significant amount of aggressiveness, but every now and then I experienced perverse fantasies about him. After a time, I came to realize that these were a kind of revenge for being the object of his passivity. With this realization, I was able to return to him in a meaningful and equilibrating way. The fantasies subsequently disappeared. From then on, a more benign atmosphere was established between myself and Osvaldo.

I agree with Bion's famous statement:

When two personalities meet in the analytic setting an emotional storm is created. If they make sufficient contact to be aware of each other or even sufficient contact to be unaware of each other, an emotional state is produced by the engagement of these two individuals. The resulting disturbance is not necessarily to be regarded as an improvement on the state of affairs had they never met at all. But since they have met, and since this emotional storm has occurred, the two parties to this storm may decide to "make the best of a bad job."

(1979, p. 321)

Unfortunately, this is not always possible.

My patient Floriana was an exceptional and bright girl. Despite this, she attempted the entrance test to a Department of Medicine several times, failing it, but then with great ease went into another scientific department. She came to me after a first analysis which she felt was a failure because it was loaded with prohibitions related to her sexual and social exuberance which, in her opinion, were only due to the "old bitch's" (her former analyst) envy. When she entered my office, she was taken by the furniture. She said, "This is Freud's office, this really is a psychoanalytic consulting room, marvelous, exceptional! I will get well by just breathing the air of this room."

I immediately perceived her seductively and erotized transference. I kept a kind but detached attitude and, in a few months, the field was cleared of this obvious resistance to analysis. True analytic work began. Floriana made ample associations, lying on the couch, reporting in detail her sexual performances. I realize (but I don't say it) that she has never had a real orgasm. I am also surprised to learn that she is well known among her colleagues, running a sort of "consultation office" where the most uncool, naïve, or promiscuous ones come to her for advice and suggestions. She makes me think of Lucy in the Charlie Brown strips.

"Read here," says one of these friends, showing her a cell phone screen. "Do you think he cares about me or just wants to fuck me?" On one side I am impressed by her caring ability, on the other I consider it a transference resistance, which shifts onto her friends the erotized relationship she has with me. I am given an opportunity by an apparently *en passant* comment, comparing her present analysis with the preceding one, "You are also a good-looking man, say like my father." It was not difficult to put things back into the right place with an interpretation that was not mortifying but actually gratifying to her Oedipal request.

At a certain point, she tells me of her self-cutting activity. She pulls up her sleeve (for the first time I realize that she has never arrived in short sleeves, not even in the summer), and I see a left arm covered with scars. She tells me openly of her continuous poking at her skin with a pocketknife, while she decides whether to do it or not. When she is most anxious, she lets the blade sink into her skin until she sees blood coming out. The depth of her elaboration on this topic surprises me. She says literally, "You see, when you feel psychic pain, it does not go away, it stays inside, you can bang your head against a wall or go fuck around to San Lorenzo, but anyway it stays; you come home and it's the same. Only when you see the blood slowly coming out of your arm you feel psychic pain dissolve; calm descends upon you, like when it starts to snow. The wound is not important, what do you care about a sign on your arm? What you want is peace with yourself."

Perhaps it is not necessary to elaborate the point I am trying to make here, but it was clear at this stage in Floriana's analysis that she felt her psychic pain could not be explored or thought about. The only solution was physical, an act of blood-letting, suggesting she was stuck in a pattern of concretely acting out her difficulties (also evident in her dissatisfying promiscuity), but also that her only goal was to expel pain, for the pain to be 'dissolved.' She believed 'peace' could only be achieved by these means.

Conclusion

The crash of bodies, much like the coming together of atoms, causes an explosion of psychic energy. The analyst must try to survive this explosion and put back together the fragments of his and his analysand's bodies so they are separate entities which can communicate symbolically, rather than through blood-sucking, transfusion, penetration, or the creation of wounds.

Notes

1 To be accurate, Winnicott describes the infant who "reacts" to a prematurely timed impingement of the mother-environment. Even though the concept is totally Winnicottian in its essence, Martin James (1960) introduced this fortunate terminology based on Winnicott 's observation in his undervalued paper, 'Premature Ego development: Some Observations on Disturbances in the First Three Months of Life.'
2 Dante, *Inferno*, Canto V, 142, "E caddi come corpo morto cade."

References

Bion, W. R. (1977). *Two Papers: The Grid and Cæsura*. London: Karnac, 1989

————— (1979). Making the best of a bad job. In: *Bion in New York and São Paulo*. London: Karnac.

Bollas, C. (1987). *The Shadow of Object*. London: Free Association Books.

Bonaminio, V. (1993). Una nota su "La pazzia della madre che appare nel materiale clinico come fattore ego-alieno" di D.W.Winnicott". *Richard e Piggle*, 1:141–147.

————— (2015). On Anna Freud's work on 'notes on a connection between the states of negativism and of emotional surrender' (1952). In: *Studies on Passivity. Indication for Child Analysis and Other Papers 1945-1956*. London: The Hogarth Press and the Institute of Psychoanalysis.

Freud, S. (1913). The claims of psycho-analysis to scientific interest. *The Standard Edition of the Complete Psychological Works of Sigmund Freud*, XIII, 165–190.

_____ (1915). The Unconscious. *The Standard Edition of the Complete Psychological Works of Sigmund Freud*, XIV, 159–215.

Green, A. (1980). The dead mother. In: *On Private Madness*. London: The Hogarth Press and The Institute of Psychoanalysis. Original publication: La mère morte. In: *Narcissisme de vie, narcissisme de mort*. Paris: Editions de Minuit.

_____ (1995). Has sexuality anything to do with psychoanalysis? *Int. J. Psycho-Anal.*, 76:871–883.

Gutton, P. (2013). *Le Pubertaire*. Paris: Presses Universitaires de France.

Haggis, P. (2004). *Crash*. Lions Gate Films.

James, M. (1960). Premature ego development: Some observations on disturbances in the first three months of life. *Int. J. Psychoanal.*, 41:288–294.

Laufer, M. & Laufer, E. (1984). *Adolescence and Developmental Breakdown: A Psychoanalytic View*. New Heaven: Yale University Press.

Klein, M. (1946). *Love, Guilt and Reparation*. Reprinted: New York, Simon & Schuster, 1975.

Lemma, A. (2010). *Under the Skin: A Psychoanalytic Study of Body Modification*. London: Routledge.

_____ (2014a). Off the couch, into the toilet: Exploring the psychic uses of the analyst's toilet. *J. Am. Psychoanal. Assoc.*, 62:35–56.

_____ (2014b). *Minding the Body: The Body in Psychoanalysis and Beyond*. London and New York: Routledge.

Little, M. (1960). On basic unity. *Int. J. Psychoanal.*, 41:377–384.

Meltzer, D. (1973). Routine and inspired interpretations: Their relation to the weaning process in analysis. In: *Sincerity and Other Works, Collected Papers of Donald Meltzer*. Edited by A. Hahn. London: Karnac, 1994.

O'Shaughnessy, E. (1992). Enclaves and excursions. *Int. J. Psychoanal.*, 73:603–614.

Quinodoz, J. M. (2002). Dreams that turn over a page. *Paradoxical Dreams in Psychoanalysis*. London: Routledge.

Rosenfeld, H. R. (1987). *Impasse and Interpretation. Therapeutic and Anti-Therapeutic Factors in the Psychoanalytic Treatment of Psychotic, Borderline and Neurotic Patients*. Hove and New York: Bruner and Routledge.

Steiner, J. (1993). *Psychic Retreats. Pathological Organization in Psychotic, Neurotics and Borderline Patient*. London: Routledge.

Tustin, F. (1990). *The Protective Shell in Children and Adults*. London: Karnac.

Winnicott, D.W. (1948). Reparation in respect of mothers' organized defence against depression. In: *Through Paediatrics to Psycho-Analysis*. London: Hogarth/Inst. of Psychoanalysis, 1975, pp. 91–96.

_____ (1954). Withdrawal and regression. In: *Through Pediatrics to Psychoanalysis. Collected Papers.* London: Tavistock Publication, 1958.

_____ (1968). Interpretation in psychoanalysis. In: *Psychoanalytic Explorations.* Edited by C. Winnicott, R. Shepherd & M. Davis. London: Karnac, 1989.

_____ (1989). A point in technique. In: *Psychoanalytic Explorations.* Edited by C. Winnicott, R. Shepherd & M. Davis. London: Karnac, 1989.

For Product Safety Concerns and Information please contact our EU
representative GPSR@taylorandfrancis.com
Taylor & Francis Verlag GmbH, Kaufingerstraße 24, 80331 München, Germany

www.ingramcontent.com/pod-product-compliance
Lightning Source LLC
Chambersburg PA
CBHW050335270326
41926CB00016B/3464

9 781032 132556